AF326544

Exploring Compatibility

Foundations of a Theory

by

Vladimir Morozov

Published in England

by

Quickstone Publishing UK

Exploring Compatibility

by

Vladimir Morozov

ISBN: 978-0-9927357-0-8

First published in Russian, entitled
Совместимость социально-экономических систем
(ISBN: 978-5-282-03283-3)

PUBLISHED IN ENGLAND

BY

QUICKSTONE PUBLISHING UK

This book is dedicated to shaping the fundamentals of compatibility theory – a mega theory directing the progress of knowledge acquisition in science, and various areas of life and the operation of society. Alongside defining the principles and criteria of compatibility, the book offers a concise exploration of compatibility patterns, classifications and approaches to studying this phenomenon.

The central focus of the book is the comprehensive development of the human being in tandem with society as a single whole. It explores the compatibility processes affecting the environment in which society develops by examining interactions of human, organizational and societal subsystems and groups of social institutions — intermediate levels of compatibility uniting humanity into a multi-level dynamic whole.

The book is aimed at a broad range of specialists, including business people, economists, sociologists, politicians and cultural figures, as well as all thinking people who ask themselves "Just how do things interact with each other?"

ISBN: 978-0-9927357-0-8

Contents

INTRODUCTION

The degree of intelligence manifested in nature is so high that the whole significance people ascribe to their thinking seems absolutely trivial and insignificant in comparison. This realization is at the core of a scientist's life and his quest... The more knowledge about the universe that science affords us, the clearer I see the hand of God in control of the Universe.

Albert Einstein

The compatibility theory is currently the most significant enigma of contemporary society, a society that is constantly growing, expanding, developing and becoming more globalized – geographically, economically, socially, politically and in terms of its cultural world view. Not enough research work has been done and not enough research papers have been published making it possible to formulate and provide a proper foundation to this theory, which stands as an "uncharted black hole" for many separate and applied theories that describe the daily life and development of humanity and its place in the Universe.

The author attempts to put together isolated components and procedures into a technically efficient, harmonious, structured descriptive framework, a compatible model of the operation and development of society based on scientists' frameworks and constructs: hypotheses, concepts, strategies and theories of development from different areas of human effort and scientific inquiry. Compatibility theories are already available for psychology (psychological compatibility), interpersonal and group level; in technology, where the interaction methods between technology and technology, human being and machine, and technology and society have been systematically explored; in medicine, which has been studying the human body and the ways it is impacted by the environment for thousands of years, assessing their compatibility or incompatibility, as well as in cybernetics, computer science (informatics), ecology and so on.

Society is developing towards establishing a rational order. This is why this book is based upon the capabilities of the human mind and its needs, the better to understand all aspects of compatibility in the world around us which human beings are continuously working to comprehend. Many scientists have attempted to formulate general, comprehensive, unified theories (for example, the theory of everything, or the unified field theory, the theory of time and space, the unified theory of matter, the unified systems theory, the unified theory of economic relations, the unified theory of natural phenomena, and others), and yet, various parts of these theories are still lacking firm, robust links between them, or are divided and seen as belonging to independent fields of enquiry, independent dimensions. This could be an attempt, one of several, to link these separate parts into a compatible, consistent chain from a humanities perspective, because, without something like this, it becomes progressively more difficult for us all to understand one another, find consensus, make plans and identify long-term interrelations, let alone coordinated interactions (the main subject of this book) satisfactory for all participants. These participants currently number more than 6 billion.

Thousands of years ago people believed that they could create an atmosphere of prosperity and happiness and attract luck to their household by organizing the living space around them in a certain way. Recent US studies have shown that regular loneliness, isolation and lack of communication with others frequently become reasons for premature deaths; however, these days, the connection is becoming evident even to the naked eye.

Compatibility between people and within society is a topic of great interest to every one of us. If one of the ways of determining compatibility between people in the Orient is the principle of compatibility of the five elements, then what scientific ways and mechanisms are there (and how does one make use of them) for the purposes of our investigation? The subject matter is divinely profound and relevant, apparently in every field, in every way. Consequently, a book like this cannot possibly contain all the characteristics of compatibility elements and compatibility parameters or perform a comprehensive, full-fledged study of material and spiritual aspects of compatibility. For this reason, the author asks readers to be understanding of his use of idiosyncratic phrases and chosen symbols (to avoid, for example, construing the content of this book as being of a kind with the compatibility of signs in Oriental and Western astrology).

This book draws analogies with attributes of the human being in its exploration of the structure of various systems, system types and formats to identify their underlying structural and fixed parameters as well as adjustable properties. We can also observe rigidly-determined, inert and dynamic properties of the human being while analyzing groups of socioeconomic systems, evaluating spiritual and cognitive, economic and legal interactions, organization management styles, etc.

Contemporary research literature proposes a large number of concepts explaining the social nature of societies and what kind of a future they can expect. Among them, *evolutionary* concepts are based on the premise that significant progress can be achieved in society by slow, organic change (i.e. through reform), while *revolutionary* concepts are based on the assumption that qualitative change in society is achievable through conflicts, crises and revolutionary change.

The concept of sustainable development of society promulgated at the 19th Session of the UN General Assembly (in 1997) has received broad formal recognition and is based on the following principles:

- The human being and his or her inalienable right to a healthy environment should be at the core;
- Governmental responsibility for the sustainable development of society should come in different grades;
- Advanced societies should share their benefits with those less advanced and less developed, to ensure the survival of the latter;
- Full integration of environmental and economic policy to achieve the main objective of this concept – the eradication of poverty.

Although rich, developed nations are paying lip service to this concept, they are not ready to share their benefits.

Some countries have recently seen the emergence of the movement for the liberation of the human mind. One can see in this attempt the first timid signs of realization that deep underlying forces of a spiritual and intellectual nature influence economic drivers and the causes of social and historical development.

This is where contradictions arise between the underlying forces and their economic and other material manifestations. Dialectic contradiction, clashes and struggles between opposites are the most general driving forces of development and also the most fundamental.

One can observe contradictions in nature and in society. Contradictions involving society arise between society and nature, between production and people's needs, between parties, nations, between the old and the new in all their manifestations. Societal contradictions can be either antagonistic or not.

Throughout this book, we will be looking at contradictions by level (or the intermediate, meso-level) of compatibility of society's life and operation. Contradictions – incompatibilities at a certain level of their development, or escalation, can lead to crises. As Goethe wrote, poetically: "...The sensible stops making sense, / And good turns to evil..."

Life resolves contradictions either in a negative way (by destroying the affected system, e.g. by causing the death of a living organism), or in a positive way, through transformation of the system in a way that releases it from incompatibility.

In social economics, our future is determined by the laws and theories of society's development. The law of accelerating historical time enables us to see ordinary things in a new light, including changes in the society's social structure or a snapshot of its status structure.

Sociocultural theories of societal development see changes in the sociocultural realm – the world view, religion, values and mindsets of a social group, society, and whole eras – as most important. Philosophical doctrines by Auguste Comte, Max Weber, and Sorokin are among those described as sociocultural theories.

Socioeconomic theories see changes in the system of economic relationships as the core defining factor. Karl Marx, Karl Bucher and Bruno Hildebrand founded some of the best-known socioeconomic theories.

Compatible societal systems are a new direction society is taking in its course of development. A set of effective objective social laws closely associated with a comprehensive theory of social development and the potential compatible paths of societal development that would have a solid foundation in science are required for the existence of humanity and successful development of societal systems.

The need arises to become active about creating new international laws of societal interaction that would be interlinked and operate efficiently together. Without this, continued societal contradictions are inevitable between countries and peoples.

It is important to have a common hierarchy of goals defining the compatibility of society's development across a broad spectrum of ways to achieve it, including an international system of society metrics (a set of society cost metrics, metrics for the most important proportions of the state and metrics for development of relationships within society in realms that go beyond the purely material level), common objective metrics of administrative performance in different aspects of interaction within society (economic, social, political, cultural and worldview-related, as well as scientific and educational).

The theory of societal development, the directions of this development and the operating laws of society should form a consistent system, be free of contradictions, contain mandatory requirements as well as recommendations, requirements for the reciprocal usefulness of individuals and their usefulness for society, for constructive and peaceful ends, and should operate within the objective limits of available regional and global life-sustaining resources. People, their interactions, and societal systems of all kinds and levels should be based upon and conform to cultural values rather than to the unbridled elemental forces (crises) of the free markets and to maximizing material consumption as the ultimate goal (which leads to the mass degradation and decay of society).

If one were to focus on the compatibility of systems of supreme values, rather than on the similarity between them, their cohesion or identity, one would notice that while supreme value systems may differ, they are not necessarily incompatible. In a modern society, citizens may follow different religions, espouse different political views, have different social ambitions and different tastes and preferences, which, however, does not result in civil war. This is further corroborated by the progress of history, when extended isolation of peoples and their values would invariably be resolved by bloody war (for religious, political and economic reasons). However, ethnic groups living in complete isolation nearly disappeared in the 19th century.

Institutions of marriage, private property, God – all these values are being questioned, become uncertain. Anarchy in society reaches an apex where values are no longer a powerful deterrent. Lust, egoism and biological urges are on the rise in society. Brute force and deception become the prevailing behavior modes. Importantly, when the moral and legal differences and contradictions increase in society, the number and severity of punitive actions of one part of society towards the other also increases: other things being equal, the greater the disparity in their values, the more extreme is this growth. It is a known fact that sustainable development is possible where the opposites and contradictions do not reach the level of antagonism, where the overall system remains capable of self-organization.

I take this opportunity to express my gratitude to everyone who helped me prepare and put together material and write this book – first of all to my wife, Olga, my "brothers in arms" Doctor of Economics, Bauman Moscow State Technical University Professor *O.N. Melnikov*; Doctor of Economics, Moscow State University Professor and Chair *E.V. Egorov*; Doctor of Economics, State University of Management Professor, Director of SUM School of Marketing, State Prize Winner *G.L. Azoev*; Doctor of Economic, Professor, Scientific Secretary of the Russian Academy of Economic Sciences' Economics and Social Science Section *Sh.M. Magomedov*; Researcher with the Russian Academy of Science's V.A. Trapeznikov Institute for Management Issues *D.V. Semenov*; Graduate Student of the MSU Physics Department *A.S. Voloshin*, and to all author-researchers exploring the compatibility theory.

CHAPTER 1

COMPATIBILITY AS A CATEGORY OF SOCIETAL DEVELOPMENT

1.1. Perception of the World as a Whole and Compatibility

Formulating the scientific and philosophical problem of a cohesive world is characteristically difficult, because it is based on the assumption of a knowable world that would entail combinations and unities. The question is: combinations and unities of what? What is there anyway? A world giving rise to never-ending questions about organization, origins, functions and development.

The manifold worldviews of different cultures and the tremendous variety of human activity imply a certain continuity of the whole, the entire horizon of world outlooks and philosophies, creating an illusion of a certain uniformity of concepts, which are seen as coming exclusively from a closed, finite set, be it ideas of substance, or being, or matter, or fire, good, time, text, power, existence, will, idea, knowledge, etc. Inevitably, there is a contour of cohesion holding together reality in all its manifold manifestations.

The problem of the world's unity cannot in principle be reduced to one single ultimate definition, but it can be hinted at, on the one hand, by the inevitable paradox between the impossibility of embracing completely the infinite inexhaustibility of the universe, and, on the other hand, by the ineradicable interconnection of everything with everything, constantly manifesting itself, and by the tentative implication, just as ineradicable, that everything that can be grasped by any concept is originally a single, cohesive whole.

The manifold connections ensure the cohesion and unity of the universe, its various fragments and components, and should be considered from at least two complementary aspects: as a snapshot at a single moment in time/as a process unfolding over the course of time, and from a time-and-space perspective.

While the spatial and synchronous aspect (representing a snapshot of spatial phenomena at a given point in time) relies exclusively on symmetrical, isotropic relationships, the processional, diachronous, temporal aspect (which observes processes as they unfold over a length of time) depends predominantly on vectoral, asymmetrical, anisotropic evolutional and historical relationships. The former aspect helps to reveal the static snapshot of the universe, with all change assumed to be perfectly reversible, and therefore immaterial – in a sense, there is no development in this case. The significance of the latter aspect is defined solely by making a different set of basic assumptions of a pervasive dynamism creating the construct of a mobile, variable, and, at the same time, virtual and irreversible reality. The new, neoclassic worldview model includes a baryon asymmetry of the Universe observable on the metagalactic scale: the overwhelming predominance of particles over antiparticles, as well as the different versions of the anthropic principle, which directly tie together the mutual inter-correspondence between fundamental physical constants and the potential driving forces behind the emergence of life and intelligence, and, finally, the existence of general, universal evolutionary principles of coherent mutual agreement and self-organization that manifest themselves across a wide range of different spheres of reality – in both inanimate and living nature, in sociocultural mechanisms and structures.

Non-conservation of the baryon charge resulting to the obvious baryon asymmetry of our metagalaxy is apparently indicative of the need to look at the Universe as a combination of a number of metagalaxies with their different conditions and symmetries, as well as of characteristic features of processes which, in the early stages of the Big Bang, sowed the seeds that determined the emergence of the situation we observe today. Baryon symmetry is disturbed in the course of bosonic decay under condition of a precipitous expansion of the spatial scale (the stage of inflationary expansion of the Universe), which results, among other things, in instability of protons. This way, the specific path of change, of the flow of time, of the irreversible evolution of the Universe is inevitably determined – and in this sense, even the general and universal cosmogonic oscillations and possible development cycles of cosmological objects will be substantially irreversible.

Apparently, any processes of self-organization isolate and carve out their own development path, which invariably goes hand in hand with disturbances in and destruction of undifferentiated homogeneity of the original substrate.

General objective laws and patterns of development of nature inevitably raise questions about the direction of ongoing universal evolution. The general trend, observable at different levels, is towards an exponential increase in complexity and systematic organization of matter-and-field combinations, despite the relatively frequent instances of destructive processes, destruction and simplification.

Alongside our extant universe which we accept by default, we cannot but also take into consideration possible universes – a potentially infinite number of hypothetical, conceivable variations upon/versions of the universe within the immediate grasp of our perception.

Modern science is rapidly developing towards embracing not only the immediately perceivable (the "real," actual) world (universe), but also other worlds (universes) – through theories of quantum mechanics, synergetics, inflationary cosmology and others. This serves to expand the conceptual space needed for thought experiments and constructing strategic planning projects to explore and "colonize" the virtual realm.

Resource virtualization makes it possible to shed the limitations imposed by their physical location and specific configuration. Computer technologies have made it possible not only to simulate various artificial realities, but also given us a way to interact with these realities. Rapid development of the Internet has gained a great significance, as the online realm has become the venue where the various social networks and communication and information-sharing communities take shape, giving any user a way to get involved interactively in their operation via a virtual personality (an avatar). The history of humanity has to be viewed primarily and mostly as a living multi-aspect process of dynamic change in the whole multi-dimensional culture while maintaining the compatibility of mutually complementary areas, spheres and domains, and also from a snapshot (synchronous) and progressive (diachronous) perspective, in the continuity of cross-sections and lines of regional and global reach of the entire sociocultural system. Inasmuch as we have no way of directly perceiving the world around us as it is "in real life," except through the medium of our senses and cultural frameworks, we are forced to use the entire variety of incompatible or even mutually excluding constructs illuminating the various sides, aspects and cross-cuts of what is going on around us. The great multifarious variety of different versions, components, aspects and angles reflects the unity of the universe in the most compatible way possible by human culture via the whole range of mutually complementary world outlooks, constructs, strategies and arguments.

The operation of human groups, and reproduction of social structures requires fairly specific restrictive conditions which serve as the stable framework of society, including material production, civic life, and the existential and mental sphere, with a certain compatible optimal set of parameters providing the best fit with universal social constants taking center stage in this entire system in any of its variations and modifications, with all the possible deviations from this optimal set filling in the periphery and border areas. The common desire of all people to have guaranteed access to living essentials, decent conditions for working and improving themselves are transformed into a set of common human values which usually include humanity, reasonableness, morality, compliance with the law, capability for critical thinking, tolerance and environmental friendliness.

This could be one of manifestations of a coherent self-organization ensuring expanded self-reproduction of the body public, which generates and constantly supports the trend for optimization of all social interactions. Sociocultural universals constituting the quasi-stationary framework of the human mindset are what ensures the very possibility of interaction between different peoples and language groups through communication, as well as the tools for projecting, translation, re-coding, interpretation and understanding of local and regional cultural bodies.

The distinction between the artificial and the natural is one of the fundamental binary oppositions used in discussion of compatibility in the context of classical philosophy going back to Plato and juxtaposing the cultural and the civilized (something invented and intentionally created by human beings) with the natural (extant independent of human beings and only discovered by them). This approach is productive in that it makes it possible to draw a consistent, systematic distinction between the artificial and the natural: artificial and natural language, classification, selection, material; identification of a natural premise, natural religion, theology, natural right and natural monopoly, just as the identification of artificial intellect implies the existence, or, at least, a possible existence of the opposites. However, this juxtaposition is neither absolute nor universal: mystical, religious and theological theories and constructs, for example, juxtapose the natural with the supernatural, i.e. the transcendental, from the realm above the material nature (a realm that includes gods, demons, spirits, the Absolute, the higher power, powerful beings, etc.). And since human beings are not gods and cannot create something out of nothing, since everything artificial is something natural that has been transformed, in a compatible manner, to a certain degree, using fundamentally natural processes that follow the laws of nature. Therefore, for a detached, outside observer, the difference between "man-made" artifacts and natural objects is not obvious. This may be the explanation of the astrosociological paradox (the so-called "Silence of the Universe/Silence of the Cosmos" phenomenon) — the absence of observable signals generated by extraterrestrial civilizations and/or the signs of astro engineering (a "cosmic miracle"), despite many years of attempts to identify these signs under the Search of Extraterrestrial Intelligence (SETI) Program.

The assumption of relative autonomy or even perfect isolation of each individual sociocultural area on any dimension seemingly goes against the very possibility of any overall cultural compatibility, representing instead fundamental fragmentation and the mosaic-like existence of very different components. Manifestations of this include Friedrich Nietzsche's aphoristic (on the surface) writing style, full of mythological symbols, strange characters and unusual plots; Marcel Proust's text structure representing a stream of consciousness, as well as constructs of local and regional cultures – civilizations conceived by Danilevskii[1], Spengler[2], Toynbee[3], the Sapir-Whorf hypothesis of linguistic relativity[4] and others. Incomparability and incompatibility of different world images and world outlooks can be

---

[1] Н.Я. Данилевский. Россия и Европа. М., 1991.
[2] Spengler, O. Der Untergang des Abendlandes. Russian edition: Vols. 1–2. Moscow, 1993–1998.
[3] Toynbee, A.J. A Study of History. Russian edition: Moscow, 1991.
[4] Languages as an image of the world. Moscow, 2003.

overcome by adapting (and therefore distorting) projection, by transferring the original meaning into a new environment of meanings and concepts, to a foreign framework of categories. This kind of interference of different approaches and views generates new meanings, the crossing of different sociocultural "relay races" brings forth discoveries and unexpected ideas.

Every cultural object, whether it is a work of art or a machine, is a certain whole entity representing the human culture in a certain whole compatible flow.

Interaction of cultures results in a compatibility of world outlooks that presumes understanding of similarities and differences.

"It was noted: cultures meet each other and adjust to each other just like people, in two stages. First, they have to notice something in common in each other – something initially compatible, otherwise meeting and getting to know the other culture would be impossible. Then, they would have to notice the dissimilarities in each other – things that are complementary, otherwise the acquaintance of cultures would be boring. In real life, this often leads to extremes: if a culture should notice something similar in the other culture, it tends to jump to a conclusion that it is not a partial similarity, but rather a complete identity down to the last detail, and would take offence, if this is not the case; if a culture sees something dissimilar in the other culture, it tends to look down on it and dismiss it as barbaric."[5] Understanding the differences as a condition of one's own possibility of existence requires fundamental compatibility, without which no communication would have been possible in principle.

Culture has very clear fractal properties. Synthesis in art is an organism, in which every part performs its designated function, and all parts together form an aesthetically whole compatible combination of parts – i.e. a unity. The more complex the inner life of a work of art is, the broader the circle of phenomena it comprises, the more symphonic are the sentiments, the greater the number of parts, the greater the variety. And yet, this is a variety united by the original energy of the author's concept. This is why a good book, good music or an ensemble of sculpture and architecture is a microcosmos in its own right. This is why separating the defining properties of architecture, sculpture, painting and other art forms in principle (and viewing them as incompatible) appears to be not only counterproductive,

---

[5] М.Л. Гаспаров. Историзм, массовая культура и наш завтрашний день // Вестник истории, литературы, искусства. Т. 1. М., 2005. С. 29.

but also incorrect."[6]

The universal nature of sociocultural mechanisms currently in effect is very clearly manifested in the various subcultures, some isolated trends towards the fragmentation of overall society notwithstanding. A subculture is usually defined as a relatively autonomous, more or less stable local or regional area, part or subsystem of the overall culture, as represented, expressed and followed by members of specific, marginal to some degree, social strata, groups, communities and/or adherents of popular causes and movements. Subcultures stand out in their own unique language features (argot or slang), values, customs, standards, traditions, their own folklore, symbols, rituals, clothing styles and behavioral scenarios.

A subculture takes shape as an addition or an alternative to the dominant mainstream culture, which is accepted by the majority by default, supported by authorities and widely disseminated, which cannot but be a mass culture in the modern times. In this strict sense, the classical high culture, the "elite" culture, which sets the values, the ideals and the standards of compatible human development, is also a type of a subculture, which emerges early on, just as does the subculture of the underworld, the criminal community. Subcultures can vary in terms of how well developed their world view is and how deeply and completely they control the lives of their followers — covering the range from full control of totalitarian cults and sects to occasionally playing a social role at various get-togethers, with the extremes rarely absolutely incompatible with each other. Unlike national (ethnic) cultural identity, following a certain subculture is a matter of free choice. Subcultures cannot exist on their own, independent of the underlying culture and, unlike the counterculture, are not attempting to destroy and supplant the underlying broader culture.

The best-known subcultures are those of sailors, the military, Afro-Americans, artistic Bohemians, the gay and lesbian community, the fashionable crowd, dissidents, yuppies, hippies, beatniks, punks, metal heads, bikers, environmentalists, nudists, Satanists, skateboarders and snowboarders, skinheads, goths, drug addicts, computer hackers, sports fans, as well as science fiction fans, amateur singer-songwriters, RPG and computer/video gamers, lovers of rock, hip-hop, rave, rap, techno electronic dance music and funk music. Other subcultures include sociocultural

---

[6] Э.И. Неизвестный. О синтезе искусств // Вопросы философии. 1989. № 7. С. 74–75.

practices like *samizdat*, graffiti art, flashmobs, hitch-hiking, the clubbing scene, communes, performance art and happenings. Radicalized subculture can become a counterculture.

Counterculture is a blanket name for the subcultures that are in direct and conscious conflict with the prevailing mainstream, default culture, which is supported by authorities and widely disseminated by fundamental institutions of family and public education, i.e. the mass culture. Counterculture is always a result and manifestation of a social and cultural crisis, it seeks to find a new authenticity, a new life, a new organic harmony, replacing common sense and logical calculation (including the Protestant work ethic, etc.) with irrational sentiments as the main guiding principle (hedonism and others). Counterculture does not represent a united, uniform front, its fundamental variety arising from the broad range of proposed alternatives and different directions of ideologies. Countercultural revolt may lead to escape from reality (e.g. escape into virtual worlds), to creating a separate milieu unique to the counterculture (communes, social circuits, etc.) or to attempt to achieve radical change in society (examples include extreme left- and extreme right-wing political agendas, social, psychedelic and sexual revolution). Counterculture may borrow from ancient oriental philosophies and various practices: mystic, artistic, political and religious. Its potential charges the space for renewal of the broader society, which sometimes works by cultural adoption and absorption; although initially counterculture tends to prefer non-commercial methods of dissemination, as it becomes more popular, it begins to operate as a separate market segment. However, counterculture is not anticulture, because it inevitably uses cultural tools to develop and promote its ideas. "Anticulture" would be a fundamentally impossible attempt to live in primal nature restored to its original condition, using neither clothes nor tools, nor language nor any acquired knowledge.

The mass culture removes the traditional opposite extremes of "high" culture and "low," "elite" and "popular" (as well as many differences between national (ethnic) cultures) both by consistently expanding the range of samples replicated (gradually assimilating the entire varied range of subcultures, including the counterculture) and through adaptation of classical masterpieces (by reproduction, making new arrangements on the basis of, or remaking old works of art) or by using double coding in postmodern art (when the same work of art is meant to be read differently at different levels).

Perception of mass culture and attitudes towards it should not be understood only directly; it also has multiple manifestations of meaningful effects of unity.

Some scientists hold that there are five different identifiable domains (independent "realms") among the various cultural areas and spheres: philosophy, science, religion, art and mysticism — because each tends to embrace the entire universe, in its own way, from its specific perspective, and use its own tools and means to build its own image of the universe. Each of the dominions (in its components) then reflects not only the universe but also all the other dominions, with their unique images of the universe.

One could similarly place the "mirrors" of every type of culture (reflecting the universe in its own unique way) in a single large room: then one could expect (assuming the reflections would be superimposed over one another) a sort of a holographic image resulting from interference of the overlaid cellular mosaic structures. We would get more than a system of multiple reflections: we would get multiple reflections that constitute an element of the system itself and produce variety in their turn. The development of a community should be explored not only as a history and strategy of military, political and socioeconomic events and processes, but first and foremost as a history of the dynamic development of the culture as a whole.

The presumed unity opens up a productive perspective. An exploration of the national – pertaining to one ethnic group – can benefit from an understanding of the Combined Unity — as an interaction of different members within a single compatible body of humanity, viewing it as an objective, and individual ethnic groups and peoples – as instruments. And every single one would be irreplaceable, making its own unique contribution. Only through interaction of different ethnic groups can a common human culture emerge – an invariant manifested in different variants, a unity through multiplicity and variety. So, while Occidental thinking is typically based on juxtaposing concepts ("either A or B"), Oriental thinking tends to find a way to bring concepts closer and Russian thinking can take both approaches at the same time ("both A and B"). In the globalized world, individual states, especially those spanning a great area and including a large ethnic population, such as Russia, can be seen as a compatible model of society.

1.2. Compatibility and Unified Field Philosophy

The philosophy of unity[7], also known as the philosophy of everything, or unified field philosophy, is a new area of philosophy that should provide an "ideology foundation" for unified field theory (the theory of everything). Unified field philosophy and unified field theory are essentially the same thing: the former deals with the subject of research from more of a humanities perspective; it is broader and touches upon aspects beyond the scope of purely mathematical models. Unified field philosophy can also consider issues pertaining to art, religion and ethics. Unlike unified field philosophy, unified field theory deals with its subject using formulas and specific calculations; it is narrower and relatively limited in its scope. Although unified field theory is primary to unified field philosophy, it is the framework, the "bone structure," whereas unified field philosophy fleshes it out, is the flesh on the skeleton provided by the theory. Together, they form a whole living body.

Unified field philosophy can essentially be a synthetic combination of materialism and idealism. The practice of contrasting materialism and idealism dates back to the early 19th century, and it is now disappearing from serious scientific literature. This new trend has become clearer since the collapse of Marxist ideology. Philosophers are increasingly of the opinion that separating the external from the internal, form from substance, is essentially impossible. Max Weber had a characteristic approach, essentially viewing everything as a combination of the material and the ideal.

To "combine" these two aspects, humanity had first to reach a certain level of technological and ethical development, and second, to invent the new unified field theory. While humanity was in a state of disconnection, when the variety of the world around people made them focus narrowly on the study of form and promoted the institution of multidisciplinary studies, global deduction and narrow in-depth digging, essentially eliminating the very possibility of investigating unified field philosophy.

---

[7] Study of compatibility, discussion and polemics about its perception and place in philosophy with illustrative charts are covered in writings by O. Bondarenko (the author of a series of books on the subject) published in 2000 in Bishkek in the Russian language under the title "Philosophy of Unity" ("Философия Единства").

But, as the Bible says, "To everything there is a season, a time for every purpose under heaven..." (Eccles. 3:1). Many "orthodox," traditional philosophers find the idea shocking that the philosophy of the future should be expressed in broad mathematical terms. And yet, conversion to mathematical terms makes it possible to achieve a standardized philosophical approach, translating philosophy into the universal language of charts, formulas and equations — which, to an extent, is what is required of unified field philosophy. It is unified field philosophy that is apparently destined to become the applied philosophy truly combining theory and practice, and it will be up to it to come up with development models (including computer models) for any systems by levels, up to a multilevel development model for philosophy itself.

Unified field philosophy represents the synthesis, the Hegelian negation of the negation. Negation of what exactly? Evidently not the new approaches emerging from the depth of obsolescent, traditional narrowly-focused fields of inquiry.

At present, science as a whole is already aware of the need for integration, and, in principle, it is prepared for this kind of integration (involving the creation of a single metascience) that will merge philosophy with science.

If we (as O. Bondarenko suggests) were to combine the initial and final stages of the entire integration process and introduce a knowledge coefficient (with 1 for knowledge and 0 for none in the binary system, with transitional sub-levels), we would get the following (Fig. 1.1).

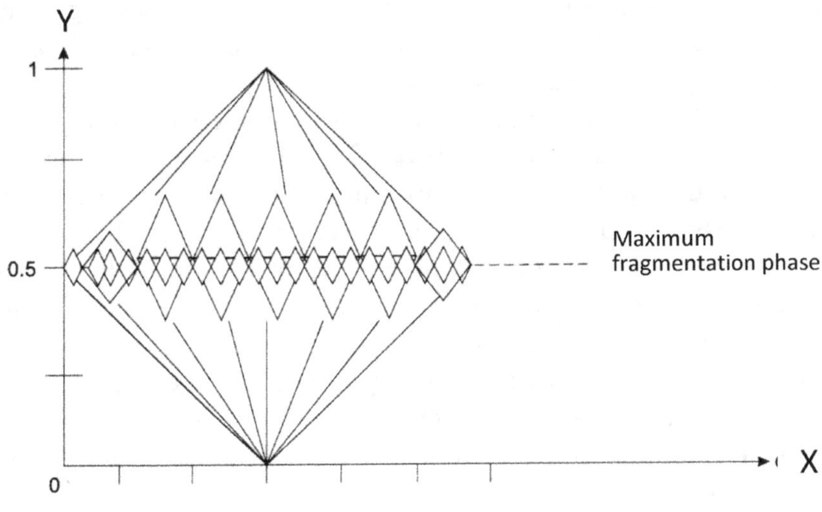

Fig. 1.1

Let us assume that we expand this schematic to development of humanity as a whole.

Levels of knowledge here are plotted on the Y axis. The X axis represents all the possible structural components of knowledge. The ordinate (Y) axis reflects process quality, while the abscissa (X) axis represents the number of components in a system engaged in a process.

As the outlook of man expands, the tree of knowledge expands laterally relative to the X axis. This automatically results in a qualitative leap on the Y axis: the more knowledge someone has, the freer this person becomes, the more self-assured and relaxed he feels, and, ultimately, the more he is in control of his environment.

What we need is a greater intensity of accumulation of knowledge. Greater intensity implies integration. Now everything progresses from details to generalities, shedding the external shells (forms) from available knowledge and penetrating into the essence, the depth of phenomena and processes, i.e. paying much greater attention to the inner contents. The age of synthesis has arrived.

This leads us to think that processes can be easier to describe using non-Euclidean Riemannian differential geometry, which also does not have parallel lines. The whole of history (for example, the history of architecture) has followed the same rules: from simple (a hut, a tent) to complex (palaces, Gothic cathedrals) and on to simple, but functionally simple, exaltedly simple, where the seeming simplicity conceals a huge amount of human knowledge (as in the ultra-modern city building of glass and composite concrete). In science, progress has moved from the all-knowing shaman at the dawn of humanity to the modern narrow specialist and on to the specialist with broader expertise who "does not pursue a specific science, but rather is looking for solutions to specific problems." Examples of this can be found in ethnology, anthropology and sociology, as well as economics and production (from making everything in one's household under the early self-sufficient household economy — to the division of labor and mass production of everything in the present to fully customized individual production and the creation of anything using computer technology with delivery over the Internet).

Therefore, we can allow that development of any systems according to the rules of Riemannian geometry is strictly speaking a universal phenomenon, and there is no area where it would be subject to other consistent patterns.

This point is of particular importance for understanding unified field philosophy. As we can see, the difference between the primeval "philosophy of unified existence" and the unified philosophy of the future is qualitative growth, as the progress from zero to one is first and foremost a qualitative increase.

We emphasize that the stage of taking things apart (the analysis) must be followed by a stage of combining things (the synthesis). To be able to come back, one must first go away. To be able to reunite, things must first fall apart. If we do not undergo the negation (falling apart) stage, we cannot appreciate the benefits of coming back together (the negation of the negation stage). The preservation and reproduction of the universe is ensured by the unification of its components; we could also present it through the prism of the Hegelian triad (Fig. 1.2).

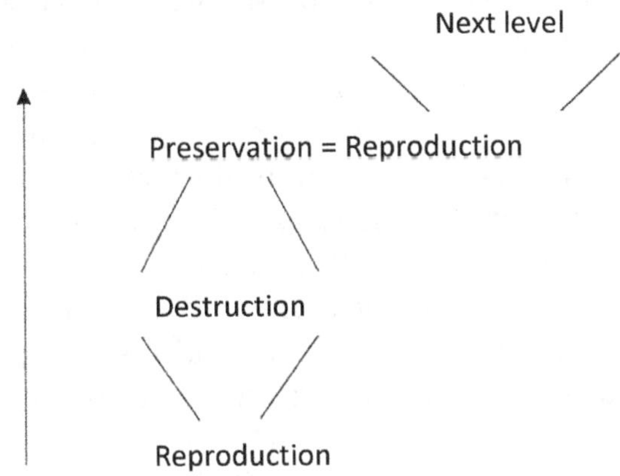

Fig. 1.2

Consequently, destruction is needed for the preservation of the cycle because it selects the most compatible viable forms, which jointly adapt for continued operation.

Conclusion: no cycle would be complete if the infinite variety of form could not eventually be reduced to something completely compatible and uniting. Positing a question about unity and variety involves the paradoxical idea: how should we relate to unity and variety?

There can be a uniform theory of matter that should reduce the whole variety, the whole range of its constituent particles to certain universal principles. While physicists allow for this eventuality, we should turn to the modern humanities, rather than sciences. The key basic premise in psychology is: the human being is extraordinarily complex, his psyche is unique, his inner world is infinitely nuanced and cannot be reduced to universal formulas. Other humanities, including culturology, deal with a multitude of human cultures that "should not" be reduced to a common denominator. Linguistics will stand by language diversity, and literature — by the unique, inimitable world of human feelings and perceptions (claiming the intimate nature of feelings, experience, the mystery of the human soul, which is in direct conflict with the idea of identity, which is the standard of universalism).

Therefore, we have natural and hard scientists agreeing to the idea of unity, while humanities scholars have a fundamental problem with that. And whoever disagrees with unity is not going to achieve unity. So one needs to look for compatible development.

We have already mentioned the prospects of creating a single metascience (see Fig. 1.1). It can only emerge from inter-disciplinary approaches; essentially, it has the idea of universal principles and integrative patterns at its very core. Until humanities scholars espouse positions of mandatory preservation of the great variety of form, the incompatibility and impossibility of unification can only increase, because unity and variety that are brought together without proper reasons for unification will be in antagonism with each other.

Society currently takes this for granted, because in this antagonism it sees only the exterior "harmony," the "behind-the-looking-glass world" of different forces. Materialists describe this harmony as a unity and conflict of opposites.

Humanities scholars use a more exalted idea — the idea of multiple levels. While they preach the ideal, in fact they break it into half-tones, modifying it until it becomes unrecognizable. Natural scientists, on the other hand, do not recognize half-tones and any internal process hierarchy, and yet allow for the concept of hidden everything. This can be represented by the following schematic (proposed by O. Bondarenko):

	Unity	Diversity
Natural sciences	1	0
Humanities	0	1

In this case, we only provide the general trend, but things can also be different. The very idea of unity can be interpreted in two different ways:

1) A unity is the starting point, an original substance that generates a diversity of form;

2) A unity is a compatibility concept permeating all extant types of form and making it possible to see substance in these forms, and also, if so desired, to ignore the form entirely. In this case, unity serves the role of a skeleton for compatibility of processes. As Lev N. Gumilev wrote, "The end and a new beginning."[8]

We must realize that matriarchal unity is not identical to skeletal, framework unity. And yet, an identity between them is possible, if we take into account the multiple levels of processes, in which the ultimate unity at one level can be seen as the starting unity of a completely different level (Fig. 1.3).

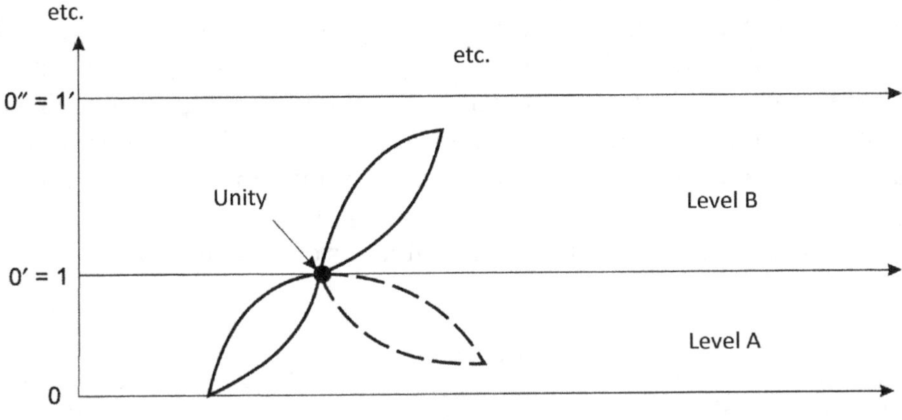

Fig. 1.3

The process can go upwards, i.e. reaching another, higher level (according to Artshuller, a system can become part of a super-system). However, development is frequently reversed (Fig. 1.3 shows the development dynamic as a dotted line); on the whole, you can see the possible directions of development represented as a wave within a single level. The point representing unity is the bifurcation point — the decision point from which development may take two different routes: up or down.

---

[8] Л.Н. Гумилев. Конец и вновь начало / Гумилев Лев Николаевич. М.: Дик-Дик, 1997. С. 544.

One should not blame humanities scholars for their instinctive escape from unity, as they prefer to see in everything an infinite variety of form and process. One must not demand of psychologists and psychiatrists that they see something uniting in the multifaceted and unique human individuality and human psyche. There is no reason to try to get historians and culturologists to reduce the great variety of cultural and historical processes to a common denominator. It would make no sense at all to try to convince sociologists that, besides a great variety of external features of social systems and people representing them, there are also internal features, hidden from casual observation (for example, the ethnic unconscious). It would be no use trying to reassure literary authors that not only unique facets of the human soul can be of interest, but also the human team as a whole, which is itself a facet of something huge, something of which it is a component.

The English author and philosopher C.S. Lewis wrote[9]: "...If movement is faster, then that which moves is more nearly in two places at once... But if movement were faster still... if you made it faster and faster, in the end the moving thing would be in all places at once... Well, then, that is the thing at the top of all bodies – so fast that it is at rest, so truly body that it has ceased being body at all." This is the highest form of compatibility, merging into a single unity.

Fig. 1.4 seeks to represent the different levels of compatibility.

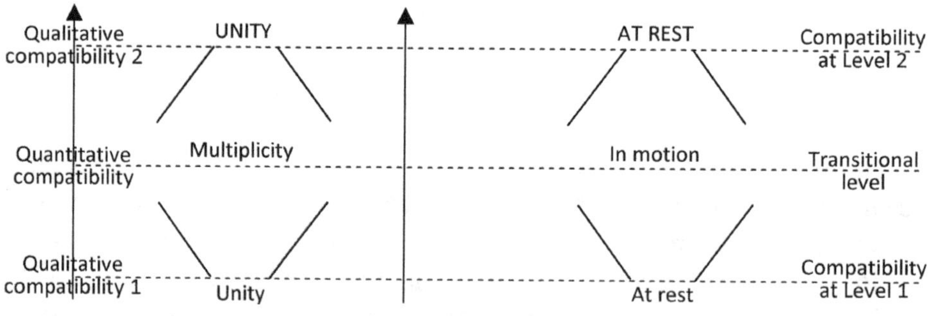

Fig. 1.4

---

[9] Lewis, C.S. Out of the Silent Planet. Quoted from the Russian edition: Льюис К.С. За пределы безмолвной планеты. Т. 1. М.: ЛШ, Вече, 1993. P. 103.

The meaning of unified field philosophy is to see any process in progress based on certain universal principles, abstracting from form, without losing sight of them entirely, but instead subjecting them to the needs of contents. The ability to combine – to find compatible points and trajectories on a plane – is the core of the philosophy of unity (compatibility of variety).

The universe is subject to rigid determination, which is to say everything in it is inter-related and inter-dependent, and any disruption of this extant order of the universe is about as likely as a disruption of the law of preservation of energy: if part of energy has ceased to be mechanical, but never became heat, simply disappearing from our universe! Things simply do not work this way. The third law of thermodynamics states: the effect cannot ever be greater than the cause, but it is always trying to reach the level of the cause, approach it, and therefore the effect becomes a cause, as a result of this "trying," this compatible action. Until the effect reaches the cause, the difference between their levels – the scissors of cause-and-effect – cannot be filled by something compatible, which does not necessarily fit into the cause-and-effect connection, which, for example, is part of the undefined. However, this holds true only until the effect becomes equal to the cause (see Fig. 1.5).

As we can see from the above, the undetermined area is constantly shrinking, until, in theory, it disappears altogether. The cause becomes one with the effect, and everything in the universe will become one enormous cause, and at the same time, an equally enormous effect. In other words, the universe would achieve full compatibility and would from then on generate itself.

Attainment of absolute compatibility is indicative of multiple levels of the universe. Its linearity shows us the visible universe, while its multiple levels are the actual universe. The visible does not equate to the actual!

Let us turn to the lists of content levels from the lowest up (following the anabolism process): the level[10] of elementary particles, the starting level – the atomic level – the level of molecules and crystalline grids and whole crystals[11] — the level of individual chemical substances, constituent parts of

---

[10] One would be justified in using the word "quality" instead of the word "level."

[11] The list is subjective and in many ways provisional and tentative. Its main point is to make the idea of levels clear: the living is on a higher level than the inanimate, the highly organized living is on a higher level than single-cell organisms, human beings are on a higher level than animals, intelligent human beings are on a higher level than the unintelligent, the spirit and spiritualism are higher than mere human mind, etc., moving

inanimate systems – the inorganic level — the organic level, and so on, up the progression of levels, up to and including various biological species from unicellulars to the highly-organized, then on to Homo sapiens as a species, human society as a whole, and finally, non-material, spiritual human systems, the entire noosphere level, and so on, up until the only system left is the Universe in its entirety. In other words, with each progressively higher level, the number of constituent components declines, while their quality or cohesion increases (following the law of transition of quantity into quality).

While at the bottom much is left to chance, at the top, we are creating the processes ourselves, we are managing it, we control for any eventuality! That is, we can move to an even higher level and be in control of the second law of thermodynamics (an observable law supported by statistical data). In other words, things that are unassailable or completely impossible at lower levels can be controlled at higher levels, at which the actions are better controlled, better coordinated and more cohesive.

The higher the level, the lower the expenditure of matter or energy. At the highest level – for the Universe in its entirety – there is no expenditure of energy and entropy is eliminated completely, which makes it possible to observe the law of energy conservation, the ultimate beneficial state from an energy perspective – the state of full, absolute compatibility of the environment.

The species of Homo sapiens has its own sublevels. It is expedient from an energy perspective to be developed rather than feral. In line with the principle of the smallest possible effort, the human being strives for development: the higher the development level, the greater the activity. Consequently, a more active human being is more economical in his energy consumption. Activity follows the principle of the smallest action. We see the supreme activity as the Universe in its entirety, as the highest-level activity, control, order and determination. As we understand it, the system of the Universe is a living organism.

It makes sense to take another look at the cause-and-effect links and the interactions among these links. If at the initial, lowest, zero level the whole universe was one enormous Cause, it follows that there would be no room for chance in this universe, with everything by necessity subjected to strict cause-and-effect relations (the ideal origin).

Things that appear chaotic and unpredictable from the perspective of

---

up to progressively higher levels.

one level, are fully ordered from the perspective of the previous level (the next one down). In this sense, the cause could easily end up being the effect. We face the question: how do we present a model for development of any process[12]: in shape of a cone standing on its sharp apex or as an upturned cone with its apex pointing up? The above leads us to the idea of superimposing the cones as shown in Fig. 1.5, replicating O. Bondarenko's suggestion.

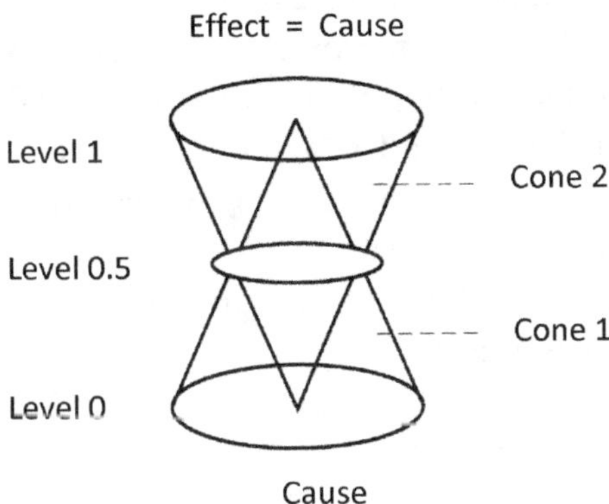

Fig. 1.5

According to the third law of thermodynamics, the effect can never be greater than the cause: therefore, the down-pointing Cone 2 cannot exist, unlike Cone 1. The entire field of physics exploring material phenomena with their fading oscillations is based exclusively on the lower cone. In the field of the non-material, for example, in the spiritual field, the upper cone would be a perfectly normal, natural model: if you add two smart brains, you would end up with combined brain power, resonating from their joint operation. In other words, the following equation would be typical of the material worldview (which focuses on external attributes):

$$m + m + m + m + ... + m \geq M, \qquad (1.1)$$

where m represents constituent parts of a given system, and M is the simple arithmetic sum of all the m's.

For the world of non-material phenomena, if we were to focus on internal attributes, the equation becomes:

---

[12] There are four different types of processes: harmonization, reproduction, metabolism and evolution, which will be considered in greater detail in subsequent sections.

$$m + m + m + m + \ldots + m \leq M \qquad (1.2)$$

In other words, the total sum of internal attributes is smaller than, rather than greater than, the combined internal attribute; any deficiency in the external (material) mass should always be matched by an increase in the internal (non-material) mass: $\Delta m_{ext.} = \Delta m_{int.}$. Paradoxical though it may sound, this equality is in full agreement with the law of conservation of energy, if we extend the meaning of this law to include both external and internal energy, as well as the interconnected unity of one and the other.

To get a better understanding of the idea of increasing internal mass, let us assume that, if all the people from one very large country were to come together to address their burning issues, we could say that the external space they occupy has been reduced to several square kilometers. As for the biomass of all these people, it would remain unchanged:
- For the people's biomass:

$$m + m + m + m + \ldots + m = M,$$

where m is the biomass of a single human individual, and M — is a simple arithmetic sum of biomass of all people;
- For the geographic space occupied by all the people:

$$s + s + s + s + \ldots + s > S, \qquad (1.3)$$

where s is the space occupied by one human individual apart from others; S is the space occupied by all individuals when they come together.

At the same time, the inner strength of compatibility of individuals and their desire and ability to solve problems, on the contrary, increases, and for a closely-knit, single-minded community:

$$f + f + f + f + \ldots + f < F, \qquad (1.4)$$

where f, F are, respectively, the inner strength of one individual and that of a group of individuals when they come together.

This is the way it should be in social life, at the very least: any consolidation reduces the external, but increases the internal. At this juncture, you might want to recall the law of transition of quantity (the external) into quality (the internal)?

Clear compatibility is essential here, because the external and the internal are always in balance, the material cannot exist without the non-material.[13] Quantity will be transformed into quality sooner or later and it will be quality that will make it possible to create quantity'. What is required for creating the additional quantity (quantity' — quantity = Δ quantity)? Nothing but quality, i.e. the compatible energy of the shaping environment. Full compatibility (unity) of development can work wonders. Unity comprises potential resources that an essentially divided humanity cannot yet understand and appreciate.

We must learn to understand that any process of cognition presumes gradual progress from the external to the internal, or from zero to 1. As the old (Russian) adage goes, "One greets people by the way they are dressed, and one says good-bye in a way matching their intelligence." This process within the scope of our study matches Hegelian dialectics (Fig. 1.6).

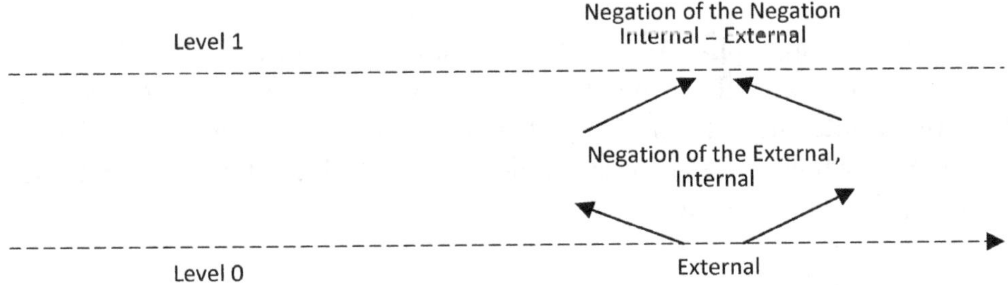

Fig. 1.6

From the external to the internal (the external $\rightarrow$ the internal is the conditional formula of any movement), from the apparent to the actual, from the borders towards the center. Because the formula "the external $\rightarrow$ the internal" is universal, and gravitation is a universal phenomenon, since, after all, both are different aspects of the same essence.

The above discussion makes it clear why unified field philosophy views all processes first and foremost as progress from the borders towards the center. The material Cone 1 (see Fig. 1.5) shows a progression of levels. As one moves from one level to the next, the number of components declines, while the quality increases. The cross-sectional circles grow progressively

---

[13] The external and the internal are complementary, if one uses N. Bohr's terms. At the same time, they are incompatible and both are in denial of each other. This is convenient for the purposes of cognition, since we only need to know what we have to find out.

smaller under the influence of forces vectored towards the center, which make the circles shrink. The shrinking, the compression takes place in accordance with Newton's law of universal gravitation. In the process, energy is released (the energy of action), which augments the energy resources of the collapsing object, i.e. the quality, which increases even as the quantity shrinks.[14]

The process is reversed for Cone 2 (see Fig. 1.5). It represents the development of non-material systems. As quality increases, the number of components increases. This is not a violation of the law of transition of quantity into quality, but rather a confirmation of this law. The full formula for this process is:

quantity $\longrightarrow$ *quality* $\longrightarrow$ *quantity'*
or, in alternative terms:
the external $\longrightarrow$ *the internal* $\longrightarrow$ *the external'*.

This notation applies to a multi-level, non-linear universe.

As you can see, the cones (1 and 2) have essentially merged together into the whole multi-level string. Dividing the material and the ideal is impossible, which is a sign of continuous compatibility of mutual processes in time (Fig. 1.7) and space.

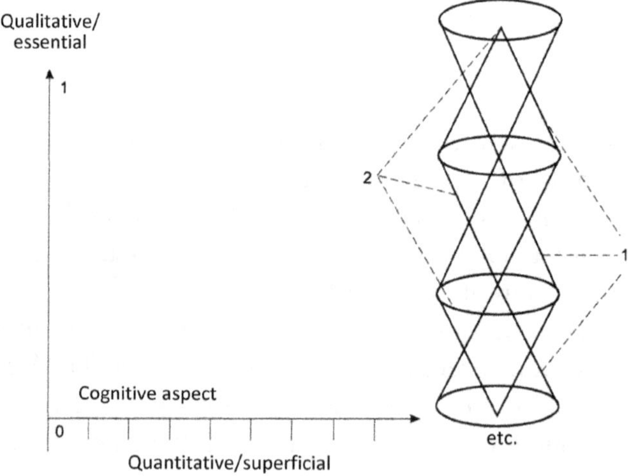

Fig. 1.7

---

[14] If compatibility is lacking, the inverted cone does not grow, resulting in a slowdown, stagnation, distortion, hypertrophied development and even a possible reversal.

The more the objects are subjected to cognition around us, the higher we climb on the Y axis. Until the external around us is completely noted, classified, and described, the internal will remain in a secondary role. Some scientists and thinkers operate with the internal, but the great majority are dealing only with the external. The best effort, the best energy goes towards extensive absorption of the external.

Apparently, an era of research focused on the internal is on its way.

How does one study the internal, the content? Possibly by ignoring the form, by looking past it. To be able to do this, we should raise and educate a cohort of broadly-trained specialists who would represent a negation of narrow specialists. Essentially, both "cohorts" are not completely compatible (they are complementary, in the words of N. Bohr)[15]. Broadly-educated specialists would emerge on their own because of the computerization/globalization of society and the increasing integration of areas of scientific inquiry.

Narrow specialists as an institution on the whole will shrink, while their significance will decline. In the period of transition, according to O. Bondarenko, they may even become something of a threat.

The meaning of the history of the internal lies in the following: at first human beings, attracted to the external, consciously narrow down the potentially open area of the internal, replacing the internal with the external; then, upon reaching the level of 0.5, when the crisis of the external is in full swing, human beings realize their bias and excessively narrow depth of concentration, and from that point on, pull back, catching up on breadth.

The history of the external and the internal can be represented as an addition of the material lower cone to the non-material upper cone (Fig. 1.8 overleaf).

We see the "given" only within a single cycle. Given the great number of levels inside and outside, we can draw the conclusion that the form (the exterior) is asymptotic, approaching zero, while the content (the interior) approaches infinity.

---

[15] A question arises of a complementary nature, adding to stages of compatibility. (R. Moore. Niels Bohr: Man and Scientist. (in Russian) Moscow: Nauka, 1981).

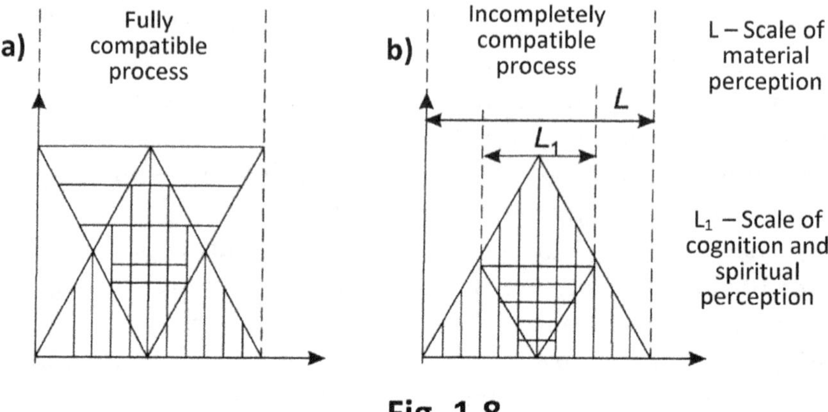

Fig. 1.8

We will illustrate this discussion with more specific examples of compatibility of human needs, institutional subsystems of the environment and its constituent organizations in subsequent sections.

1.3. Terms and General Conditions of Compatibility

Dictionaries name compatibility as a required mandatory condition for a postulation or a hypothesis to match not only the factual material on which it is based and which it is posited to describe and explain, but also the laws and theories in the relevant area. For example, if someone is proposing a design for a perpetual-motion machine, his opponents would primarily be interested in whether the author is familiar with the conservation of energy law before asking him any questions about the design or its originality.

Although the condition of compatibility is of paramount significance, it does not necessarily mean that every new postulation absolutely must be completely and passively adapted to what is currently seen as a "law." In a similar manner, compliance with currently accepted theories should not be blind or slavish.

New knowledge sometimes sheds new light on what was accepted previously, causing experts in the field to revise their understanding, refine or even delete portions of the "old" knowledge. Bringing new developments into line with the accepted theories makes sense until they aim at finding the truth, rather than upholding the established position of the old theory. The proposed hypothesis must take into account the entire body of relevant material and match it. However, if there is any conflict, the new hypothesis must show that things that have been accepted as established fact or proven theory are not true. In any case, if this is not the case, it must make it possible to look at facts and their theoretical interpretation in a new way.

The proposed new postulation must be in accordance not only with well-established theories, but also with certain general principles that have taken shape in the practice of scientific research. These principles are different in nature, they are different in generality of application; some are more and some are less specific, and compliance with them is desirable rather than mandatory.

We see the simplicity principle as the first of these: it requires using as few independent assumptions as possible to explain the phenomena being explored, and these assumptions must be as simple as possible.

The simplicity principle has been important throughout the history of natural science. For example, Isaac Newton made a special requirement of "no more causes of natural things than such as are both true and sufficient to explain their appearances." Simplicity is less of a fundamental requirement than matching the experimental data or previously accepted theories. It is sometimes the case that generalizations are formulated in such a way that precision and correspondence with empirical data are to some extent sacrificed to attain an acceptable level of simplicity, especially simplicity of mathematical calculation.

The next general principle frequently used to evaluate the proposed postulations is the principle of familiarity (or conservatism). This principle advises avoiding unjustified innovation and trying as much as possible to explain new phenomena using already known laws. If conflicting recommendations follow from the principles of simplicity and conservatism, the simplicity principle takes precedence.

The third principle is the universality principle, which presumes that the new postulate would be tested for applicability to a broader range of phenomena than those on which it was originally formulated. If a statement that is true for a certain field is proven to be universal and leads to new conclusions not only in its original field, but also in several adjacent fields, its objective value increases perceptibly. The quantum hypothesis, originally proposed by Max Planck only to explain the radiation by a black body, is a typical example.

The beauty principle states that a good theory should produce a special aesthetic impression, should be elegant, logical and, possibly, romantic.

In addition to those named here, there are a great number of other principles used to evaluate new ideas and theories. Some of these principles are unclear and others are even misguided and detrimental.

Every area of expertise has its own standards against which a new theory is tested for validity. Not only do they depend on context, but they also are governed by convention. These standards approved by the scientific community have to do with the general nature of things that are researched and explained, the quantitative precision of measurements, rigor of argumentation, breadth of data and other aspects.

It follows from the above that the new scientific statements are not evaluated using universal or unchanged criteria. The rules of validation accepted in science, the requirement for consistency, general principles and standards of validity are not set in stone. The boundaries of the "scientific method" are fairly vague and, to some extent, a matter of convention. Any significant changes in a scientific theory result in changes also in the combination of methodologies and tools used within the scope of the theory.

We propose taking a closer look at the requirement for consistency, which states that new hypotheses should be logically consistent with earlier recognized theories. At the same time, this requirement can be unreasonable because it ensures that the older theory remains in place, rather than the better of the two theories. Hypotheses that contradict confirmed theories give us evidence that could not have been obtained in any other way.

At first blush, the requirement for consistency can be described very concisely. It is common knowledge that Newton's theory is inconsistent with Galileo's freefall law, as well as Kepler's laws; that statistical thermodynamics is inconsistent with the second phenomenology law; that wave optics is inconsistent with geometric optics, and so on. Please note that this is not about inconsistencies between, for example, Newton's theory and Galileo's law, but rather about the inconsistency of certain corollaries of Newton's theory with Galileo's law in the area where the latter applies. In this particular case, the situation appears to be particularly clear-cut. Galileo's law states that free fall acceleration is constant, while Newton's theory as applied to conditions prevailing on the surface of Planet Earth provides an acceleration that, instead of being constant, decreases (if gradually) as the distance from the center of Earth increases.

In more abstract terms, let us consider theory X which is successful at describing the situation within a certain field of inquiry. Theory X is consistent with a finite number of observations (this class of observations would be denoted M), and this consistency lies within the margin of error L. Any alternative that contradicts Theory X, lies outside Class M within L, is backed by exactly the same observations (empirical data) and would therefore be acceptable, if Theory X was acceptable on the assumption that all observations (empirical data) are in Class M. The consistency requirement is far less accommodating, disregarding and eliminating a certain hypothesis from consideration because it diverges from another theory relying on the same empirical evidence as the new hypothesis, rather than because of its inconsistency with facts. This is why it makes the untested part of this theory the measure of its validity. The only difference between the old and the new theories are their age and how well they are known. If the more recent theory had been the first to emerge, the requirement for consistency would have been working in its favor. The earlier valid theory therefore has priority over equally valid theories that were introduced at a later time. The other theory has no edge over the theory it has replaced. The only real improvement is that it has added new facts. New facts contribute to real progress. Therefore, a truly scientific procedure would instigate a clash between the accepted view with as many relevant facts as possible. Eliminating alternatives helps scientific progress in the best possible way. The requirement for consistency eliminates fruitless discussions and makes a researcher focus his attention on facts a set of which is ultimately the only corroboration of the theory. This would protect the validity of a certain theory and motivate the decision not to consider any empirically possible alternatives to it.

In other words, the reasonable essence of this is that theories should not be replaced until there are compelling reasons to do so, and the only compelling reason for replacing a theory with something else would be its inconsistency with facts. This is why a discussion of facts inconsistent with a theory results in progress, whereas a discussion of hypotheses inconsistent with a theory does not. Consequently, it would be reasonable to increase the number of relevant empirical facts, whereas increasing the number of factually valid, yet inconsistent alternatives would be unreasonable. Certainly, more formal improvements by improving elegance, simplicity, degree of generalization and logic, according to the other principles listed above, are admissible. However, if these improvements are made, the researcher has nothing to do but collect facts to test the theory.

This is possible on condition that facts exist and are available regardless of whether any alternatives to the theory being tested are considered. We are going to call this assumption, whose validity defines the reasoning above, an assumption of relative autonomy of facts, or the autonomy principle. This principle does not deny that discovering and describing facts depends on any theories, but claims that facts providing empirical content of a certain theory can be obtained regardless of whether any alternatives to this theory are considered. This assumption deals with confirmation and testing in a vast majority of all studies. All these studies rely on a model that compares a single theory against a class of facts (or observational assumptions), which are seen as "data," or "evidence."

In real life, facts and theories are connected to each other much more closely than the autonomy principle suggests. Not only does the description of every individual fact depend on a certain theory (which can be very different from the one being tested), but also there are facts that cannot be discovered without recourse to the alternatives, and which become inaccessible as soon as we eliminate the alternatives from consideration. This leads us to the idea that the methodology unit we should consider when discussing tests and empirical content is generated by the whole set of partially overlapping, relevantly valid but mutually inconsistent theories.

Relevance and the contradictory nature of key facts can only be supported by other theories, which are inconsistent with the concept being tested, although they may lack immediately relevant validity. This is why coming up with and exploring alternatives comes before the identification of contradictory facts. The empirical approach, at least in some of its best developed versions requires that the empirical content of any knowledge we have should grow as much as possible. Consequently, coming up with alternatives to points of view under discussion is a substantial part of the empirical method. And the other way around, the fact that the requirement for consistency eliminates alternatives demonstrates that it is in conflict with not only scientific practice, but also with the empirical approach. By eliminating important tests, it reduces the empirical content of "approved" theories (as noted earlier, these are usually theories which were the first to emerge); among other things, this condition reduces the number of facts that could demonstrate the limited options of these theories. This last outcome of using the consistency principle is of particular interest. Quite possibly, if we stay with physics as our example, rejection of uncertainties in quantum mechanics would require just such an inclusion of contemporary theory into a broader context, which is in conflict with the idea of complementarity, and could therefore lead to decisive tests. It is equally possible that defense of the consistency principle by several leading contemporary physicists, if successful, would protect uncertainties from rejection. Therefore, this requirement may eventually result in a certain point of view becoming an unassailable dogma, completely entrenched against any possible criticism, allegedly all for the sake of testing.

We propose taking a closer look at an "empirical" defense of a dogmatic viewpoint. Let us assume that physicists – intentionally or not – have completely accepted the idea of complementarity and have agreed to develop the orthodox point of view, refusing to consider any alternatives. This can be completely harmless initially. Eventually, however, an individual or even a whole influential research school can devote some time to the single-minded development of a theory that interests them rather than one they may find unattractive.

Let us also assume that development of a given theory has been successful and provided a satisfactory explanation for circumstances that were previously mysterious or confusing. This will lend empirical support to an idea that until then had only one strength: being interesting and exciting. From now on, obligations to pursue this theory will increase, while tolerance for alternatives will decline. If the idea that many facts can be obtained only using the alternatives proves correct, discarding the alternatives would be to discard potentially contradictory facts. Among other things, facts would not be obtained which by their discovery would have demonstrated the general and irreparable lack of validity of this theory. These facts would be unattainable; the theory would appear free from faults, creating the impression that all the evidence patently and definitely indicates that all processes, including unknown interactions, are consistent with the fundamental quantum law.

This would result in a further increase in certainty that the accepted theory is unique and assure scientists that any attempts to do research along alternative paths would be futile. Deeply convinced that only one kind of microphysics is valid, physicists would attempt to explain facts potentially conflicting with it in its terms, without worrying too much if these explanations were not entirely convincing. Then, the general public will become aware of this scientific accomplishment. Popular science books (including many books on the philosophy of science) increase the fame of the theory's fundamental postulations, helping to expand its area of application, with orthodox scientists receiving funding that its denied to their opponents. Empirical support for the theory appears immense. The chances of considering any alternative theories becomes exceedingly slim, while the ultimate success of fundamental assumptions in quantum theory and the concept of complementarity appear assured.

And yet, clearly this apparent success cannot be seen as confirmation that the theory is a true and accurate reflection of natural phenomena. Besides, a suspicion arises that lack of significant difficulties is a result of shrinking empirical content caused by elimination of alternatives and facts that could have been discovered through them. The assumption begins to take shape that the success achieved is determined, that, over the course of its development, the theory has gradually become a rigid ideology. This ideology is "successful" not because it matches facts convincingly, but rather because its success rests on a biased selection of facts in a way that would preclude any chance of verification, with some facts eliminated from consideration completely. It therefore follows that this "success" is completely artificial and spurious. Once the decision has been made to stick to certain ideas at all costs, these ideas would naturally be preserved. If this decision is forgotten at a later point, or has ceased to be obvious, becoming more of a habit, the survival of these ideas becomes independent support for them, reinforcing the original decision or making it obvious. Eventually, the circle is complete. In this way, empirical "evidence" may be created by a certain procedure that is reinforced by the evidence it generates.

At this stage, an "empirical" theory of the type described above becomes practically indistinguishable from a second-rate/secondary myth. To illustrate this point, let us consider a myth; for example, the myth of witches and demonic possession developed by Catholic ideologists that was prevalent in the 15th – 17th centuries across Europe. This myth represents a complex system of explanations with a great number of ancillary hypotheses, which serve to explain special cases, helping it to get a high degree of confirmation by observation very easily. It was refined over a very long period of time; its content was instilled in people's minds by fear, ignorance and superstition, as well as by the efforts of zealous and fanatical clergy. The constituent ideas of this myth found their way into the most widespread means of expression, infecting all ways of thinking and leaving their stamp on many crucial decisions of human life. This myth provides handy models for explaining away any possible events – which were available to those who accepted the myth. The key terms of the myth were clearly and rigidly established, and any idea that they could be copies of unalterable entities and that changing their meanings, if it had occurred, would have been the result of human error, by then became entirely plausible. Conviction of its truth reinforces and justifies all actions used to preserve the myth (up to and including physical elimination of the myth's opponents).

The toolbox of concepts of a theory and emotions associated with their use permeate all communication media, all actions and the entire life of society, ensuring the success of methods like transcendental deduction, analysis of word choice and use, phenomenological analysis, or, in other words, methods contributing to further ossification of the myth. This only confirms that all methods typically used by different schools of philosophical thought – both historical and contemporary – have one thing in common: they all try to preserve the status quo of spiritual life. Observation results will also support the given theory, because they would be formulated in its terms.

The impression is created that the ultimate truth has been found. At the same time, it is clear that all contact with the outside world has been lost, while the stability promoted as the absolute truth is nothing more than the result of absolute conformism. Indeed, how can one possibly test or improve a theory if it is structured in a way that any imaginable event can be described and explained in terms of the theory's principles? The only way to explore these all-embracing principles would to be to compare them to another set of similarly general principles, which we discussed earlier (Fig. 1.9); however, that route was eliminated at the outset.

Consequently, a myth has no objective meaning, and exists solely through the efforts of the community of myth believers and their leaders – be it priests or Nobel prize winners. Apparently, this is the decisive argument against any method upholding uniformity – empirical or any other. In any case, any method of this kind is a method of deception: it perpetuates a conformity of ignorance, even as it speaks of truth; it undermines and corrupts spiritual ability and weakens the power of imagination, all the while talking about deep understanding; it destroys the most valuable gift of a young age – the immense power of imagination, even as it speaks of education.

One can make the reasonable assumption that it is the church that needs uniformity of opinion, or, in the political sphere, the frightened or personal gain-seeking victims of myths (ancient or modern) or a tyrant's weak and voluntary followers. Objective cognition requires, first and foremost, a variety of opinion. And a method encouraging this variety would be the only one consistent with a humanist position. In the extent that the requirement for consistency restricts this variety, it contains an element of theology, which is certainly at the basis of the cult of "facts" so typical of all new empiricism.

As an outcome of this discussion, we propose a schematic model for understanding the coexistence of compatible/consistent and incompatible/inconsistent requirements for the development of cognition and understanding of truth in our living environment.

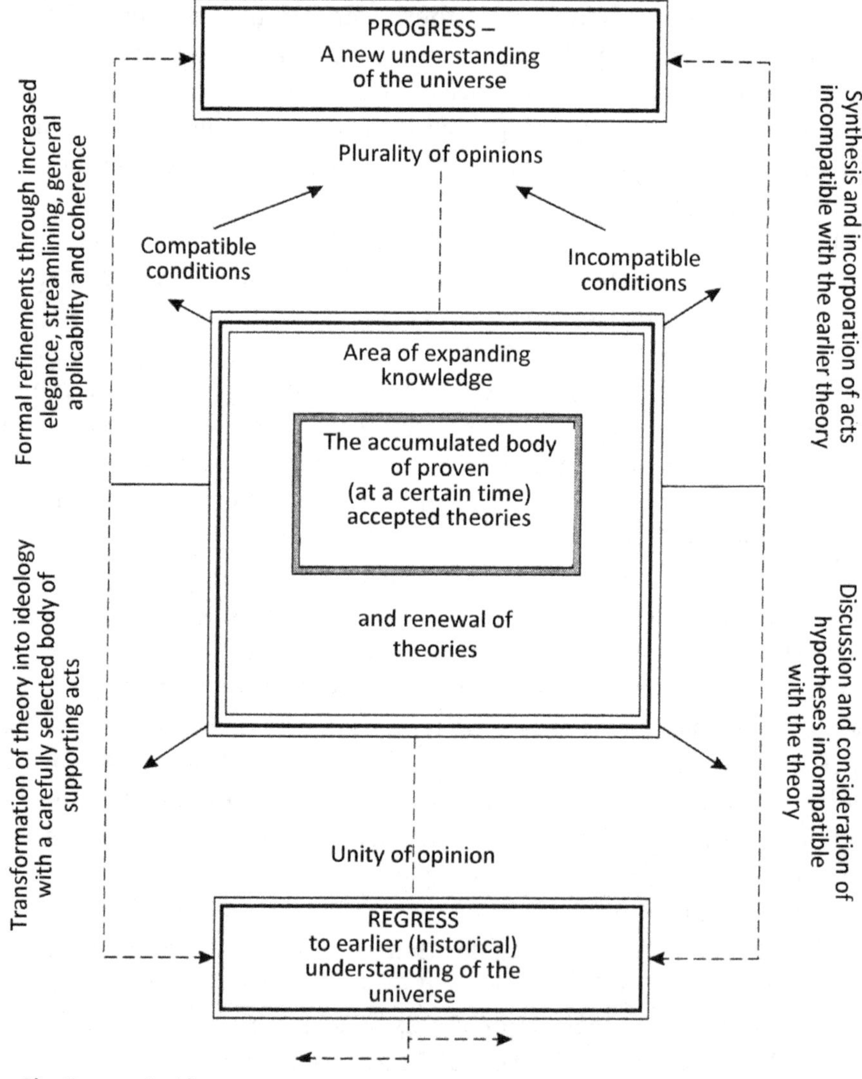

Fig. 1.9

A method encouraging a variety of opinion for objective cognition (of the universe), is still the only one compatible with the humanistic position:

$$Z = S_d \times R_m,$$

where Z is a compatible general solution, which is characterized through a variety of opinions — R_m (the greater the variety of opinions R_m, the higher the compatibility Z with components of the system C_i); S_d is the compatibility of actions (for a simple majority of participants);

$$R_m = \sum_i f(C_i, Z)$$

with C_i representing the ith fraction of the system, and $f(C_i, Z)$ — the function of correspondence of a general solution to every person involved.

1.4. Definitions, Classifications and Criteria of Compatibility

The dictionary definition of compatibility comprises: combinability; lack of contradiction; ability to be physically joined together; communicability; ability or capability to match or be superimposed. Some possible expressions are: compatibility of notions (concepts) or compatibility of symmetrical shapes. In the case of animate beings, compatibility is a set of qualities, abilities and character traits in two or more individuals enabling them to achieve full coordination of their joint work or other joint activity.

The meaning of compatibility in the context of logic represents a type of relationship between concepts and statements. Two notions (concepts) can be described as compatible if they have matching of partially overlapping scopes, i.e. if they have at least a single component in common. For example, if we consider the concepts "politician" and "competitive athlete," they have overlapping scope: there are people who are both politicians and competitive athletes and are personifications of both these concepts, which makes these two concepts compatible. However, the concepts "grade school student" and "politician" have no common components in their scope, since there is not a single individual who can be a grade school student and a professional politician at the same time; and, therefore, these concepts are incompatible.

Compatible concepts can be of equal scope, subordinate or subordinating, or overlapping. Statements are also described as compatible if all of them are true, i.e. if the fact that one of them is true does not prevent the other from being true as well. For example, the statements "Some people have brown hair" and "Some people do not have brown hair" are both true, which makes them compatible. Traditional logic views as compatible: a general affirmative and a specific affirmative statement, a general affirmative and a specific negative statement, a specific affirmative and a specific negative statement. Mathematical logic views as compatible statements that are true at even a single set of values of their variables. For example, statements A & B and A -> B are compatible, because they hold true whenever both A and B are true.

The concept of compatibility today is actively studied and used not only in technology and psychology, but also in medicine, biology, cybernetics, and other areas of scientific inquiry. Systems theory views compatibility as "the kind of relationship between two systems that reveals a relationship between two systems that manifests a similarity of or something in common between the systems on certain parameters or in essence, making interaction between the systems possible."[16]

We propose to begin with looking at the key terms and definitions of compatibility using the definitions of technical compatibility as an example; the relevant terms are presented in the most compete manner in general terms in GOST 30709-2002[17] and GOST 30372-95 (GOST R 50397-92) inter-governmental standards[18].

The following general concepts are defined in the Standard:

• *compatibility* is suitability of products, processes or services for combined use without causing undesirable interactions (interference) in assigned conditions for performing at a specified performance level;

• *technological compatibility* is compatibility of product, their components, structural materials, fuel and lubricants, technological production and monitoring process;

---

[16] Н.Н. Обозов. Три подхода к исследованию психологической совместимости // Вопросы психологии. 1981. № 6.

[17] Межгосударственный стандарт. Техническая совместимость (термины и определения). Минск: ИПК изд-во стандартов, 2003.

[18] Межгосударственный стандарт. Совместимость технических средств электромагнитная (термины и определения). Минск, 1995.

- *technological compatibility objects* — two or more objects the compatibility of which is evaluated and ensured to accomplish a specific task;
- *combined objects* are an object produced by combining or close interaction of two or more objects;
- *combinable objects* are technologically compatible objects joint use or interaction of which can ensure meeting the requirements of relevant standards of technical documentation for combined objects;
- *incompatible objects* are objects joint use of or interaction between which fails to meet at least one of the requirements set in standards or technical documentation for combinable objects;
- *technological compatibility for technological compatibility objects* is a type of technological compatibility for which the technical documentation states the technological compatibility objects;
- *technological compatibility for requirements for compatible objects* is a type of technological compatibility for which requirements are set in applicable standards or technical documentation which are to be complied with for combinable objects.

A.L. Gorelik[19] provides a noteworthy definition of technological compatibility, describing it as the capability of technological devices and systems to operate effectively while interacting with other devices. He also makes a distinction between functional and interference (noise) compatibility. According to Gorelik's definition, functional compatibility describes the capability of a certain technological system to work in conjunction with other systems and is relevant because of the need for combining systems into larger, more complex assemblies that would still be effective. Interference compatibility describes the level of interference (noise) in technological devices and systems running at the same time, but not linked for their function.

A simple overview of available definitions shows that more than 50 kinds of technological compatibility are currently known. However, these different kinds have yet to be structured and there is a lot of overlap and contradiction.

The first step towards structuring the general knowledge of technological compatibility is its categorization. Any categorization W can be performed under proper conditions:

---

[19] А.Л. Горелик, В.А. Скрипкин. Построение систем распознавания. М.: Сов. радио, 1974.

$$D = \int [Q(D)] \cap K(D),$$

where $Q(D)$ is the set of objects to be categorized; K(D) is the set of categorization criteria (attributes).

There is a minimum of categorization conditions for technological compatibility. The process of categorizing technological compatibility can be likened to creation of a set of sets $\{X_j\}$, where $j \subset J$, and J is a certain set of categorization criteria (attributes). This operation is expressed in mathematical terms as partitioning set X. In this case, X is the set of objects (things, notions, source data, etc.) to be categorized. For our purposes, X is a set of varieties of technological compatibility of scientific and practical interest.

The procedure of partitioning set X can be seen as performed correctly if the following conditions are met:

$$X_j \in X \ for \quad all \quad j \in J$$

$$X_j \neq O \ for \quad all \quad j \in J$$

According to A.A. Nosenkov[20], several categorization groups of technological compatibility can be identified at present.

1) By type of objects combined: compatibility in a technology-technology system, a technology-human being system, and a technology-nature system.

Compatibility in a technology-technology system is purely technological compatibility. Compatibility within a technology-human being system can come in two varieties: ergonomic compatibility in a human being-machine system, and compatibility in a technology-society system. As the latter describes the level of fit between technology and the requirements of society, it can be described as compatibility between technology and consumer. Compatibility within a technology-nature system can be appropriately described as ecological.

2) By essential nature of compatibility: physical, chemical, mathematical, psychophysiological, organizational compatibility.

Psychophysiological compatibility will be considered in greater detail later in this book. It indicates how well a human being is suited

---

[20] А.А. Носенков, В.И. Медведев. Теория технической совместимости как новая дисциплина системного анализа // Вестник САА имени академика М.Ф. Решетнева. Вып. 2. Красноярск, 2001. Р. 231–236.

for work within a human being – machine system.

3) By factors being combined: electromagnetic, electrical, thermal, information, size, algorithmic, software and other compatibility.

This categorization group includes most known types of technological compatibility, with new types added to it all the time that are established during various engineering and scientific research endeavors.

4) By lifecycle stages: design, technology, operational compatibility.

Every compatibility type in this categorization group has a generic character. Sets of constituent specific compatibility types overlap.

5) By "territory": external, internal compatibility.

6) By type of manifestation: stable — unstable, obvious – unobvious, recoverable – unrecoverable compatibility.

7) By degree of implementation: full, partial (local).

8) By degree of randomness: deterministic, stochastic.

9) By predictability: forecastable, unforecastable.

10) By degree of independence: dependent, independent.

11) By place of implementation: hardware, communication compatibility.

12) By type of connection between objects: direct compatibility and compatibility by proxy.

The set of compatibilities being categorized (including groups 1–4) can be represented as a multi-level hierarchic structure:

$$C_1 \rightarrow \left\{ C_2^1, C_2^2, ..., C_2^m \right\} \rightarrow ... \rightarrow \left\{ C_r^1, C_r^2, ..., C_r^n \right\}$$

where C_1 is compatibility of the first, highest order; C_2, C_r are compatibilities of second through r[th] order.

Exploration of compatibility between people has a rich history in both Russian and international social psychology. The concept of compatibility here is eminently insufficiently precise, overlapping other concepts, which makes it fuzzy and likely to be substituted in certain cases.

Dictionaries of psychological terms define and categorize compatibility as follows:

1) Group compatibility is "a sociopsychological characteristic of a group, manifested in its members' ability to coordinate (make uncontradictory) their actions and optimize their relations in different types of joint activity"[21];

---

[21] Краткий психологический словарь / Сост. Л.А. Карпенко / Под общ. ред. А.В.

2) Interpersonal compatibility is "a mutual acceptance of partners in communication and joint activity based on optimal combinations of values, social attitudes, interests, motives, needs, character, temperament, pace and rhythm of psychophysiological reactions and other personal psychological attributes relevant for interpersonal interaction"[22];

3) Psychological compatibility is "the effect of interaction between people characterized by their highest possible satisfaction with each other"[23].

According to A.L. Svenitsky, psychological compatibility is the ability of members in a group to engage in joint activity based on their optimal matching.[24]

B.F. Lomov defines compatibility as a phenomenom arising in the process of mutual regulation of behavior.[25]

According to K.K. Platonov, psychological compatibility is realized by interaction through behavior (by movements, actions and acts). The compatibility process itself becomes increasingly complex as more psychic and social processes are added to it. There can be not only positive and negative compatibility (incompatibility), but also compatibility of different degrees and types.[26]

N.N. Obozov defines compatibility as the "effect of combination and interaction between individuals, characterized by maximum subjective satisfaction of partners with each other with a significant (above-average) expenditure of emotions and energy".[27]

According to V.V. Boyko, A.G. Kovalev and V.N. Panferov, compatibility of people presumes an optimal combination of their attributes which ensures the greatest effectiveness of their activity within a group. This covers all personal attributes describing the structure of personality.[28]

Петровского, М.Г. Ярошевского. М.: Политиздат, 1985.

[22] Психология. Словарь. 2-е изд. / Под ред. А.В. Петровского и М.Г. Ярошевского. М.: Политиздат, 1990

[23] Коллектив. Личность. Общение. Словарь социально-психологических понятий / Под ред. Е.С. Кузьмина, В.Е. Семенова. Л.: Лениздат, 1987.

[24] Основы социально-психологической теории / Под общей ред. А.А. Бодалева, А.Н. Сухова. М.: Международная педагогическая академия, 1995.

[25] Ломов Б.Ф. Методологические и теоретические проблемы психологии. М., 1984.

[26] К.К. Платонов. Личность как объект социальной психологии // Методологические проблемы социальной психологии. М.: Наука, 1975.

[27] Н.Н. Обозов. Межличностные отношения. Л.: Изд-во ЛГУ, 1979.

[28] Межгосударственный стандарт. Совместимость технических средств электромагнитная (термины и определения). Минск, 1995

E.S. Kuzmin and V.E. Semenov believe that people can be "considered compatible when they are in a sense, inseparable (indivisible), i.e. one cannot be without the other, autonomous (in the sense of internal self-management). The most significant attribute of wholeness and compatibility on the same level in a hierarchy is the existence of inner unity of the subjects in communication."[29]

N.I. Shevandrin describes as compatible people who are "situationally indivisible in terms of their inner unity and self-management," while the consequences of incompatibility, according to him, are predisposition to conflict, inability to understand each other, lack of synchronization in psychomotor reactions, differences in attention, thinking and other processes.[30]

At the same time, A.A. Leonov and V.I. Lebedev define psychological incompatibility as an "inability to understand each other in critical emergencies, lack of synchronization in psychomotor reactions, differences in attention, thinking and other innate and acquired attributes of a person which hinder or preclude joint activity."[31]

Analysis of labor psychology reveals that compatibility is understood as a result of combining individuals that yields the greatest possible effect under the circumstances with the smallest possible expenditure of energy by interacting members within a group.

"Compatibility can be evaluated by results of work, energy expenditure (based on data on psychophysiological shifts in the process of joint work), subjective satisfaction derived from joint activity. Compatibility creates the basis for mutual sympathies, comfort and unification of psychological and physiological functions."[32]

According to F.D. Gorbov and M.A. Novikov, compatibility can be understood as the mutual match of attributes among members in a group.[33]

Scientists A.N. Sukhov and N.N. Obozov propose looking at compatibility from two perspectives: as a process and as a result of

---

[29] Социальная психология: история, теория, эмпирические исследования / Под ред. Е.С. Кузьмина, В.Е. Семенова. Л.: Изд-во ЛГУ, 1979.

[30] Н.И. Шевандрин. Психодиагностика, коррекция и развитие личности. М.: ВЛАДОС, 1998

[31] А.А. Леонов, В.И. Лебедев. К проблеме психологической совместимости в межпланетном полете // Вопросы философии. 1972. № 9.

[32] Методология исследований по инженерной психологии и психологии труда / Под ред. А.А. Крылова. Л.: ЛГУ, 1974. Ч. 1.

[33] Ф.Д. Горбов, М.А. Новиков. Краткий психологический словарь-хрестоматия. М.: Наука, 1974.

interaction. "Compatibility as a result is the degree of the partners' satisfaction with each other (with their thoughts, feelings and behavior). When we consider compatibility as a process, we isolate the processes of adjustment, "fine-tuning the match" between character, needs, behavioral motives."[34] "An optimal match of personal qualities (temperament, character, needs, interests, values, etc.) of a couple or members of a group is a condition for compatibility as a process. Coordination of behavior, emotional experience and mutual understanding in which the entire personality of interacting people manifests itself is the compatibility process." As a result, "compatibility is the effect of matching and interaction between individuals. Interaction, rather than combination, is a

process that results in compatibility or incompatibility of people."[35]

International scientists, including US psychologists, distinguish between two approaches to interpersonal compatibility: need-based and behavioral. Correspondingly, compatibility is understood mostly as the greatest possible degree of mutual satisfaction of needs and coordination of behavior among members in a group.[36]

All definitions in Russian psychology provided here treat compatibility as group compatibility, interpersonal, psychological compatibility or simply compatibility. It is manifested in the interaction process, in the result of interaction, in a characteristic of a group, as well as the interaction effect and combining effect, and the ability for joint actions, and simply as a phenomenon.

This multifaceted understanding of the nature of compatibility has to do either with the complexity of this phenomenon and the great varieties of approaches to it (for example, when describing a large object, people with perception disorders only notice one part or aspect of the object), or with its multiple different manifestations (the fact that there are separate different types and kinds of compatibility), or substituting other phenomena for compatibility, or confusing compatibility itself with its causes and effects.

To understand what compatibility is, let us select the essential attributes from these definitions and categorize and analyze them. These descriptions can be divided into groups according to understanding compatibility as, primarily: a) a behavioral phenomenon (coordinated actions and behavior,

---

[34] Основы социально-психологической теории / Под общей ред. А.А. Бодалева и А.Н. Сухова. М.: Международная педагогическая академия, 1995.

[35] Н.Н. Обозов. Межличностные отношения. Л.: Изд-во ЛГУ, 1979.

[36] Р.Л. Кричевский. Проблема межличностной совместимости в зарубежной социальной психологии // Вопросы психологии. 1979. № 5.

mutual regulation of behavior, ability to act together, synchronous psychomotor reactions); b) an emotional phenomenon (satisfaction with each other, mutual sympathies, satisfaction with the process and result of interaction); c) a cognitive phenomenon (understanding each other, mutual understanding); d) a systematic phenomenon (the effect of combining individuals, matching, the optimal combination of attributes of group members); e) the degree of how close people are to each other (situational indivisibility, internal unity and integrity).

When people interact, they undoubtedly mutually adjust their behavior, and this is why compatibility may be defined through behavior, although it also goes beyond that.

Compatibility and emotional manifestations? Yes, interactions between people involve emotions, therefore compatibility may be manifested in this way, but it is more than simply emotions. You can better define compatibility as a coordinated set of emotional experiences (not always positive). Satisfaction from relations or interactions frequently coming up in definitions of compatibility is a result, a consequence, of compatibility (people interact first, become compatible later, and satisfaction from this may only come at a subsequent time) and has more to do with the psychological climate than compatibility (compatibility being one of the reasons for a certain psychological climate to emerge).

Compatibility and cognitive manifestations? Indeed, cognitive processes play a role in interactions between people, therefore compatibility can be manifested in that way, but it goes beyond mutual understanding.

Compatibility and combination of attributes in interacting people? Indeed, people with certain attributes (qualities, characteristics) are more compatible than others, but a combination of qualities is a condition (a reason) for compatibility, rather than compatibility itself.

Compatibility and proximity of people in space and time? Indeed, compatible people voluntarily tend to be together and are capable of being together for an extended period of time, creating a certain unity. This understanding of compatibility is the closest to the truth and is a phenomenological, rather than structural definition, because it describes external attributes of compatibility rather than its essence.

Therefore, the compatibility phenomenon is definitely identified as having three aspects typical of many psychological processes: behavioral, emotional, and cognitive. This structure of three components is quite useful for describing and explaining relations, including the phenomenon of internal compatibility.

Drawing conclusions, we can say, with some degree of certainty, that:

1) Compatibility is the result of relationships;

2) Compatibility is manifested externally in the desire and ability to interact with each other voluntarily for an extended time;

3) Internal compatibility is the coordination of behavior and mutual influences, but it also goes beyond that;

4) Internal compatibility is the coordination of emotions, relationships and interactions, but it also goes beyond that;

5) Internal compatibility goes hand-in-hand with mutual cognition and mutual understanding, but it also goes beyond that;

6) Its origin lies in a certain combination of people's qualities;

7) Compatibility leads to other psychological phenomena (love, friendship, unity and loyalty to a cause, psychological climate, and others).

These differences in descriptions and definitions of compatibility as a phenomenon are a result of confusion of different types of compatibility. We propose identifying two types of compatibility based on the size of the group within which interactions between people are taking place:

1) Group compatibility — the result of interactions within a group of three or more people and 2) Interpersonal compatibility — the result of interactions between two people. Group compatibility arises from a combination of interactions between a number of pairs of people, but is different from those interactions.

When we talk about the phenomenon of compatibility in several branches of psychology (social psychology and psychology of labor), it is frequently confused with the phenomenon of well-adjusted teamwork or the process of developing it. Well-adjusted teamwork is seen as more significant than compatibility in a workfloor setting.[37] We are providing definitions of well-adjusted teamwork to achieve a more complete analysis of the correspondence between these two concepts.

Dictionaries generally define well-adjusted teamwork as a "metric of interpersonal coordination in the context of a specific common activity," which is characterized by high productivity and adequate subjective satisfaction by the process and result of working together[38]; as a "result of interaction among people characterized by the greatest achievable success

---

[37] Основы социально-психологической теории / Под общ. ред. А.А. Бодалева, А.Н. Сухова. М.: Международная педагогическая академия, 1995.

[38] Краткий психологический словарь / Сост. Л.А.Карпенко; под общ. ред. А.В. Петровского, М.Г. Ярошевского. М.: Политиздат, 1985.

of joint activity with a small expenditure of emotions and energy."[39] According to N.N. Obozov, well-adjusted teamwork is "the effect of combining individuals and their subsequent interactions characterized by the highest productivity possible (in their joint work) with the smallest possible expenditure of emotions and energy (on the main activity and interaction) in the context of adequate (close to average) subjective satisfaction. Success is the main component of well-adjusted teamwork."[40]

Therefore, well-adjusted teamwork, just like compatibility, is a result of human interaction; but, unlike compatibility, well-adjusted teamwork targets workplace objectives, productivity (success in the workplace), minimization of energy expenditure, coordination or working tempo and building work skills.[41]

While evaluating the optimal combination of qualities (characteristics, features, aspects) of those involved in communication and interaction as conditions and reasons for compatibility, psychology sources most frequently refer to two laws. First, many authors believe that compatibility is determined by symmetry (a similarity) of qualities in people. However (second), compatibility does not necessarily imply a similarity or full identity of some properties (qualities); it is still achievable when people's properties (qualities)

are quite different, among other things, through compensation of lacking or weak qualities in one person by another. This also brings up the idea that compatibility may be determined by interacting people having complementary qualities and skills.

Just as defining compatibility presents a problem, its criteria are also rather poorly defined, because the fuzziness of the concept of compatibility makes it hard to pick compatibility indicators (criteria). Satisfaction with the result and process of interaction is widely seen as a key criterion of compatibility. Other aspects are named as compatibility criteria: satisfaction with interpersonal relations, satisfaction with a joint activity, effectiveness and efficiency of a joint activity, effectiveness and efficiency of a group activity; effectiveness and efficiency of interaction, high cohesion of a group, a group's stability over time, low proclivity for conflict, high level of

---

[39] Коллектив. Личность. Общение. Словарь социально-психологических понятий / Под ред. Е.С.Кузьмина, В.Е.Семенова. Л.: Лениздат, 1987.

[40] Н.Н. Обозов. Межличностные отношения. Л.: Изд-во ЛГУ, 1979.

[41] Социальная психология: история, теория, эмпирические исследования / Под ред. Е.С. Кузьмина, В.Е. Семенова. Л.: Изд-во ЛГУ, 1979; Шевандрин Н.И. Психодиагностика, коррекция и развитие личности. М.: ВЛАДОС, 1998.

mutual understanding between people, the degree of role coordination, similarity of character and personal features, choice of partner for communication, positive inter-personal emotions, etc[42]. However, none of these compatibility criteria is either well grounded or universal[43].

The criterion of satisfaction with an interaction is subjective and context-dependent (compatibility is a long-term phenomenon, while the level of satisfaction may fluctuate rapidly over time) and is probably more of a consequence of compatibility, characterizing the sociopsychological climate in a group of people rather than compatibility[44]. Satisfaction with interactions and relations is also a criterion of both well-adjusted teamwork and friendliness, as well as group cohesion (just like emotional appeal)[45]. Nor is low proclivity to conflict a very precise criterion of compatibility, because it can be the product of well-adjusted teamwork and even indifference, and is more of an aspect of the prevailing psychological climate. Stated criteria like effectiveness and efficiency of interaction (or joint, group activity) are also criteria of well-adjusted teamwork. Group cohesion is a separate psychological phenomenon and can be a consequence of compatibility as well as other factors. The choice of partner for communication can be a criterion of compatibility in the context of the theory of interpersonal appeal if free choice of partners is available, but there can be other reasons for selection. Stability of a group over time is determined not only by compatibility, but also by the pressures of society, external socioeconomic and intra-group factors.

Any criteria of compatibility in relations between people are vulnerable to criticism and are more of a consequence of compatibility of separate psychological phenomena overlapping the concept of compatibility.

We propose categorizing the criteria based on which interaction component they reflect. Therefore, all compatibility criteria can be divided into three groups: 1) Behavioral (choice of partner for communication and relationships, efficiency of interaction, low proclivity to conflict, coordination or role behavior, etc.), 2) Emotional (satisfaction with the

---

[42] Н.Н. Обозов. Межличностные отношения. Л.: Изд-во ЛГУ, 1979; Психология: Словарь. 2-е изд. / Под ред. А.В. Петровского, М.Г. Ярошевского. М.: Политиздат, 1990.
[43] Н.Н. Обозов. Обозова А.Н. Три подхода к исследованию психологической совместимости // Вопросы психологии. 1981. № 6.
[44] Социальная психология: история, теория, эмпирические исследования / Под ред. Е.С. Кузьмина, В.Е. Семенова. Л.: Изд-во ЛГУ, 1979
[45] Ibid.

interaction result and process, interpersonal relations, positive interpersonal feelings, etc.) and 3) Cognitive (high level of mutual understanding, positive perceptions of interaction, etc.). Besides, emotional and behavioral criteria will be mostly situational and context-based, while emotional and cognitive criteria will be primarily subjective. In this light, behavioral and cognitive criteria are more objective. The choice of a criterion is determined by the researcher's preferences, as well as by parameters of relations and specific details of methods used.

The criteria will be distinct and different from one another: for each type of compatibility, for every approach to compatibility, for every variety of compatibility. Thus, two realms – inanimate (technology) and animate (relations between human beings) – have been used to systematize and order significant attributes of compatibility; definitions were given, and a typology of compatibility has been proposed on this basis. This study deals with compatibility as a whole and as an individual type of compatibility – the result of multi-level relations. We have partially analyzed compatibility criteria and made the assumption that they are defined by participants in the interaction and would be distinct and different for every approach to, type and variety of compatibility.

Later on, we will consider compatibility as an ability of coordinated interaction and long-term voluntary mutual development defined by an optimal combination of complementary properties. Coordination is understood as lack of contradictions, matching expectations with people's (and technological) actions.

Chapter 2

STUDY OF COMPATIBILITY

2.1. Approaches to the Study of Compatibility

Compatibility has been studied from theoretical and practical angles in the realm of the animate – human society. Extensive historical experience enables us to look at key approaches to the study of compatibility in modern psychology in greater detail at the beginning of this section. Three approaches are currently the most common:

1) Structural — oriented towards achieving an optimal combination of various parameters and qualities of partners at different stages (in different types) of interaction;

2) Adaptive — oriented towards improving communication processes within groups and refining interpersonal relations;

3) Functional — oriented towards the study of group dynamics, functions, goals and objectives.[46]

The structural approach aims at searching for optimal combinations, matching features in people who are partners in cooperation, with each individual viewed as a stable combination of certain properties. The

---

[46] Обозов Н.Н., Обозова А.Н. Три подхода к исследованию психологической совместимости // Вопросы психологии. 1981. № 6. P. 98–101.

attributes of such partners have to be either symmetrical or complementary, depending on the level (type) of compatibility being studied.

The methodology of the structural approach makes it possible to identify and describe certain relatively independent levels (layers, strata, types, etc.), at which people interact.

The number of these levels fluctuates between two and five according to different authors, for example:

1) Psycho-physiological: a certain similarity in psycho-physiological aspects of individuals that provides a basis of consistency in their emotional and behavioral response;

2) Sociopsychological: an optimal combination of behavioral types within a group, people with common social standards and values, interests and needs.[47]

A.A. Bodalev and others, including Yu.A. Kolomeitsev[48] and A.V. Petrovsky[49] identify three levels of compatibility:

1) Personally (individually) psychological;

2) Sociopsychological;

3) Sociocultural.[50]

N.N. Obozov and A.N. Obozova, Yu.N. Oleinik,[51] K.K. Platonov[52] and N.I. Shevandrin[53] identify four compatibility levels:

1) Psycho-physiological: level of interactions between temperament features and needs;

2) Psychological: level of interactions between behavior characters, motives and stereotypes;

3) Sociopsychological: level of coordinating functional (role-based) expectations and actions;

---

[47] Основы социально-психологической теории / Под общ. ред. А.А. Бодалева, А.Н. Сухова. М.: Международная педагогическая академия, 1995.

[48] Ю.А. Коломейцев Взаимоотношение в спортивной команде. М.: Физкультура и спорт, 1984.

[49] А.В. Петровский Возникновение и сущность стратометрического подхода к психологии коллектива // Психологическая теория коллектива. М.: Педагогика, 1979.

[50] Основы социально-психологической теории / Под общ. ред. А.А. Бодалева, А.Н. Сухова. М.: Международная педагогическая академия, 1995.

[51] Ю.Н. Олейник Исследование уровней совместимости в молодой семье // Психологический журнал. 1986. Т. 7. № 2. Р. 59–67.

[52] К.К. Платонов Общие проблемы теории групп и коллективов // Коллектив и личность. М.: Наука, 1975. Р. 6–11.

[53] Н.И. Шевандрин Психодиагностика, коррекция и развитие личности. М.: ВЛАДОС, 1998.

4)   Sociological: level of matching or similar interests and values.

I.V. Grebennikov, unlike the previous authors, identifies five types of (marital) compatibility:

1)   Social (as represented by commonality of worldviews. Values, ideals, interests);

2)   Spiritual (spiritual direction, ideas of life);

3)   Psychological (interaction between characters, temperaments, and personal attributes and attributes of the will of the married couple);

4)   Sexual (including psychological as well as biophysical components, affecting interactions and mutual attitudes of a husband and wife, as well as other compatibility types);

5)   Family and household-based (identity of ideas and views of the meaning and style of family life, roles and responsibilities within the family).[54]

When we use the term "level" in this book, we are referring primarily to the quantitative degree of compatibility. The term "type" is used to mean the content, the nature of a certain variety of compatibility and its difference from other compatibility types. Thus, compatibility at a certain level may comprise different types of compatibility (for example, psycho-physiological compatibility when seen at a certain level of compatibility, may comprise qualitatively different compatibility types such as compatibility of needs, temperaments, sensorimotor responses and other types of compatibility). This is why we propose focusing on distinctive qualities of compatibility types.

Some of the compatibility types discussed in the available literature, for example, psycho-physiological and spiritual compatibility, are conceivably real enough, but lie on the frontier between psychology and other fields of scientific inquiry (psycho-physiological compatibility also pertains to the realm of biology and physiology, while spiritual compatibility is also a subject of sociology and philosophy), and their study requires an inter-disciplinary angle as well.

We can identify relatively independent and distinct compatibility sub-types. For example, For example, compatibility of needs, temperaments, and sensorimotor responses can be identified within psycho-physiological compatibility, while compatibility of roles and social needs lies within the

---

[54] И.В. Гребенников Основы семейной жизни. М.: Просвещение, 1991.

broader socio-psychological compatibility. Isolating sub-types can be something of a challenge in other types of compatibility (for example, in psychological compatibility).

The structural approach has both its downsides (it makes no distinction in significance of features identified, ignoring the principle of integrity of the personality)[55] and benefits: the ability to make a clear distinction by compatibility levels and types.

The adaptive approach is fairly common and is geared more towards practical applications. It explores the results of compatibility, i.e. positive interpersonal relationships, effective communication and other phenomena, rather than compatibility in its own right. The analysis focuses more on individuals rather than groups. The adaptive approach has the purpose of improving communication processes and interpersonal relationships. The level of partners' compatibility will increase based on their personal development and changes in their interpersonal communication skills.

The adaptive approach to compatibility is based on concepts of a group or relationships between people as a system in flux, going through natural development crises that make participants in the relationships incapable of resolving new problems in the old ways (which creates the need for adaptability).

S.I. Golod's[56] concept is a prominent example of the adaptive approach, with interactions between spouses (which are measured by stability of their marriage) relying on the spouses' adaptability, which depends on factors such as intimacy (liking, fondness and erotic attachment of the spouses) and autonomy (independence of spouses relative to each other that presumes that they have needs and pursue types of communication outside of their relationship as a couple). S.I. Golod identifies seven adaptability niches: spiritual, psychological, sexual, information, familial, cultural, and one steeped in everyday life. These niches are hierarchical, with changes decided by the stages in family development.

J.Å. Stets and P.J. Burke explored processes of human adaptation to the environment. Their research focused on the mechanism whereby an individual strives to control the environment in his or her interactions with it. The researchers made the underlying assumption that controlling urges

---

[55] Н.Н. Обозов, А.Н. Обозова Три подхода к исследованию психологической совместимости // Вопросы психологии. 1981. № 6. P. 98–101.

[56] С.И. Голод Стабильность семьи: социологический и демографический ас- пекты / Под ред. Г.М. Романенковой. Л.: Наука, 1984.

directed towards others come back to the originator of these urges in a modified form. The researchers studied young married couples to identify the effect of controlling urges on the partner's behavior as well as the individual's own.[57]

D. Olson's concept presumes two relatively independent metrics to "gauge" relationships within a family: a) the ability to present a common front as a manifestation of emotional attachment between family members (which can be measured by engagement, emotional commitment, and family boundaries); b) adaptivity as a manifestation of the ability of a married couple or a family to change its internal structure and roles in response to changes in their environment (defined by specifics of leadership, decision-making, nature or roles and rules within the family). Empirical research indicates that as unity and adaptivity approach extreme values on their respective scales, the relationship in the family begins to crumble.[58]

The adaptive approach is better suited for analyzing interactions within small groups of three people or more than in couples, as it implies a study of group dynamics over time (through longitudinal research, among other things).

The functional approach is geared towards social psychology and group dynamics. It treats a small contact group as a union created with the purpose of dispensing certain functions. Group members are correspondingly seen as representing specific functions (or roles in social psychology). The degree to which the different roles are aligned is the measure of compatibility. The exploration completely ignores exactly which properties of an individual are responsible for the assumption and acceptance of certain roles by the individual. The functional approach presumes the exploration of functions, goals and objectives of a group.[59]

The functional approach is currently rarely used in psychology and is more frequently used to analyze interactions within small groups of three or more people.

Out of all the theoretical approaches that we have looked at in modern psychology, we see the structural approach as the most suitable, as it allows

---

[57] Stets, J.E., Burke, P.J. Inconsistent Self-Views in the Control Identity Model // Social Science Research. 1994. P. 236–262.

[58] Основы социально-психологической теории / Под общ. ред. А.А. Бодале ва, А.Н. Сухова. М.: Международная педагогическая академия, 1995.

[59] Н.Н. Обозов, А.Н. Обозова Три подхода к исследованию психологической совместимости // Вопросы психологии. 1981. № 6. P. 98–101.

the researcher to identify and explore specific compatibility types differentiated by quality. The structural approach also makes it possible not only to identify the relevant factors (i.e. individuals' properties and other qualities affecting compatibility), but also to evaluate their significance, finding their optimal combinations (symmetrical or complementary). At the same time, this approach makes it possible to build a more rigorous structure for empirical research.

An integrative systemic approach is used to explore technological compatibility based on the concept of a system understood as a combination of elements interlinked in certain way.[60] The unique nature of a system is manifested through its structure and operation over time, which tend to go hand in hand: when a system has a complex structure, this usually implies complexity of its operation as well. Therefore, one can describe the complexity of a system by the variety of its reactions (operations) to external stimuli.

The theory of technological compatibility relies on three categories to describe systems (just as modern psychology does): structure, function and process (adaptation). One apparently has to address every one of these categories to provide a systematic description of technological compatibility, of which every one features its own set of parameters and values defining its level of content and interactions with other categories. This can be done using the premises set out by V.I. Ivanov and V.V. Cheshev[61] if viewed in conjunction with technological compatibility.

Every system can be described in three different ways: 1) from a natural-science perspective; 2) in terms of function and technology; and 3) in terms of its structure and morphology. The first way would ultimately result in identifying a set of physical variables (from the realm of natural science) and associations between them. Since a range of natural characteristics is a set $E = \{E_1, E_2, ..., E_n\}$, the mathematical description of a system is a set of variables linking its physical (natural) parameters:

---

[60] В.И. Иванов, В.В. Чешев Становление и развитие технических наук. Л.: Наука, 1977; Ф.И. Перегудов, Ф.П. Тарасенко Основы системного анализа. Томск: Изд-во НТЛ, 1997; Системный анализ: Проектирование, оптимизация и приложения / А.Н. Антамошкин, М.А. Воловик, А. Торн и др.; Под общ. ред. А.Н. Антамошкина; Сибир. отд-ние междунар. инженер. акад.; САА. Красноярск, 1966; В.Н. Спицнадель Основы системного анализа. СПб.: Бизнес-пресса, 2000.
[61] В.И. Иванов, В.В. Чешев Становление и развитие технических наук. Л.: Наука, 1977.

$$\int_i \left(E_1, E_{2,} ..., E_n \right) = 0, i = 1, ..., n \qquad (2.1.1)$$

These equations directly describe the process rather than the structure. They only offer an ambiguous and indirect reflection of the structural details. Morphologically different structures can result in the same process format. The first type of description is relevant for research on the topic of this book because the nature of technological compatibility is usually physical.

Functional features of systems are reflected in the second way of describing them, which comes with its own set of features. A system's function is put into effect through its definite action on other systems, and, conversely, a functional and technical description can be recorded as a set Y = {Y_1, Y_2, ..., Y_m } of its descriptor variables and a series m of equations linking these variable together:

$$\varphi_j \left(Y_1, Y_{2,} ..., Y_m \right) = 0, j = 1, ..., m \qquad (2.1.2)$$

Although the first and second descriptions are similar on the surface, the difference between them in principle is that while the first way reveals the content of a physical process irrespective of the system's operation, the second way has its main purpose in reflecting the process of the system's operation. Consequently, a functional and technical description is closely linked to functional technical compatibility, but should also take the noise component into account.

The third way to describe a system focuses on formulating a set of constructive (morphological) parameters K = {K_1, K_2, ..., K_p }, which serves as the foundation for a structural / morphological description. This description uses technical terms and a natural language. The technical terms denote specific elements and morphological links between them. Each technical theory gives its core subject a special idealized image. The subject's morphological links have to be introduced by relatively precise numerical morphological characteristics of properties inherent in the subject and specific to it: the physical property of its constituent material, its geometric shape and its three-dimensional features, the properties of its surface, details of placement of its components relative to each other, its electrotechnical properties, features of physical fields, etc. This is why the structural / morphological description lies at the core of many types of technological compatibility and at the core of the theory of technological compatibility as a whole.

The third way to describe $M(S)$ has no generalized mathematical representation in equation form, unlike the first (2.1.1) and second (2.1.2) ways, and can only be written down in mathematical terms as:

$$M(S) = M(K, J, R, B), \qquad (2.1.3)$$

where K stands for a set of constructive parameters $K = \{K_1, K_2, ..., K_p\}$, J represents a set of terms $J = \{J_1, J_2, ..., J_l\}$, R is the set of links $R = \{R_1, R_2, ..., R_k\}$, B represents a set of verbal interpretations $B = \{B_1, B_2, ..., B_r\}$.

The links connecting the three descriptions of a system set out above are also of interest.

Let us look at the links between the natural-science and functional / technical descriptions in sequence by their constituent variables.

This means in mathematical terms that we need to derive equations that tie together the natural (physical) variable E and technical variables J, from natural-science and functional/technical descriptions respectively:

$$\psi_\nu(E, J) = 0, \nu = 1, ..., k \qquad (2.1.4)$$

We can derive these links by plugging in J variables into equations used to describe natural processes. This is possible because each technical variable has a physical meaning and value, and is therefore no different from the variables in the new description. When establishing the connection between the first and the third descriptions, we take into account that the morphological structure represents the details of the natural process, while the general formats of cause-and-effect connection between physical variables and properties, size and other characteristics are established within the realm of natural science, and take on specific manifestations when a system is described in this way.

We can represent all equations linking together the constituent variables as

$$V_V(E, K) = 0, \qquad (2.1.5)$$

where $\qquad v = 1, ..., l,$

and the inter-dependent connection between the second and the third descriptions as the equation

$$И_v(J, K) = 0, \qquad (2.1.6)$$

where $g = 1, …, q$.

Equation (2.1.6) connects technical features of a system under exploration as a whole with parameters of its constituent components.

The objective here is to make sure that all parameters in Equations (2.1.1) – (2.1.6) are compatible in any system:

$$C_p(E, J, K) = 0, \qquad (2.1.7)$$

where $p = 1, …, l$.

Ultimately, the overall description of a system is

$$D_\gamma \big[C_p(E, J, K) \big] = 0, \qquad (2.1.8)$$

where $\gamma = 1, …, u$.

The conditional, even abstract nature of equations (2.1.1) — (2.1.8) makes it possible not only to give a more rigorous format to the descriptions above than would have been possible with purely verbal descriptions, but also provide a graphic way to represent the communicative and associative power and other links of a system (in the context of its compatibility).

The adaptive approach described above in the context of the physical process (and briefly described as part of the systemic approach) is the primary way to study compatibility in technology (just as it is in psychology); it also focuses on improving the interaction between materials, units and subassemblies in technology.

The methodology and specific schemes and solutions of adaptation of modern technology is covered very well in Russian and international research literature.[62] These books consider the possibility and role of

---

[62] Апорович А.Ф. Проектирование радиотехнических систем: Учеб. пособие. Минск: Высш. шк., 1988; Вальков В.М., Вершин В.Е. Автоматизированные системы управления технологическими процессами. Л.: Политехника, 1992; Гиттис Э.И., Данилович Г.А., Самойленко В.Н. Техническая киберне- тика. М.: Сов. радио, 1969; Дружинин В.В., Еонторов Д.С. Проблемы сис- темологии (проблемы теории сложных систем). М.: Сов. радио, 1976; Костецкий Б.И. Фундаментальная

technology adaptation, among other things, to optimize the objects of their research; however, the link between adaptation and compatibility of technology remains an open question. Since the proof for the hypothesis that adaptation is an effective way to ensure and improve technological compatibility lies in the semantics of the adaptivity concept defined as adjustment, modification for the purpose of preservation, improvement, or acquisition of new properties for available technology under changing conditions. Adaptivity comes into play when a system has a certain mechanism for changing its parameters, a strategy of operation or a control structure based on information obtained during operation of the system, i.e. during its interactions with other systems and/or the environment. Effective adaptation hinges primarily on the system's capability for automatic adaptation and its focus on improvement (and ultimately on optimization) of the operation process. This is where adaptation is linked to functional technological compatibility.

B.I. Kostetsky's research[63] looks at stabilization of the wear process described as structural adaptation of materials to friction. It is associated with the natural and fully expected change of structure and properties of the outer layers of material in a manner that is energy-efficient under the circumstances, resulting in a stable dynamic state of the material in terms of its reduction to wear and friction.

However, cyberneticists, to pick one area of expertise, who would tend to associate the idea of self-organization with artificial intelligence, would object to physicists that a simple phenomenon of this kind is categorized as the highest class of adaptation.

This phenomenon is an important condition for ensuring compatibility of wear surfaces and is certainly a matter of great interest for engineering and for experts involved in operating a fleet of machine tools, vehicles or other equipment.

Adaptation of electronics devices and systems has been the subject of

---

закономерность самоорганизации технических трибосистем: Докл. Академии наук УССР // Физико-математические науки. Сер. А. 1989. № 4; Лапко А.В. Непараметрические методы классификации и их применение. Новосибирск: ВО «Наука». Сибирская изд. фирма, 1993; Семенкин Е.С., Семенкина О.Е., Коробейников С.П. Адаптивные поисковые методы оптимизации сложных систем/СиБУП. Красноярск, 1996; Флейшман Б.С. Элементы теории потенциальной эффектив- ности сложных систем. М.: Сов. радио, 1971.

[63] Костецкий Б.И. Фундаментальная закономерность самоорганизации тех- нических трибосистем: докл. Академии наук УССР // Физико-математические науки. Сер. А. 1989. № 4.

extensive research.[64] This field of inquiry has yielded a classification of adaptation types: by location of devices and systems being adapted (adaptation at the receiving or transmitting end and adaptation of entire systems), adaptation by incoming signal, by range, by reliability of reception, adaptation when changing modes of operation, as compensation for or a way to eliminate radio interference.[65]

And yet, the largest amount of research literature on adaptation of technology has been written about the realm of cybernetics technology.[66] The body of research in this field is extensive and deals with many different aspects of the subject. Methods of the theory of malfunction identification are among the most advanced. Identification of malfunctions as a diagnostic task is essentially identification of the state of an object (observing the state of an object) and categorization of it as one of the predetermined types of technical condition (categorizing the state of an object).

Researchers use physical or mathematical modeling (simulation) of different types of malfunctions. For this purpose, individual defects (malfunctions) are introduced into each part (assembly) of a system (and object) which is known to be in good working order, the values of each control output signal y_i are measured and recorded as input signals are fed into the system to imitate outside perturbations.

As we analyze identification of adaptation elements in malfunction identification systems, we observe them in two different manifestations: first, their suitability for better performance in achieving their objectives; and second, their learning capability as yet another manifestation of

---

[64] Апорович А.Ф. Проектирование радиотехнических систем: Учеб. пособие. Минск: Высш. шк., 1988; Гуткин Л.С. Проектирование радиосистем и радиоустройств. М.: Радио и связь, 1986.

[65] Апорович А.Ф. Проектирование радиотехнических систем: Учеб. пособие Минск: Высш. шк., 1988.

[66] Гиттис Э.И., Данилович Г.А., Самойленко В.Н. Техническая кибернетика. М.: Сов. радио, 1969; Горелик А.Л., Скрипкин В.А. Построение систем распознания. М.: Сов. радио, 1974; Дмитриев А.К. Распознание отказов в сис- темах электроавтоматики. Л.: Энергоатомиздат, 1983; Дружинин В.В., Еонторов Д.С. Проблемы системологии (проблемы теории сложных сис- тем). М.: Сов. радио, 1976; Лапко А.В. Непараметрические методы класси- фикации и их применение. Новосибирск: ВО «Наука». Сибирская изд. фирма, 1993; Медведев А.В. Элементы теории параметрических систем управления // Актуальные проблемы информатики, прикладной матема- тики и механики. Ч. 3. Информатика: Сб. научн. тр. / Отв. ред. В.В. Шайдуров; СО РАН. Новосибирск-Красноярск, 1996. С. 87–111; Семенкин Е.С., Семенкина О.Е., Коробейников С.П. Адаптивные поисковые методы оптимизации сложных систем. Красноярск, 1996.

adaptability in a malfunction identification system; and also in both manifestations at the same time, as their functional compatibility increases.

As in psychology and technology, compatibility is explored in medicine using combinations (a structural approach), i.e. simultaneous administration of two or more treatment factors. The synergistic effect of heat and electrical current (galvanics) in a four-chamber galvanic bath and galvanic mud baths is just one of many examples of such a combination. However, combinations of two powerful stimuli should be only used in moderate dosages, commensurate with the patient's condition and endurance. Inductive heat electrophoresis is an example of galvanic treatment relying on more than two simultaneous factors.

For example, simultaneous use of induction, heat, and electrophoresis to administer Ethonium on the chest is indicated for patients suffering from chronic bronchitis at the mildly acute stage or during a partial remission.[67]

At the same time, many physical and balneological treatments cause a significant long-term reaction in a patient. Therefore, administering several treatments with a powerful effect on the same day is usually inadvisable. A cumulative effect of multiple powerful additive stimuli can result in various functional disruptions in the nervous, cardiovascular and other essential systems within the human body, which makes them incompatible for simultaneous (combined) administration.

An adaptive approach is also used in medicine. For example, a flare up of a localized reaction can become especially strong when several factors are combined, some producing a primarily local and others a primarily general effect. It is an established fact that a local response can be augmented if a general procedure (a bath, a shower, etc.) follows a local treatment. However, physicians should work on a case-by-case basis, assigning doses corresponding to the condition of each patient after alternating treatments have been administered.[68]

For example, massage therapy when combined with exercise and physical treatment can be administered either before or after an exercise session, and can be administered in conjunction with all types of physical treatments except for ultraviolet treatments in erythema dosages applied to the same area of the body. However, it usually makes better sense to

---

[67] А.А. Шатров, С.Я. Троценко, Б.А. Соколов Методические рекомендации методов лечения НИИ им. Сеченова. Ялта, 1986.
[68] Ibid.

prescribe massage therapy on every other day, alternating it with hydrotherapy, ultrasound, medicinal electrophoresis and other electrophysical and light treatments. When assigning massage therapy and medicinal electrophoresis on the same area of the body on the same day, the physician should take into consideration that massage administered before electrophysical treatment would increase electrical conductivity of body tissues and promotes deposits within the skin of drugs administered by direct current. Administering massage after medicinal electrophoresis would tend to retard the accumulation of such deposits, but would speed up delivery of drugs to internal organs.

The adaptive approach is closely intertwined with functional in the study of compatibility in medicine, because the focus here is also on the study of group dynamics, and the degree of match of each procedure is closely linked to the patient's condition (state of health). This explains restrictions on the multifunctional treatment of patients depending on the compatibility or incompatibility of such treatments, for example:

- dosages of physical and balneological treatments (medicinal electrophoresis, magnetic therapy, laser irradiation, heat treatments, acupuncture, medicinal inhalations, etc.);
- relative shares of exercise, climatic and physical treatments in a treatment plan;
- gradation and dosages of treatment factors and drugs, etc.

2.2. Some Patterns of Compatibility

Seven specific patterns of technological compatibility have been established and manifest themselves in the process of perfecting modern technology.[69] Every new generation of a product with the same function is known to emerge as a result of implementing more advanced versions and types of compatibility. The following three aspects are of especial interest:

1) the material and moral essence of the new, and the way it can be accomplished;

2) the overall effect of the new on the world outlook, its new properties;

3) economic and social expedience of practical implementation of the new.

---

[69] ГОСТ 21-03. ЕСКД. Стадии разработки. М.: Изд-во стандартов, 1977.

The first pattern is a transition from a less advanced to a more advanced version of a direct cause-and-effect link.

The physical essence of the new in technology may lie in a change of distance between interacting systems or devices, in use of increasingly interference-proof components and increasingly more efficient lubricants on components producing friction; the introduction of more forgiving modes of operation for the product, designing the product based on a new physical principle.[70]

In other areas of science, this is a change in the state of inter-related (interacting) objects without a deterioration of this state, but resulting instead in the mutual improvement of the objects through a reduction in tensions, disagreements, and the development of a potential/dynamic perspective of joint operation or interaction.

In various fields of technology resulting from human activity, the effect of the new leads to higher power output, speed, productivity, an increase in the resource, etc. The economic sense of implementation of a new design or development is evaluated by:

$$\sum_{i=1}^{m} Э_i \succ \sum_{i=1}^{m} E_i \qquad (2.2.1)$$

where $Э_i$ is the benefit (incremental additional revenue) of the ith innovation; and E_i is the cost of the ith innovation.

The second pattern has to do with the transition from direct to indirect compatibility. Indirect compatibility is manifested indirectly, through an intervening medium, including peer relationship between objects (subjects), or within a class of objects (subjects), intersecting relationships overlaid in certain situations (positions), and a subordinate relationship, when an object lies completely within another object, but the other object's content is not limited to the first object (the relationship of genus $\geq$ species $\geq$ individual).

For example, the essence of something new in technology may have to do with installing intermediary devices, e.g. to introduce units sensitive to interference, to change the structure of the assembly (the system), to switch to a new principle of operation, and to achieve greater economic efficiency.

---

[70] Носенков А.А. Техническая совместимость: практика, наука, проблемы. Красноярск, 2005.

The third pattern is a transition from indirect to direct compatibility (when the intervening medium has outlived its usefulness and two objects have become fully compatible without it). In this case, the new essentially has to do with the elimination of the intermediary device because a better design has been achieved, the structure has been modified to reduce weight, size, or to improve other parameters to achieve a higher economic efficiency.

The fourth pattern has to do with the transition from less to more advanced modes of mediated compatibility. In technology, this applies primarily to the use of more advanced materials and components in transitional / intermediary devices, making it possible to achieve a higher quality level, a better (e.g. more ergonomic) layout, enabling, for example, the use of other devices and units of the product, etc.

The above has a similar meaning in other fields of science, but when talking about human interactions, we may have to go back to classic, fundamental principles: the pillars of human interaction.

The content of the first four patterns represents the full range of possible transitions from direct to indirect (mediated) compatibility and vice versa. The next three patterns – the fifth, the sixth and the seventh – represent the full range of possible changes in the amount (level) of specific compatibility types.

The fifth pattern represents a transition to fewer different compatibility types: e.g. designing a new product based on a new principle of operation and relying on fewer physical and technological effects, resulting in less variety of technological compatibility.

The technological effect of the new can be extremely diverse. Economic efficiency is defined by the following:

$$\left.\begin{array}{l} \sum_{j=1}^{l} Э_{j}^{[н]} \geq \sum_{i=1}^{k} Э_{i}^{[n]} \\[2em] \sum_{j=1}^{l} E_{j}^{[н]} \leq \sum_{i=1}^{k} E_{i}^{[n]} \end{array}\right\}$$

(2.2.2)

where $Э_{j}^{[n]}$, $Э_{i}^{[n]}$ are effects (benefits, or incremental revenue) of the new and the old product, respectively; and $E_j^{[n]}$, $E_i^{[n]}$ are the unit costs of the new and the old product, respectively.

The formulae (2.2.2) must hold true for any commercial product, because they guarantee economic well-being of both producers and users of these products. Products manufactured for government use may be still acceptable at suboptimal values (2.2.2), because the government may have to have certain facilities or products no matter what, for example, it would have to have current defense technology at any cost.

The sixth pattern deals with transition to an expanded range of different compatibility types when the material and moral essence of something new (a product, a material, a service, a management solution or approach, etc.) is based on a new principle involving a greater number of compatibility functions than the operating principles of a previous version of the product, service, or solution necessitated, which entails a greater variety of compatibility types. The overall effect can be very diverse. The economic and social value of the sixth pattern is similar to that of pattern five.

The seventh and final pattern represents a change in compatibility types while the amount (level) of compatibility remains the same, i.e. when the material and spiritual essence of the new is based on a new principle of operation which comprises the same number of functions as the underlying principle of the old solution, with some aspects of the compatibility type becoming different. The effect can vary. The economic and social value is similar to that of the fifth and sixth patterns. We note that is is absolutely impossible in principle to replace absolutely all the compatibility types. For example, compatibility of structural design as a type of technological compatibility has to be present in any technological device, and only its level of quality may vary.

Compatibility in different spheres of our life tends to deteriorate, age, and degrade in other ways, despite the most advanced methods of preventing this and ensuring continued compatibilty; these processes being an inevitable corollary of human evolution.

Many scientists see loss of material compatibility of products and commodities as a random event subject to the laws of probability, just like any other random process, which are thoroughly explored by the probability theory. These laws are widely used by applied science and technology, and their approaches and methods are applicable to the theory of technological compatibility as well. This cross-applicability works first and foremost for books and papers on reliability theory, among which A.S. Pronikov's[71] work stands out especially for the purposes of this study. Several postulations of Pronikov's book, for example, the analytical graphic model of buildup towards gradual breakdowns, can be used for interpretation of the compatibility loss process.

What are the rules of probability distribution for loss of compatibility $Q(C)$? Some elements of the reliability theory would apply here as well. A standard probability distribution would be adequate to describe the processes of compatibility loss through wear and tear and obsolescence, i.e. processes leading to gradual destruction (loss) of compatibility. Weibull-Gedenko distribution, gamma distribution or Rayleigh distribution would be suitable for a study of these processes. Exponential probability distribution would be suitable for describing a sudden loss of compatibility.

For example, A.A. Nosenkov calls the law of compatibility loss that applies to all technology "a monism law,"[72] which states that the reason of any malfunction of any machine lies in the loss of compatibility by one of its components. A manifestation of this monism can be described in both physical and mathematical terms. We can write down the probability of compatibility loss by two components of a machine (k^{th} and r^{th} components) at the same time, assuming that compatibility loss by any one component is an independent event, as:

$$Q(C_k, C_r) = Q(C_k) \times Q(C_r), \qquad (2.2.3)$$

where $Q(C_k)$, $Q(C_r)$ are the probabilities of loss of compatibility by k^{th} and r^{th} components respectively.

The probability of complete loss of component compatibility (malfunction) in machines (systems) of the new type lies within $Q(C_i) = (1 \times 10^{-6}) \div (1 \times 10^{-4}), i = 1 \div N$, where N is the number of components in a product.

In this connection, the probability of (2.2.3) is very small and can be safely ignored.

To explore compatibility processes and make any associated forecasts it is essential to build models of different kinds of systems, including technological systems (which are usually subjected to physical or

---

[71] А.С. Проников Параметрическая надежность машин. М.: МГТУ им. Баумана, 2002.
[72] А.А. Носенков Техническая совместимость: практика, наука, проблемы. Красноярск, 2005.

mathematical modeling).[73]

The level of a system's complexity would depend both on the type of compatibility and on how detailed any specific objective is. Studies of electromagnetic compatibility are the most complex in technology. Mathematical models of general compatibility of technological systems are essentially topological models used solely to describe a situation and demonstrate the possibilities.

Subsequent sections will look at changes in and modeling compatibility of subjects, their inter-relationships and interactions in other realms of science.

2.3. Key Compatibility, Theories, Hypotheses and Principles

Development of scientific fields and sciences is becoming ever more intricately intertwined, and this overall combination gives us a better understanding of the structure and development of the universe and us.

Because compatibility is an abstract concept, the empirical side of understanding and "knowing" it traditionally comes from (as is the case with other abstract concepts) basic empirical knowledge, processed using the tools of logic and mathematics, categorized into groups as common patterns identified for groups and generalized into scientific laws. The components of this process are observation, observation tools and measurements to obtain more advanced empirical knowledge.

The next step of empirical knowledge includes analysis, synthesis and systematization of experimental data and categorization of phenomena which are the subject of research.

A scientific categorization (classification) is based on an all-around investigation of real properties and relationships of phenomena, reflecting objective distribution of phenomena across groups. The main objective of empirical research is to reveal the nature of each of the groups of phenomena being categorized, provide an empirical generalization and establish an empirical pattern (a natural law).

An empirical generalization (as a research method) uses logical

---

[73] Г.М. Гнедов Об актуальности и проблеме создания теории технической совместимости. Л.: Ленинград. электротех. ин-т, 1979.

induction, analysis, synthesis, abstractions, comparisons and equations to increase the quality of cognition by extending the knowledge (data) of one group/sector to a multitude of similar groups/sectors. As the essential nature of phenomena in the group/sector being explored manifests itself, it makes it possible to establish a certain empirical pattern (an empirical natural law).

After the empirical stage, scientific cognition goes to the next – theoretical – stage.

The theoretical component of scientific cognition, the very possibility of its development, depends on meeting a range of certain preliminary conditions, including: establishing a theoretical foundation; creating one's own scientific theory on this foundation; using the theory so created to interpret certain phenomena from a scientific perspective in the context of a developing realm of knowledge.

1. The stage of establishing the foundation involves forming a scientific view of the world in the context of the new theory, general concepts, scientific principles and hypotheses of the new theory being created.

A study of compatibility as a phenomenon of natural science as well as applied science and technology requires accepting, in general terms, the following two concepts of a scientific worldview:

• as a system of high-level generalized concepts of the world around us arising from knowledge accumulated in a specific scientific field;

• as a general concept of the world around us, i.e. combining all scientific knowledge.

Applied science and technology serve the purpose of expanding knowledge about technology as a part of the world around us, while natural sciences serve their purpose by adding to our knowledge of the world outside the realm of technology. Any discussion of compatibility in technology would focus on physical manifestations of compatibility.

The concept of a principle in the context of cognition denotes the starting point, the bedrock foundation for any theoretical "superstructure," any theoretical constructs. For the purposes of this discussion, it is important that some, possibly a majority, of principles have a universal significance for the theory we are building. For example, electromagnetic compatibility in physics (and similar concepts) is based on the principles of energy conservation, momentum (and angular momentum).

Scientific hypotheses interpreting theoretical postulations that explain previously unknown phenomena corroborated by evidence become solidified into a principle.

2. The essence of a scientific theory and its structure are shaped at the theoretical research stage and comprise assumptions specific to this scientific theory, which has a structure of its own and is constructed using specific methods.

The unique structure of a specific scientific theory can be represented as a logical system reflecting dialectic laws (which can be expressed in formal terms to ensure a more profound understanding).

3. The final stage of theoretic research serves to find out whether the new scientific theory can be used to explain phenomena, after which the theory's assumptions are tested and adjusted. In our case, the study of compatibility in the broader sense is based on a very abstract theory that comprises many disparate aspects and can open up truly amazing, far-reaching forecasts and predictions.

At the same time, a theory's effectiveness can be tested by comparing conclusions reached on the basis of the theory against reality.

A methodological principle that is common for the entire realm of scientific knowledge is a necessary condition for corroborating a scientific theory. Thus, A.A. Nosenkov[74] uses several hypotheses for the theory of technological compatibility which is currently in development. Let us review them in brief.

The first hypothesis. Technology usually relies on the common principle that provides for both technology makers and technology users a certain sufficient internal and external compatibility of technological solutions (devices).

This can be written down as:

$$C_{\text{suff}i} = \int (T_w, T_{wt}, T_{obs}, F_c) \qquad (2.3.1)$$

where $C_{\text{suff}i}$ is a level of ith compatibility type sufficient to meet the requirements for quality of technological solutions; T_w, T_{wt}, T_{obs} are the warranty (guarantee) period, the time over which a solution is lost to physical wear and tear and the time after which the solution reaches obsolescence. F_c – unique things that need to be done to ensure Type I compatibility of technological devices or machines.

---

[74] Носенков А.А., Медведев В.И. Теория технической совместимости как новая дисциплина системного анализа // Вестник САА имени академика М.Ф. Решетнева. Вып. 2. Красноярск, 2001. P. 231–236.

The independent variables T_w, T_{wt}, T_{obs} and F_c cannot be formalized as they depend on a combination of different factors: the experience of designers, the customer's requirements, market conditions, the corporate policy of the manufacturing facility, the physical essence of the ith type of compatibility, etc.

Therefore, $C_{suff i}$ is achieved as a compromise between the customer's requirements on the one hand and the manufacturer's capabilities as defined by relevant circumstances. In some cases, the nature of F_c can be the defining factor – it can be either the allowed geometrical tolerance (for mechanical compatibility) or the noise level (for electromagnetic compatibility).

The second hypothesis: since the principle of sufficient compatibility applies to all technology, we can presume that the principle of sufficient compatibility is typical of all technology, and therefore it is dialectic as far as the most general laws of dialectics are evidenced in technology.

Let us look at the law of unity and conflict of the opposites to test this hypothesis.

This law essentially discusses certain opposites and states that these opposites are in a dialectic conflict. Some examples of more generic or specific opposites are:

1) the interactions and interrelated impact of components of technological solutions (devices);

2) positive and negative effects of friction, temperature, and other similar (physical) factors on the performance of a technological solution (device);

3) different polarity of components of electrotechnical, electrochemical and electronic devices.

At the same time, any innovation in technology is fraught with opposites, as, although innovation tends to eliminate some problems, it also causes others. On the one hand, innovation tends to reduce the size and weight of solutions (devices), on the other, smaller devices can become more susceptible to interference, etc.

The first pair of contradictions listed above is the most noteworthy: interaction $I(T)$ and mutual influence $F(T)$. $I(T)$ in this context is seen as part of the normal operation of components of technological solutions (devices), whereas $F(T)$ is construed as an instance of the harmful mutual impact of these components upon one another. $I(T)$ and $F(T)$ have different relative weights depending on where a specific device (machine, technological solution) is in its lifecycle:

$$I(\text{T}) \ll F(\text{T}), \qquad (2.3.2)$$

$$I(\text{T}) < F(\text{T}), \qquad (2.3.3)$$

$$I(\text{T}) = F(\text{T}), \qquad (2.3.4)$$

$$I(\text{T}) > F(\text{T}), \qquad (2.3.5)$$

$$I(\text{T}) \gg F(\text{T}). \qquad (2.3.6)$$

The first correspondence may be in effect, for example, before initial adjustment of electronics, when device components are not yet properly adjusted, attuned to each other by their input/output parameters and consequently are at the greatest degree of contradiction. As electronic devices are progressively adjusted, the relation of $I(T)$ to $F(T)$ gradually passes through states formally expressed as (2.3.2–2.3.5) and may even reach the state described by (2.3.6). Most types of technology approach this last stage only after a period of wear-in at reduced operating loads. This process is well known to anyone starting to drive a brand-new car, fresh from an assembly line.

As the resource T_p is used up, the relation between $I(T)$ and $F(T)$ changes in the opposite direction, until the time comes when the condition of a device is rated as unacceptable, and it has to be written off or recycled.

Ensuring technological compatibility in the context of obsolescence is harder, because one needs to take into account the psychology of users' attitudes to technology, the field of application, and operating conditions. The benefits derived from operating a device and the detriment of its obsolescence can be viewed as dialectic opposites.

The above goes to corroborate the dialectic nature of the original principle of dialectic compatibility, which is quite evident even from a single dialectic law.

The third hypothesis. The principle of sufficient compatibility can be viewed as a methodological principle, which means that it can become the basis for a methodology and the guiding light of the theory of technological compatibility.

Methodological principles are some of special elements in a scientific theory defining its structure and development.[75]

So what is the theoretical potential of the dialectic compatibility

---

[75] Методологические проблемы научно-технического прогресса. Новоси- бирск: Наука, 1987; М.Л. Сетров Методологические принципы построения единой организационной теории // Вопросы философии. 1969. № 5. Р. 28–41.

principle? To answer this question, we are going to have to define the principle of dialectic compatibility, which says: sufficient compatibility must be maintained in the process of design (development), manufacture and operation of a technological solution; in a way, this compatibility is a compromise between internal and external contradictions of technological solutions, ultimately defining the quality of these solutions and acting as one of key starting points of technological progress.[76] This definition provides solid methodological support to the theory of technological compatibility which is now taking shape, focusing attention on the role of the theory as one of the main drivers of technological progress.

The law of bidirectional transition between quantitative and qualitative change, also known as the second law of dialectics, expresses the mechanics of any development based on interactions between quantity, quality and measure. The operation of this law results either in elimination or in transformation of an old quality.

The fourth hypothesis. Since the second law of dialectics is closely associated with the first law of dialectics and contains many of the same categories and concepts, it should also affect the process of enabling technological compatibility.

The study of the mechanism whereby the second law of dialectics affects the development of technology enabled A.A. Nosenkov to establish yet another principle, which he named the principle of maximum perfection:[77] when designing new technology, it is necessary to implement those conceptually new technological solutions that are associated with the most complete set of "perfect features" possible and are a good match for other components of the device or machine under development in terms of the main compatibility types. Essentially, the principle of maximum perfection provides a generalized set of rules for technological creativity on the one hand and the order of using innovation in technology on the other. Every new technological solution can be used in any device or machine under development if, in combination with other solutions (components) being implemented, it can give the device or machine under development more

---

[76] А.А. Носенков О методологической концепции теории технической совместимости // Микроэлектронные устройства. Проектирование и технология: Межвуз. сб. / Отв. ред. А.А. Левицкий. Красноярск, 1990. Р. 100–103; А.А. Носенков Совместимость как первооснова качества техники // Проблемы обеспечения качества изделий в машиностроении: Матер. междунар. научн.-техн. конф. КрПИ. Красноярск, 1994. Р. 423–430.
[77] Ibid.

advanced, more "perfect" parameters and features. And yet, as the adage goes, there is no limit to perfection.

The fifth hypothesis. The principle of sufficient compatibility, along with the principle of striving for maximum possible perfection, are methodological principles of the theory of technological compatibility.

On the surface, it would appear that the principle of maximum perfection applies only structurally to the technology design (development) stage. In fact, every technological device or machine is very intimately connected with the processes of its manufacture and operation, which are also in the process of innovative development according to the second law of dialectics. Furthermore, every innovation usually applies to the entire product-process. The principle of maximum perfection aims to ensure compatibility of innovation with other technological solutions implemented in a product (process). A.A. Nosenkov believes[78] that these arguments make it possible to treat the principle of maximum perfection as a methodological principle in the theory of technological compatibility.

The third law of dialectics, often called "the law of negation of the negation", focuses on the continuity and direction of development and irrevocable replacement of the old by the new. It describes the helical nature of change and development, and helps to identify elements of the old (negative as well as positive) in the new. Creators of modern technology face the task of preventing the former and maximizing the latter.

The sixth hypothesis. This composition of all the dialectic laws taken together defines the development of the world around us, including technology. Consequently, the third law of dialectics also plays a role in ensuring technological compatibility.

A detailed investigation of ways in which the third law of dialectics impacts the development of technology enabled researchers to formulate the third principle, named the principle of rational continuity,[79] which states that one needs to perform a retrospective analysis of already known technological solutions when designing (developing) new technology to evaluate whether they are sufficiently compatible and can be effectively

---

[78] А.А. Носенков, В.И. Медведев Ibid.

[79] А.А. Носенков. О методологической концепции теории технической совместимости // Микроэлектронные устройства. Проектирование и технология: Межвуз. сб. / Отв. ред. А.А. Левицкий. Красноярск, 1990. Р. 100– 103.; А.А. Носенков Совместимость как первооснова качества техники // Проблемы обеспечения качества изделий в машиностроении: Матер. междунар. научн.-техн. конф. КрПИ. Красноярск, 1994. Р. 423–430.

used in new designs. This principle implies that progressive development of technology may involve carefully combining the old or even the very old with the new (an example of a very old technology coming back would be renewed construction of airships. It is the ascending gradient of executed improvements in the technological environment that defines the degree of re-use of old technological solutions in new designs.

The seventh hypothesis. The principle of rational continuity together with the principles of dialectic compatibility and maximum perfection belong in the category of methodological principles of the theory of technological compatibility.

All arguments used to corroborate this hypothesis are expressed based on the principle of maximum perfection (maximum improvement), the only difference being that the principle of rational continuity is focused on the link between compatibility and quality in the technological creativity process that incorporates earlier, already known designs and solutions.

Interrelation of all these principles is one of the signs indicating that all these principles are systematic. Another sign of their systematic nature must be their hierarchical subordination implying that the content of higher-level principles can be transformed into lower-level principles,[80] i.e.

$$\left\{P(Var)_1\right\} \to \left\{P(Var)_2\right\} \to \left\{P(Var)_3\right\} \to \ldots \to \left\{P(Var)_j\right\} \qquad (2.3.7)$$

where $\left\{P(Var)_1\right\}$ are the principles of the first (highest) level; $\left\{P(Var)_2\right\}, \left\{P(Var)_3\right\}, \left\{P(Var)_j\right\}$ are the principles of the second, third, and j^{th} levels, respectively.

Studies of links between already known principles of technology development have shown that the general principle of technology development from less to more advanced cannot be converted to specific principles such as the reliability principle and the controllability principle.[81]

It follows that the fewer innovations and new features that are added to

---

[80] А.А. Носенков, В.И. Медведев, А.М. Мулин Совместимость технических систем. Красноярск, 2005.

[81] А.А. Носенков О методологической концепции теории технической совместимости // Микроэлектронные устройства. Проектирование и техно- логия: Межвуз. сб. / Отв. ред. А.А. Левицкий; КрПИ. Красноярск, 1990. Р. 100–103.; А.А. Носенков Совместимость как первооснова качества техники // Проблемы обеспечения качества изделий в машиностроении: Материалы междунар. научн.-техн. конф. КрПИ. Красноярск, 1994. Р. 423–430.

a piece of technology, the more reliable it is in operation, the more user-friendly and easy to operate it is. This signifies that there is another level of principles in between the principles listed above; and principles at this "unanticipated" level are more specific than the general development principle and more general than the reliability and controllability principles.

Exploration of methodological possibilities of the principles already established and described above (the principle of dialectic compatibility, principle of maximum perfection (maximum improvement) and the principle of rational continuity) leads to a natural conclusion that these levels can play the role of transition, the link between the general principle and specific principles of technology development (principles of reliability, controllability, environmental friendliness, safety, technological completeness and others). In this case, one can represent the system of principles as a hierarchic structure (Fig. 2.1).

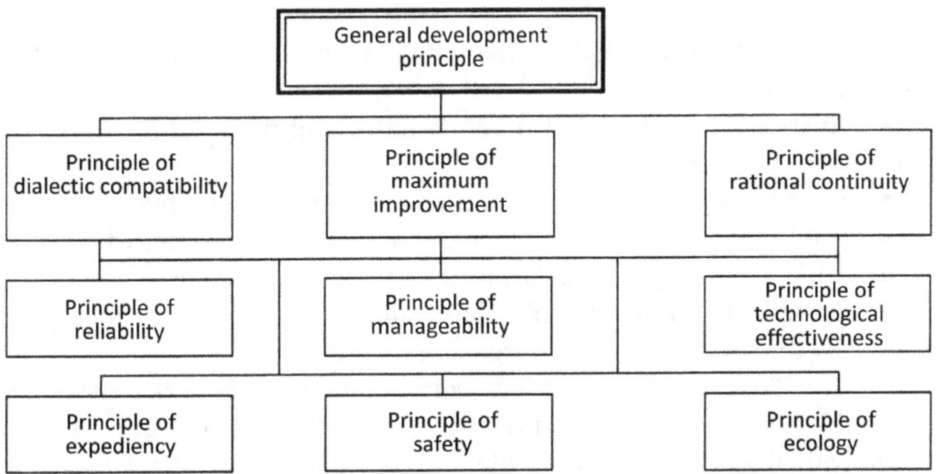

Fig. 2.1 System of methodological principles of technology development

One should also note another role of the principles we have established. Dialectic laws do not just automatically apply to technology. The human factor often plays a decisive role in this context. Academician N.N. Semenov said some four decades ago that the laws of process development for processes that include the human factor are not an absolute guarantee for their success, but rather only an opportunity to achieve success if the necessary conditions are met.[82]

These conditions also include the methodological principles listed above, along with socioeconomic, sociopolitical and organizational factors that require further investigation and improvement.

For human relationships in the community, all the existing compatibility theories, most of which were developed outside Russia, can be grouped into several fields.

The needs-based field is one of the key fields in international psychology. Compatibility in this field is defined through mutual satisfaction of needs of the interacting partners.[2] The following main theories can be identified in this field.

W. Schutz's compatibility theory was designed within a broader framework of the theory of interpersonal interactions. According to this theory, every individual has a typical way of social orientation towards other people that defines his or her interpersonal behaviour. Depending on the individual's history of interactions with the parents and the degree of satisfaction of his or her interpersonal needs, there are four behaviour types:

• excessive behaviour, where the individual constantly strives to satisfy his or her needs;

• deficit-based behaviour, where the individual does not try directly to satisfy his or her needs;

• perfect behaviour, where the needs are adequately satisfied;

• pathological behaviour, the result of a failed relationship, which leads to alienation, isolation, various forms of regressive behaviour.

The details of interpersonal relationships in W. Schutz's theory are defined by three fundamental interpersonal needs.[83]

1. The need for inclusion (communication) (I) is the striving to establish and maintain good relations with other people both from the individual towards other people (becoming involved in relationships, establishing contact with others) and the other way around (ensuring that others establish relationships with the individual). The need for inclusion manifests itself in the desire to feel that one is a valuable,

---

[82] Н.Н. Семенов Наука и общество. Статьи и речи. М.: Наука, 1973.

[83] Р.Л. Кричевский Проблема межличностной совместимости в зарубежной социальной психологии // Вопросы психологии. 1979. № 5. Р. 161–170; Общая психодиагностика / Под ред. А.А. Бодалева, В.В. Столина. М.: Изд-во МГУ, 1987; А.А. Рукавишников Опросник межличностных отношений. Ярославль: НПЦ «Психодиагностика», 1992. Р. 47.

significant personality, in the desire to be liked, to attract attention and interest, cooperate with others and join various social groups.

2. The need for control (C) is the striving to establish and maintain relationships with other people relying on control and power. These relationships include psychologically acceptable two-way relationships with people: from the individual towards other people (constant control or lack of control over behavior of others) as well as from other people towards the individual (defining whether or not others control the individual's behavior). The need for control is manifested as dominance, influence, competence, responsibility, decision-making, authority.

3. The need for affection (love) (A) is the striving to create close emotional bonds with other people, to be liked, to be loved. These relationships include psychologically acceptable two-way relationships with people: from the individual towards other people (establishing close personal relationships with everyone or not establishing a close personal relationship with anyone) as well as from other people towards the individual (whether others often or very rarely establish close personal relationships with the individual). The need for love manifests itself in growing closer to a partner, the ability to love, establishing a friendly relationship and the striving for close emotional contact with other people.

The three areas of relationships can be briefly defined as follows: a) inclusion: inside – outside, b) control: above – below, c) affection: close – distant.

An individual's interpersonal orientation within each area is determined by the difference between the actual (expressed) behavior (E) and the desired behavior (W). The greater the difference between these two terms, the higher the probability of internal conflicts and frustration in that area.

W. Schutz defines interpersonal compatibility in a group of two people (a duo) as a specific character of relationships involving two or more individuals that leads to mutual satisfaction of interpersonal needs and co-existence of the people involved.

An individual's behavior is evaluated across three areas of interpersonal needs: inclusion (I), control (C) and affection (A) by three compatibility types:

1) Mutual compatibility implies a degree of demonstrated (overtly expressed) behavior by one person matching the expectations of

another one in a given field of needs (i.e. the case of complementary expectations and demands);

2) Initiator compatibility implies a match between the initiative and active approach of one individual and the passivity of another in a given area of needs (i.e. the case of complementary activity and passivity);

3) Compatibility of mutual exchange implies a match between the frequency of change in a given field of needs of one individual and the expectations of another (i.e. the symmetry of two individuals' ideas of the desired intensity and frequency of contacts).

Even though W. Schutz's theory has been criticized (for substitution of the individual for the social, isolating these three specific needs as "fundamental" and orientation towards psychoanalysis), the existence of the phenomena he described is beyond any doubt.

E. Altmann and V. Haythorne's theory of compatibility of needs explores the interactions between duos of newly recruited navy sailors in conditions of social isolation. The duos were categorized by their degree of homogeneity in the following variables: the need for achievement, the need for affiliation, the drive for dominance and dogmatism. The degree of compatibility within duos was determined by sociometric methods, through observation, and measurements of stress and emotional symptoms. The results obtained indicate that duos symmetrical in their dogmatism, need for achievement and need for affiliation, and complementary in their need for dominance are more compatible.[84]

Robert F. Winch's theory of complementary needs assumes that individuals with complementary basic needs are more likely to marry each other. The theory explores two types of complementarity: (1) where the needs of one individual are different from those of another individual in their quality; and (2) where the needs of two individuals are of different intensity.

R.F. Winch identified four frequently seen combinations in married couples (seen as complementary from the dominance vs. subordination perspective):

1) Families modeled on the conventional, stereotypical relationship between "mother and son", where a strong and capable woman takes

---

[84] Р.Л. Кричевский Проблема межличностной совместимости в зарубежной социальной психологии // Вопросы психологии. 1979. № 5. P. 161–170.

care of her husband who needs someone he can reply on;

2) Families in which a strong, capable husband takes care of a passive and yielding, accommodating wife, who resembles a little doll in many ways, looking to be coddled and taken care of;

3) Families in many ways similar to the conventional (stereotypical) model of a master and maid servant relationship, in which a capable woman looks after a condescending husband;

4) families in which an active woman reigns over a frightened and disappointed husband.[85]

Subsequent testing of R.F. Winch's theory led to heavy criticism of the theory and found no empirical proof for it.[86]

Theories of interpersonal attraction. Many studies of interpersonal compatibility have been carried out from the perspective of the theory of interpersonal attraction.

C. Izzard studied friendly and spousal relationships for different degrees of inter-dependence and differences in relationships between same-sex and heterosexual couples, using the EPPS questionnaire that identified 15 types of needs. The results have shown that more than half of all needs (8 out of 15) for two spouses have a significant correlation, which implies a symmetry rather than a complementary nature of needs (the needs for dominance, upbringing, training and assistance showed no significant correlation).[87]

A study by B. Sifried and S. Hendrick[88] does not offer a clear answer to the question of whether needs are symmetrical or complementary in most couples, proposing a hypothesis of four possible different combinations of the needs of two people:

1) similar needs leading to satisfaction through interaction;

2) dissimilar needs leading to satisfaction through interaction;

3) similar needs not leading to satisfaction through interaction;

---

[85] С.В. Ковалев Психология современной семьи. М.: Просвещение, 1988; Р.Л. Кричевский Проблема interpersonaloй compatibility в зарубежной социальной психологии // Вопросы психологии. 1979. № 5. Р. 161–170; Н.Н. Обозов Межличностные отношения. Л.: Изд-во ЛГУ, 1979. Р. 149; Т. Шибутани Социальная психология. Ростов-на-Дону: Феникс, 1998.

[86] Р.Л. Кричевский Проблема межличностной совместимости в зарубежной социальной психологии // Вопросы психологии. 1979. № 5. Р. 161–170.

[87] Н.Н. Обозов Межличностные отношения. Л.: Изд-во ЛГУ, 1979.

[88] Медведев В.В. Экспериментальная установка для исследования согласованности групповых действий и рационального подбора групп // Вопросы психологии. 1967. № 2. Р. 166–169.

4) dissimilar needs not leading to satisfaction through interaction.

Many schools of international psychology understand interpersonal compatibility as a result of mutual satisfaction of needs (this understanding has its roots in psychoanalysis).

Of all the theories presented, W. Schutz's is the best developed theoretically and methodologically. At the same time, the question remains which needs are most important for interactions within a duo and what are the patterns of optimal combination of needs (symmetry or complementariness). As the overview of literature suggests, the needs mentioned belong more in the group of social needs than among the inherent physiological needs.

Behavioral psychology is seen as one of the key fields in both Russian and international psychology. Within this field, the standard assumption is that certain personal qualities determine typical behavioral models leading to either compatibility or incompatibility of people. International experimental studies (by Heyerton, Shaw, Smelser, Fry) mostly looked at dependence of group members' behavior on such qualities as authoritarianism and dominance; groups with complementary authoritarianism levels are presumably more compatible. [89]

Behavioral studies in the 1960-1970s yielded experimental methods to study the intricacies of interactions within a small contact group, including cybernometer and homeostasis to evaluate the type of compatibility.

Behavioral psychology is widespread in both Russian and international psychology. Instead of focusing mostly on building theories that define compatibility through factors and patterns in which they can be combined, as with other fields in psychology it explores the real behavior of people (the behavioral element of dependence) using objective methodological approaches.

The cognitive field. As cognitive psychology becomes more developed, various theories emerge pointing towards the role of self-appraisal and the concept of ego in a relationship.[90] For example, couples that see their relationship as successful and themselves as responsible for this, have a higher self-appraisal. The results of studies indicate that compatibility is better in couples the higher the degree of match in external factors and the

---

[89] Р.Л. Кричевский Проблема межличностной совместимости в зарубежной социальной психологии // Вопросы психологии. 1979. № 5. P. 161–170.
[90] А.Н. Волкова Социально-психологические факторы супружеской совмес- тимости. Автореф. дис. ... канд. псих. наук. Л.: Изд-во ЛГУ, 1979.

higher the inner self-appraisal.[91]

M. Preston and E. Kelly's research shows that partners in happy couples evaluate each other less objectively (less realistically) than those in unhappy couples. Furthermore, husbands in unhappy married couples judge their wives more strictly than they judge themselves.[92] S.L. Murray's studies of partner idealization in a marriage also indicate that positive illusions about a partner contribute to greater satisfaction from a marriage.[93]

Cognitive psychology is not strictly defined, is widespread primarily in international psychology (i.e. psychology outside Russia) and does not appear to have any specific theoretical approaches or an analysis focused on certain common factors. And yet, given the "young" age of this field of psychology, its development, the number of cognitive processes and phenomena involved in interaction, it has the greatest potential for "strategic" development.

Interactive psychology. J. Edwards' theory (the transaction principle) is used fairly often to analyze relationships between people; according to this theory, people try to extract the maximum benefit at the lowest possible cost. The resources (stimuli) used for this purpose can include parameters including age, education, looks and income.[94]

The next well-known theory in international psychology is B. Merstein's *filter model* (a "stimulus – value – role" model). According to this model, relationships go through several critical stages (filters) in their development that determine whether a continued relationship is possible. The first filter (the early stage in a relationship) depends on stimuli of the (primarily external) features of the partners (the process of attraction); if a couple endures as a duo and passes the first filter, the second filter kicks in (a certain similarity of values), and then the third filter (search for role adequacy, a match of interpersonal roles).[95]

---

[91] Sharpley C.F., Khan J.A. The Relationship Between Marital Adjustment and Self-Concept for Married Individuals and Couples // Individual Psycholoqy Journal of Adlerian Theory, Research and Practice. 1982. Vol. 38 (1). P. 62–71.

[92] Roland J. Psychological Patterning in Marriage // Psychological Bulletin. 1963. Vol. 60 (2). P. 98–112.

[93] Murray S.L., Holmes J.G., Griffin D.W. The Benefits of Positive Illusions: Idealization and the Construction of Satisfaction in Close Relationships // Journal of Personality and Social Psycholoqy. 1996. Vol. 70 (1). P. 79–98.

[94] Основы социально-психологическойой теории / Под общ. ред. А.А. Бодалева, А.Н. Сухова. М.: Международная педагогическая академия, 1995.

[95] Л.Я. Гозман Психология эмоциональных отношений. М.: Изд-во МГУ, 1987; Основы социально-психологической теории / Под общ. ред. А.А. Бодалева, А.Н. Сухова. М.: Международная педагогическая акаде- мия, 1995.

R. Stepchen combines the positions of symbolical interactionism and a theory of social exchange, proposing the *"hypothesis of compatible world outlook,"* according to which people, in the course of communication, make joint assumptions of the way the world is structured, the way things are connected to each other, and about their importance and the significance of the partner's behavior. This hypothesis views reciprocity as a two-directional interaction in which partners demonstrate similar behavior (either simultaneously or in succession), and complementary interaction where the partners' actions are different but complement each other.[96]

This direction in psychology — interactionism — is fairly common outside of Russia, represented by individual authors' theories and focuses on the study of couples' compatibility. At the same time, there is some overlap between interactionism on the one hand and behavioral and cognitive psychology on the other; pure interactionism is rarely if ever used to analyze compatibility.

The last field in psychology we will look at is psychoanalystics. Many authors note the influence of the parents' family on a relationship between adults. The contribution of classic psychoanalysis and E. Bern's transaction analysis[97] have made a well-known contribution to this field. According to the psychoanalytical direction in the study of spousal compatibility, the identification mechanism in boys and girls in a family helps them acquire the standard of husband and wife. Mother and father are most often the role models. So, matching the mother (the role model) and associated concept of woman in the wife's role plays an important part for men in spouse selection and determines details of the relationship.

J. Roland's numbers indicate than 94% of men who are married to women similar to their mothers in their physical parameters and temperament have been happy in their marriage. At the same time, only 33% of married men have been happy with wives unlike their mothers. Women demonstrated a different trend: they evaluate their husbands by comparing them to other comparable men they know rather than to their fathers. J. Roland makes an assumption on the basis of this that the father has but a weak influence on shaping the daughter's standard of the future husband,[98] although some researchers disagree. Outside the scope of

---

[96] К. Лийк, Т. Нийт Интимность и взаимоотношения в семье // Человек, общество и жилая среда / Под ред. Ю. Орна, Т. Нийта. Таллин, 1986. P. 154–163.

[97] Э. Берн. Введение в психиатрию и психоанализ для непосвященных. Минск: Попурри, 1998.

[98] Roland J. Psychological Patterning in Marriage // Psychological Bulletin. 1963. Vol.

psychoanalysis, many authors note the influence of the parents' family on one's own.[99]

The psychoanalytical field has a long history and is quite widespread in both international and Russian psychology as a means of exploring the gamut of relationships between people. Although psychoanalysis receives much criticism, experimental data suggest a strong influence of parent figures and relationships between the parents on relationships of their children as adults.

The key compatibility theories are distributed across a range of areas corresponding to the key schools of psychology that emerged in the 20th century. The "older" schools of psychology (including psychoanalysis and behaviorism) are represented in compatibility theories to a greater extent than "newer" schools (such as cognitivism). Thus, the study of interpersonal compatibility has been following the development path of psychology. At the same time, we note that none of the changing theories provides a complete picture of interpersonal compatibility, as the available data about the factors affecting compatibility and the patterns of optimal combination of these factors are obscure and not enough for building a clean compatibility model on their basis.

Let us take a look at the key premises of compatibility in medicine and healthcare. Modern medicine most often resorts to comprehensive treatment. Various physiotherapeutical treatments and remedies in combined use can either reinforce or reduce each other's effect. This is why, to improve the efficacy of prevention, treatment and rehabilitation of patients with various conditions one must take into account the compatibility phenomenon, including where physical treatment factors are assigned in a certain sequence.

These methodological recommendations contain data on compatibility, incompatibility and the sequence of appointment of physiotherapy (including hydrotherapy and electrotherapy), balneological, climatic and other treatment procedures, and about how they should be combined with medication.

Let us talk about the key principles of combined and concurrent use of physical treatment factors.[100]

---

60 (2). P. 98–112.

[99] Baron, R., Richardson, D. Aggression. NYC: Plenum Press, 1994; Эйдемиллер Э.Г., Юстицкис В. Психология и психотерапия семьи. 2-е изд. СПб.: Питер, 1999.

[100] А.А. Шатров, С.Я. Троценко, Б.А. Соколов, Н.П. Лещинская, В.И. Мизин Методические рекомендации Ялтинского НИИ физических

Combined use is currently understood as sequential administration of two or more treatment factors during a course of treatment. Procedures may be administered: 1) in quick succession on the same day; 2) on different days; 3) a course of treatment by one factor is replaced by another course. Concurrent use is the simultaneous administration of two or more treatment factors.

Complex physical-chemical and physiological processes lie at the heart of the way in which compound physiotherapy works, with synergies, sensitization and antagonism having especially great significance.

The synergy principle makes it possible to achieve a stronger final effect by including a set of physical factors with similar effect in the treatment plan (the addition of similar reactions from certain physiological systems or the potential of the effect of various physical factors).

Sensitization takes place when one physiotherapy treatment puts the body or some of its systems into a state of heightened sensitivity to the effects of another physical factor.

The antagonism principle most often finds practical applications when undesirable side-effects of one of the factors need to be mitigated: for example, contrast showers and baths help avoid blood vessel atony, venous hyperemeia which can be caused by the action of pure heat.

The principle of amplification of a local reaction can be manifested when factors with predominantly general and local effect are combined. It has been established that a local reaction becomes stronger if a local procedure is followed up with a procedure producing a general effect (baths, showers, etc.). According to A.A. Shatrov,[101] a correctly composed plan of physiotherapy treatments (one that may include hydrotherapy, electrotherapy, etc.) would ensure that the positive effects of several physical factors pulling in the same direction add up, while the negative effect of some components is reduced; additional effects on body systems and some aspects of the pathological process are introduced, the duration of subsequent effect of treatments administered jointly is increased. We will take the liberty to repeat that examples of synergistic effects of heat and galvanic current (according to S.Ya. Trotsenko, B.A. Sokolov[102]) are four-chamber bath and electrogalvanic mud bath (a galvanic mud bath).

методов лечения и медицинской климатологии им И.М. Сеченова. Ялта, 1986.

[101] Совместимость и последовательность применения лечебных физических факторов / Под ред. А.А. Шатрова. Ялта, 1986.

[102] Ibid.

However, this combination of two powerful effects can be used only in moderate quantities admissible given the functional condition of the patient's body. An example of an electrotherapy method using several treatment factors at the same time is inducto-thermoelectrophoresis.

An example (provided by N.P. Leshchinskaya) of the simultaneous application of inductothermy and electrophoresis is the new method of concurrent use of inductothermy and aethonium electrophoresis in the chest area, which is recommended as a way to treat patients suffering from chronic bronchitis in the weakly acute or incomplete remission stage.

Speaking of the compatibility and incompatibility of physiotherapy and balneological treatments (V.I. Mizin), one should note that these treatments produce a strong, lasting effect in the patient. Therefore, care should be taken to avoid administering several treatments with an intense effect on the same day. When the effects of several powerful factors add up, this may cause various functional disruptions in the nervous, cardiovascular and other systems within the human body.

The treatment plan must be assigned to a patient individually, on a case-by-case basis, taking into consideration the severity and stage of the illness or condition, details of the patient's overall clinical picture, the existence of concurrent illnesses and preexisting conditions, the way that physical treatment factors affect the patient and whether they are compatible. However, one must not reduce integrated therapy to polypragmasia (lumping together a great number of different treatments), as administering many treatments in quick succession or concurrently may put an excessive strain on the body and exacerbate pathological conditions.

In most cases, it is advisable to restrict a patient to only one of these treatment procedures.

When medicinal electrophoresis or other types of electrotherapy are used, a second electrotherapy procedure may be administered on the same day if it applies to a small part of the body.

Treatments with the opposite effect are usually incompatible, according to A.A. Shatrov (e.g. heat and cold treatments, soothing and stimulating), except where a contrasting reaction needs to be achieved (e.g. contrast showers or baths).

When putting together a combined therapy treatment plan and addressing the practical matters of the (in)compatibility of physiotherapy treatments, one must take into account the special aspects of the effect that separate physical factors may have.

Galvanic current produces a high concentration of accumulated medications introduced into the body through other channels in the tissues and organs in the space between the electrodes. This principle is used in so-called intra-tissue, or intra-organ electrophoresis.

A.A. Shatrov believes that ultraviolet radiation in erythemic doses (sufficient to cause redness of the skin) is incompatible with electrophoresis of the same area of the skin, inductometry therapy, microwaves, d'arsonvalization, ultrasound, massage therapy, X-ray therapy, heat and water treatments. X-ray therapy can be administered a week after the patient receives UV erythema. Sunlight treatment can be administered no sooner than a month after a course of radiotherapy.

In their study of acupuncture, S.Ya. Troschenko and B.A. Sokolov emphasize that it is more effective in conjunction with climate therapy than it is by itself to treat lung and cardiovascular disease, whereas medicinal inhalations can be combined with electrotherapy and other physiotherapy treatments on the same day.

When looking at the compatibility and incompatibility of climate and physiotherapy treatments (including hydrotherapy and electrotherapy), A.A. Shatrov emphasizes the following: "Of climatic treatment procedures, it is advisable to use at, as well as outside of, health resorts different types of aerotherapy (staying out in the open for an assigned period of time or round-the-clock, sleeping on the beach, air baths), heliotherapy (exposure to sunlight), swimming in the sea or other natural bodies of water: a river, a lake."[103] Specific combinations of climatic treatments may be assigned depending on how serious an illness and the overall clinical condition are, and on the stage in the treatment process that determine the admissible additional strain on the human body, and also depending on the season, weather and specific conditions at the resort.

Compatible and incompatible procedures are those that either do (may) not cause or (may) cause positive and negative effects, respectively, on proper functioning of the system, identical to those of the preceding climate complex, except for irradiation with natural light sources.

When using automated systems for controlling the treatment process, methodological recommendations can be included in control software algorithms in order to:

a) control to make sure appropriate treatments are assigned with a view to recommended compatibility and sequence;

---

[103] Совместимость и последовательность применения лечебных физических факторов / Под ред. А.А. Шатрова. Ялта, 1986.

b) correct treatment assignments made by resident physicians.

One example of a device that can implement the algorithms of compatibility and sequence of treatments is the Gamma 1 medication compatibility analyzer.

When evaluating the efficiency of implementation, the use of methodological recommendations at healthcare institutions and rehabilitation facilities will help more efficient use of physical treatment and rehabilitation factors for patients with various conditions, as well as in preventative physiotherapy, hydrotherapy and electrotherapy treatments.

The results of treating patients with bronchial, lung, cardiovascular, neurological and other conditions are evaluated by the dynamics of key clinical symptoms, the findings of special studies, the reduction in days of temporary disability, etc.

A.A. Shatrov[104] concludes that these principles of putting together rational treatment plans contribute to a better-differentiated, better-targeted approach in using physiotherapy, hydrotherapy and electrotherapy treatments, expanding the range of conditions where these treatments can and should be used, as well as preventing detrimental, negative reactions to these treatments.

N.P. Leschinskaya and V.I. Mizin[105] believe that using the proposal stated above would reduce the number of sick days. A differentiated approach to evaluation of compatibility (of drugs for use in treatment) helps to increase coverage of patients by physiotherapy, hydrotherapy and electrotherapy at medical institutions.

2.4. Compatibility Types

2.4.1. Psychological Compatibility, its Hierarchy and Stages in the Interaction Process

It would be hard to determine now in what field of socio-psychological inquiry the concept of compatibility began to be used first. Studies of group

---

[104] Совместимость и последовательность применения лечебных физических факторов / Под ред. А.А. Шатрова. Ялта, 1986.
[105] Ibid.

conflicts, psychological climate in a group, effectiveness of group activity, group behavior types, when exploring the processes and results of intra- and inter-group communication, dynamics of relationships between people and feelings and other socio-psychological phenomena discovered that they are determined in a certain way by the combination of properties of interacting subjects.

Researchers and people in general started describing a certain combination of features and characteristics of individuals involved in a common activity that made a positive impact on the purpose of their activity as compatibility: personal, situational, functional, etc. In this connection, a distinction emerged between compatibility types: physiological, psychophysiological, socio-psychological and ideological. Analysis of work groups is usually associated with an emphasis on psychophysiological, psychological and socio-psychological compatibility, which has come to be known under the umbrella of the general scientific term of *"psychological compatibility."*

Psychophysiological compatibility is based on a certain match of temperaments describing the dynamic characteristics of people interacting, of the biological needs of the individuals involved. Psychological compatibility is defined by interaction between personal indiosyncracies, characteristics, character and motives for certain behavior. Socio-psychological compatibility, as a more integrated compatibility type, presumes coordination of social roles, functional/role expectations, interests and core values. All these compatibility types belong mostly in the field of psychology.

Physiological compatibility takes into account age, gender and associated properties of interacting individuals and their physiological processes and belongs in the field of physiology. Finally, ideological compatibility associated with the pursuit of one's class interests belongs in the field of political science.

This division into types of compatibility is essentially a matter of convention. Neither physiological, nor socio-psychological, nor any other compatibility types manifest themselves in isolation; all of them are seamlessly integrated into people's behavior. Therefore, when speaking of any specific compatibility type, one can still use the blanket term "psychological compatibility." The most important things one has to take into account when evaluating compatibility are aspects of the mind, emotions and the will in people's behavior.

Including aspects of the mind, emotions and the will in regulation of people's interactions more or less ensures compatibility of people, which, however, comes at a cost of different types: at the cost of time, psychological effort, energy expenditure, etc. Moreover, as interconnection grows closer, as N.N. Obozov notes, increasingly more levels (types) of compatibility come into play.[106]

When determining whether people are compatible in their job environment, different levels of psychology are often invoked: the conscious and the subconscious. Compatibility is the mutual suitability of qualities of a group's members. It includes mutual sympathy, the positive nature of emotional imperatives, mutual suggestion, the existence of common interests and needs, similarity in the dynamic direction of psychophysiological reactions during operations and the absence of pronounced egocentric tendencies in a given group.[107] "Incompatibility is the inability to understand each other in a critical situation, lack of synchronization of psychomotor reactions, differences in attention level and attention span, as well as other innate and acquired personality traits that would interfere with a joint activity."[108] When discussing the nature of compatibility in work groups, one has to emphasize the interpersonal aspect of collaboration.

Interpersonal compatibility usually comes with the emergence of mutual sympathy, mutual respect and confidence in positive outcomes from future contacts. It takes on a special meaning in the difficult conditions of living and working together in extreme conditions (e.g. on an expedition, the ascent of a mountain), when a common goal is achieved given a deficit of resources (including money), time, space and a limited number of essential participants.

Compatibility within a group produces a hierarchy of levels.

The following compatibility types comprise the lowest level:

1) Psycho-physical compatibility (of temperaments and characters of group members);

2) Sensorimotor coherence of group members in performing joint actions;

3) Their solid unity manifesting itself through intensity of communication links within the group and commonality of sociometric choice.

---

[106] Н.Н. Обозов Межличностные отношения. Л.: ЛГУ, 1979. P. 93.

[107] Краткий психологический словарь. М.: Политиздат, 1985.

[108] А.А. Леонов, В.И. Лебедев К проблеме психологической совместимости в межпланетном полете // Вопросы философии. 1972. № 9. P. 18.

Psychophysiological compatibility is based on the assumption that people are satisfied with each other on the strength of such personal characteristics as reaction time, speed and intensity of psychological processes, etc. Compatibility at this level depends largely on the temperament of people interacting. (For example, if a choleric and a phlegmatic are working side by side on an assembly line, they will find it difficult to work together in sequence).

Compatibility at a higher level emerges as matching functional/role expectations — i.e. the ideas group members have what, with whom and in what order each of them should be operating while working on a common goal of import to their community.

Psychological compatibility presumes that people are satisfied with each other on the strengths of their character traits, individual qualities, skills and intellectual potential (if people have different psychological qualities, compatibility may still emerge because some of these qualities may be mutually complementary).[109]

The highest level of compatibility, which applies only to a group of people, reflects the unity of substantive-purpose and value orientation, identification with one's group, the ability to impose and assume responsibility for success and failure in the context of inter-relationships among group members.

Sociopsychological compatibility presumes a certain similarity of core values, ideals, principles, level of professional training and education. It is important for group work and is a foundation of a group's unity.

One group of researchers names compatibility as a prerequisite for group unity. Compatibility takes shape on the basis of an ability to adjust in order to work together more effectively. It arises as a result of such a fairly long interaction between people in which they are satisfied with one another.

For another group of researchers, compatibility of group members implies that a given composition of a group can ensure that the group should fulfill its function, and its members should be capable of interacting effectively.

A third group of researchers sees compatibility as a complex psychological effect of the combination and interaction of people communicating with one another. These researchers understand structural compatibility as compatibility of temperament, character and the personal

---

[109] Л.М. Каткова Совместимость персонала в организациях. М.: МОСУ, 2002.

qualities of partners; they see functional/role compatibility as a match in the partners' understanding of the interpersonal roles they will implement themselves and expect the other(s) to fill in the process of communication and interaction. If the role concepts and expectations of team members coincide, they have a strong chance of achieving harmony in their relationship based on interpersonal appeal. It has been established that compatibility can manifest itself as a similarity or contrast of the individual characteristics of group members. Compatibility is high if partners have complementary features of temperament or character traits (e.g. in pairings of a sanguine person with a melancholic one, a choleric with a phlegmatic) and similar personal goals and qualities (examples of these qualities would be gregarious, worrisome, dreamy, etc).

Most researchers state among the most general aspects of compatibility analysis that compatibility is a phenomenon associated with interpersonal relationships that presumes an optimal coordination of individual psychological characteristics of group members and includes the idea of satisfaction with a joint activity and communication. Compatibility can also be defined as the optimal combination of partners' individual psychological traits and interpersonal roles, which contribute to optimization of their communication and activity.

Group compatibility on a physiological level is associated with similarity of physiological parameters in modern individuals (their electrocutaneous reactions, pulse, tremors and the properties of their nervous systems). Russian studies[110] indicate that similarity in the temperament of partners contributes to their interpersonal compatibility. Results of international studies demonstrate that not only similarity of parameters, but also their contrast can define interpersonal compatibility. At the psychological level of compatibility analysis, researchers have observed a great disparity of empirical data. Compatible partners, according to Russian research, could manifest both similar and contrasting levels of non-verbal intellect. Psychological compatibility is defined to a large extent by partners' matching core values, interests and needs. Socio-psychological compatibility is associated with a clear-sighted evaluation of one another and mutual understanding within a group, identification with one's partner, and coinciding ego concepts, and assessment of the other's significant

---

[110] Roland, J. Psychological Patterning in Marriage // Psychological Bulletin. 1963. Vol. 60 (2). P. 98–12.

qualities. A number of Russian psychologists[111] believe that group compatibility depends on how clear differentiation within a group is. International psychologists[112] observe compatibility in groups with both homogenous as well as heterogenous roles.

A.V. Petrovsky and M.G. Yaroshevsky point out that one should look for the basis of psychological compatibility in the coordination of comprehensive joint activity rather than in performing any single operation taken by itself, where this joint activity is defined for the individual by a common goal and has a structure that reflects the combined image of participants in this activity.

One must pick as a starting point the view that compatibility as a phenomenon of human interaction and communication can be regarded as a process, as a result, and also as a condition of interaction among group members when working towards a common group goal.

Compatibility as an interaction process takes shape over a certain period of time and is characterized by the personal adaptive capabilities of group members. A group of people finding themselves in a certain environment goes through an adaptation process, during which individuals adjust to one another and to their environment.

Four different stages of group dynamics (a.k.a. "group development") have been identified which are common for a broad range of work groups and workplace situations:

1) *Group formation stage.* An early stage of group building when group members are introduced to one another and familiarize themselves with their environment;

2) *Stage of psychological tension.* A common stage in group dynamics, especially typical of groups pursuing a common goal when group members demonstrate psychological tensions, are cautious and apprehensive when approaching one another, vie for leadership of the group, demonstrating diverging opinions on some issues and other manifestations of interpersonal stress and psychological tension;

3) *Normalization stage.* The next stage after the stage of psychological tensions, which is characterized by establishing common

---

[111] Roland, J. Psychological Patterning in Marriage // Psychological Bulletin. 1963. Vol. 60 (2). P. 98–112; Леонов А.А., Лебедев В.И. К проблеме психологической совместимости в межпланетном полете // Вопросы философии. 1972. № 9. P. 18; Л.М. Каткова Совместимость персонала в организациях. М.: МОСУ, 2002.

[112] Kaufman, J. Analytical Psychotherapy. 1976. Whitmont E.C. The Symbolic Guest. N.Y.: Putnam, 1969.

values, role expectations, and behavior principles.

4) *Activity stage.* The stage when the roles of group members become clearly delineated and assigned, functional specializations have been developed, and details of functional interdependence have been identified to an extent where the group can achieve its objectives efficiently.

In the process of joint operation, communication, and under common living conditions, people reveal their individual, personal qualities to a greater, clearer extent, learning to understand and respect one another's needs and interests, and forecast partners' behavior and actions in different conditions and situations. Compatibility is achieved as a result of this joint adjustment, or, more specifically, this process of achieving compatibility.

This state of the group is described as a "good adjustment," a "solid team," a "well-oiled machine," a "united front," "group cohesion," etc. However, there is no definitive answer to the question how long it takes to reach this state, because a great number of factors come into play: material, social, psychological, physiological, and others. Available studies indicate that compatibility as a result of joint activity is not always achieved by all employees in a group, but can devolve into the creation of informal, conflicting microgroups (cliques), which often results in overall group incompatibility.

In this case, treating compatibility as a process and as a result of joint activity has to be associated with stages, or levels of team development, which manifest themselves in a common system of ideological and political values, a degree of collective mindset, and adherence to group (team) beahavior standards.

Compatibility is often a prerequisite for efficient operation and work of work groups. It defines productivity, achieving results and the degree of employee satisfaction with their joint work.[113] Whether or not joint activities contribute to the desired result would depend on whether the psychological compatibility of employees within a work group is taken into account.

It is common knowledge that group activity is inextricably associated with a lively communication process. Studies have identified certain specific "standard" communication patterns, which imply certain categories of people engaging in communication. The following personality types have been identified:

---

[113] А.И. Китов Психология хозяйственного управления. М.: Профиздат, 1984. P. 150–154.

1) People driven to become leaders who can address common tasks and act only by subjugating other group members to their will;

2) Individualists attempting to act by themselves when attempting to work on a common task of the group;

3) Those adjusting to the group, who easily follow orders and fall under the influence of others;

4) Team-minded people who try to achieve the common goal through joint group efforts.

As it turns out, an optimal group composition has members actively exchanging information among themselves to achieve their common goal. In this case, commonality of opinions and assessments contributes to identifying the most significant content of communication, and goals of joint activity. Differences in these qualities tend to reduce the integration and unity of any social group. Research indicates that social needs manifest themselves in a specific, somewhat unusual manner.

When putting together a work group, one has to pay attention to the following considerations:

1) Mutually complementary needs: interaction is based on a needs system comprising a set of mutually determinant drives. For example, when some group members are driven to lead, while others are willing to follow, the former have a need to take care of someone, and the latter need to be taken care of;

2) Mutual autonomy of needs: different people with opposite needs are inclined to cooperate. For example, people with a strong need for communication and people with a need for autonomy;

3) Complementary skills and experience: some team members' inadequate skills are compensated by a high skill level of others. For example, an experienced manager and a conscientious deputy can work together to be an effective management team;

4) Complementary knowledge: team members have non-overlapping knowledge, ensuring that everyone can teach from someone else or rely on another group member's competence;

5) Common values: group members share a common system of values and behavior rules.

All these compatibility types are closely associated with group viability, but the connection is achieved through different ways, and disregarding or undermining each compatibility type leads to different results.

When A.I. Kitov considers the conditions for achieving group cohesion, he compares them with professional and moral and psychological qualities of individuals. He proposes using the following features as the basis:[114]

1) Rational distribution of functions among people interacting with one another;

2) A match between personal capabilities and the structure and content of the activity the person engages in;

3) Combining different and complementary individual capabilities of people engaging in interaction, thus forming a unity;

4) A common understanding of the professional doctrine, i.e. the overall direction of organizational goals and the key methods to achieve those goals;

5) Deep mutual understanding based on the assumption of the desire and ability of all employees engaging in interaction to foresee the possible intentions of their counterparts and coordinate their own actions with these counterparts in advance;

6) Mutual trust of people engaging in interaction;

7) The desire to support and help each other;

8) Relative homogeneity of employees' motives and their attitude to their duties.

An analysis of available literature[115] and empirical data gathered in the course of various studies of interdependent activity would help identify several states of the mechanism of psychological (interpersonal) compatibility:

- affinity of qualities in interacting individuals;
- contrasting qualities in interacting individuals;
- mutually complementary qualities, i.e. qualities of interacting individuals are statically matching (this state also includes the two states above);
- homeostasis, i.e. the state of dynamic correspondence of qualities (and properties) of interacting individuals (this state also includes all three states listed above).

Properties that are largely determined by biology, heredity (psychophysiological, emotional/dynamic) are stable personal traits which tend to be contrasting in compatible individuals.

---

[114] А.И. Китов Психология хозяйственного управления. М.: Профиздат, 1984. Р. 150–154.

[115] В.М. Давыдов, И.Д. Ладанов Психологическая совместимость в трудовых коллективах. М., 1985.

Qualities largely defined by upbringing or acquired as a result of influences from the sociocultural milieu (core values, key assumptions and preconceptions, interests and so on) are most often similar for many individuals. Complementary nature is based on a combination of similarity and contrast between the personal qualities of interacting individuals, representing a "snapshot" produced during interaction demonstrating the degree of functional coordination of behavior and actions by participants in a group activity at a certain stage.

The state of homeostasis manifests itself in that compatible individuals create, in the process of their interaction, a mobile, dynamic, balanced system that ensures the effective two-way exchange of information and redistribution of functions. At the same time, individual personal qualities and psychological processes ongoing at this point in time and the state of group members mutually compensate and complement one another in the course of interconnected activity, ensuring a stable and efficient level of operation.

The idea of homeostasis, as described in W.R. Ashby's book,[116] is essentially internal regulation, preserving parameters of a system that is stable within certain limits. Blood temperature regulation is a classic example of homeostasis, with constant limits because of the body's ability to operate in a satisfactory, acceptable manner within certain limits. These limits are not arbitrary or imposed from the outside; they come from within.[117]

A homeostatic combination of individuals' qualities ensures the conflict-free distribution of interpersonal roles, improving a group's integrity and unity based on the members' interdependence. It would be a natural assumption to make that the homeostais principle is common for any group engaged in an interconnected activity, regardless of the sector or type of activity involved.

If we consider a group as a system with a certain structure (of group members) and functional links (representing formal and informal relationships between group members), to get a better understanding of compatibility, we would need to look at literature on systems theory, where this concept is widely used. Premises on operation of a system can be used both to put together a work group and to manage it.

The dictionary definition of a system is a unity with a certain order to it

---

[116] Ashby, W.R. An Introduction to Cybernetics. London: Chapman & Hall, 1961.
[117] Beer, S. Management Science. London: Aldus, 1967.

based on the orderly, planned positions of the mutual links of components of something.[118] A system is usually approximated as a set, and the main type of relationship defining an object as a system is taken to be the links between the parts and the whole.

A system is understood as a finite set of elements of functional states of elements united by links ensuring their interaction and making a certain whole unity out of it. As a system reaches a certain degree of complexity, groups of elements can be identified within it, the links between which are stronger or more important than their links to anything outside these groups. These groups of elements are called subsystems.

A combination of elements and subsystems taken together forms the whole system, which can have any degree of complexity. Just as the categories "element" and "structure" are relative, so is the idea of "wholeness", or unity, because a system has a certain unity when combined with another system. This relativity should be constantly borne in mind as we explore various systems.

Studies of interconnected group activity identify the key attribute of a system — its unity, without which a system would have been unable to function, i.e. a combination and interaction of different elements within the system (group members), and the establishment of different connections and relationships between/among them, leading ultimately either to the continued existence of the system in a certain dynamic stability, or to its disintegration. If a system is operational, it can be described by the criterion of its effectiveness.

F.D. Gorbov and V.I. Lebedev believe that the efficiency of interrelated group activity can be defined on the basis of whether a system has a certain balance.[119] Consequently, if a system reaches the level of dynamic stability, it begins to function as a whole regardless of the impact of any internal or external interference (perturbations) affecting it, which ultimately ensures the desired result of the system's operation, which can be successful group activity as measured by one or several metrics.

In this connection, a group's functional organization as a result of the interaction of its members can be categorized as one of the most complex system types, the entire behavior of which is subordinated to achieving a specific goal, i.e. as a goal-oriented self-regulating system capable of

---

[118] Большой толковый словарь русского языка. СПб., 2000. Р. 1189.

[119] Ф.Д. Горбов, В.И. Лебедев Психоневрологические аспекты труда операто- ров. М.: Медицина, 1985.

changing its organization and structure during its operation. These systems are often characterized by several often-conflicting goals at different levels, and by the cooperation and conflict of these goals.

The idea of unity is closely associated with the compatibility of components within a system and also between each of the components and the overall system. "Compatibility," V.G. Afanasiev writes, "is an especially typical property of social systems comprising people. First and foremost, compatibility of components ensures rational interactions among them; without such interactions a working system would have been unthinkable."[120]

M.I. Setrov believes that compatibility is the first and most important condition of any interaction between objects and phenomena.[121] In this case, correspondence is one of the possible forms of compatibility of real phenomena, reflecting compatibility between a system and its environment, or between the structure and functions of a system and the conditions in which it exists. "To ensure that a system is organized," M.I. Setrov writes, "two types of compatibility are needed at the same time: compatibility of single-level components as the necessary condition for interaction and compatibility of a single component, taken by itself, with all other components of the whole, i.e. compatibility between a component and the system of which it is a part."[122]

In this case, we are dealing with single-level compatibility, which is adequate for describing systems at a single level of development, independent and of equal importance (representing a horizontal relationship), and multi-level compatibility, associated with hierarchical correspondence, emphasizing the different significance of systems in a combination (representing a vertical relationship).

Systems theory sees compatibility as a relationship of two or more systems that helps to identify the affinity or common ground of several systems by some parameters or by their content, ensuring their effective interaction. In this context, the matter of the compatibility of two or more components becomes relevant only if these components are different.

The need for differentiating components arises from the most important principle of system construction – the principle of the necessary variety of components. Variety, or differentiation (mutual complementarity)

---

[120] В.Г. Афанасьев Системность и общество. М.: Политиздат, 1980. P. 83.
[121] М.И. Сетров Организация биосистем. Л.: ЛГК, 1971. P. 33.
[122] Ibid.

of components is a condition of a system's survivability and flexibility, and its stability under a range of different conditions.

2.4.2. Technological Compatibility Types

It was a notable manifestation of the combination of different types of technological compatibility when the makers of the world's first machine succeeded in sufficiently coordinating its components. We propose discussing the following types of technological compatibility: design, mechanical, dimensional, heat, electromagnetic, operational, information, energy, biophysical, compatibility of technology, and cognitive compatibility, as well as compatibility at the level of the entire system. All of these are reviewed on the basis of studies and conclusions by a large group of Russian scientists, including A.A. Nosenkov, V.I. Medvedev, A.M. Mullin, V.D. Tsvetkov and others.[123]

Design Compatibility

When describing the design compatibility of technological devices and machines, one should note that this is the subject of scientific and engineering books and papers as well as standards and laws. Design compatibility is defined as the coordination of content and the structure of information and measurement-taking systems which is achieved by installing and applying unified standard forms of design elements. Design compatibility is construed as a quality ensuring the coordination of design parameters, ergonomic, and aesthetic requirements and technological matches (combinations) of these elements when used together.

When designing communication satellites and similar automatic space vehicles, a special place in original data is given to a-priori $A^{[n]}$, a multi-component set of physical connections of parameters of individual onboard systems, design features, orbit path and a space vehicle's program of operations. It can be written as

$$A^{[n]} = \{A_1^{[n]}, A_2^{[n]}, \ldots, A_n^{[n]}\}, \qquad (2.4.1)$$

---

[123] Formulas and equations for key types of technological compatibility are taken from: А.А. Носенков, В.И. Медведев, А.М. Муллин Совместимость технических систем. Красноярск, 2005.

where n is the number of components $A^{[n]}$, for n communication satellites.

Every component of the equation $A_i^{[n]}$ ($i = 1,2,..20,...$), has the following:

$A_1^{[n]}$ is the speed V_i of data transfer by *Zemlya* communication satellites that depends on the distance of the satellite L_{SAT} from the point of signal reception on Earth, the onboard antenna's amplification ratio, for example, the parabolic K_{oba} and the wattage power of the onboard transmitter W_{TRNSMT};

$A_2^{[n]} - W_{TRNSMT}$ determines the mass of the transmitter M_{TRNSMT} and its electric power consumption (E_{TRNSMT});

$A_3^{[n]}$ — the power consumption defines the capacity of the onboard chemical battery E_{obCB} required to transmit data and the wattage power consumption drawn off the solar panel W_{SP} to top up the onboard chemical battery;

$A_4^{[n]}$ and so on describe other parameters of the spacecraft.

Equation (2.4.1) does not represent the whole combination of physical connections that need to be taken into account when designing communication satellites, but it showcases the complexity of the task of ensuring design compatibility. Based on the content of individual links, most of them affect, to some extent, not only the process of ensuring design compatibility, but also the task of achieving it in an optimal manner.

Considering that the parameters of all the systems depend on the orbital parameters, program of operation and design of the communication satellites, the task of ensuring design compatibility at an absolutely optimal, perfect level becomes impossible. In this connection, rational design comes into play, if in the process of development of a communication satellite's design, its physical links are analyzed to an adequate depth, and optimal or near-optimal combinations of parameters are implemented.

Mechanical Compatibility

Mechanical compatibility is understood as the ability of technological devices to operate at a required level of quality under the influence of a dynamic mechanical load (mechanical impact) in a real operational environment.

In order to achieve mechanical compatibility in modern technology, the least problematic are dynamic calculations at the design stage to determine the structural strength of a design, the resonance frequency and loads. In this case, the starting point is the selection of a dynamic (physical) model of the structure being designed (a combination of inertial, elastic and dampening elements) with spectrum components of dynamic impacts taken into account. After this, a mathematical model of the structure is developed; the model should contain a closed system of key equations, as well as defining the ways to set initial and borderline conditions. Design modeling systems used in modern technology are systems with an infinite number of degrees of freedom or systems with distributed parameters explored by the methods of mathematical physics or variation methods. Designers usually move from a complex system to a simpler equivalent system with one or a finite number of degrees of freedom, which is a system with concentrated parameters, making it possible to do research on the basis of Lagrangian equations.

When the problem is written as a physical model, designers usually look at oscillations of cores and plates, because they are the components most frequently used in load bearing structures. For example, equations of the monodimensional longitudinal oscillations of a solid homogenous core are:

$$\partial^2 \xi / \partial t^2 = c^2 \partial^2 \xi / \partial x + f(x,t), c^2 = M_y \rho \qquad (2.4.2)$$

where ξ is the shift (amplitude) of the point at the moment t; M_y is elasticity Mode; p is the density of the core material; $f(x, t) = F(x, t) / \rho$ — the density of force per mass unit; $F(x, t)$ is the external force.

The original conditions are written as:

$$\xi(x,0) = \varphi(x), \qquad (2.4.3)$$

$$\partial \xi / \partial t(x,0) = \psi(x), \qquad (2.4.4)$$

Then designers find the limited terms defined by the patterns (the "law") of movement of the end of the core and set the extreme problems for Equation (2.4.2) determined by those limited terms. Solving these equations by the separation of variables method, one can make use of a system of equations and define the desired parameters of the oscillation process.

Very precise frequency bands (sometimes several different ones) are set to calculate the vibration load in the design. Thus, for communication satellites calculations are made for frequency bands typical of transportation used to deliver the spacecraft to the launch pad (road vehicles, trains and airplanes) and the space launch vehicle.

A well-designed product must not have its own structural frequency f_0 within the frequency spectrum of external influences. Although any structure has several values of natural vibration frequency, calculations are made only for the lowest value f_0. If the lowest frequency value f_0 lies within the range of external frequencies, the structure is improved until the f_0 value is increased to lie outside the frequency band of external influences. To increase resilience in the face of vibrations, additional bracings, spars and reinforcing contours and flanges are added, and materials with high dampening capacity are used. When manufacturing communication satellites, a separate version of the spacecraft is built which is subjected to the full spectrum of possible operational dynamic loads on the spacecraft.

Dimensional Compatibility

Dimensional compatibility is based on the mutual purpose of a product's components being attached to each other which have to be of an acceptable and precisely right size to ensure an adequate connection, as well as their electrical parameters falling within acceptable tolerances. Production tolerances for a specific product restrict the spread of parameters resulting from manufacturing errors and inaccuracies under normal operating conditions. Calculation of tolerances is most important for mass production, because possible deficiencies here can lead to very serious consequences. As a rule, Gaussian distribution of random variables (parameter deviations) is used for individual components and systems, as shown in Figure 2.2.

In this case:

$$f(\Delta A) = \left[1 / \sqrt{2\pi}\sigma(\Delta A)\right] \times \exp\left\{-\left[\Delta A - m(\Delta A)\right]_2 / 2\sigma^2(\Delta A)\right\}, \quad (2.4.5)$$

$$m(\Delta A) = \int_{-\infty}^{\infty} \Delta A \times f(\Delta A) \times d(\Delta A), \quad (2.4.6)$$

Deviation dispersion

$$\sigma^2(\Delta A) = \int_{-\infty}^{\infty} [\Delta A - m(\Delta A)]^2 \times f(\Delta A) \times d(\Delta A) \qquad (2.4.7)$$

Estimates of numerical values can be derived from experiments:

$$m^*(\Delta A) = \sum_{i=1}^{N} \Delta A / N \quad_{i}, \qquad (2.4.8)$$

$$\sigma^*(\Delta A) = \sqrt{\sum_{i=1}^{N} (\Delta A_i - m^*(\Delta A))^2 / (N-1)}, \qquad (2.4.9)$$

where $\Delta A_i = A_i - A_{io}$ is the deviation from the nominal value of a parameter at the ith measurement (experiment); N is the number of measurements (experiments).

These expressions are valid for relative error in product parameters $(\Delta A/A)_i$ and error in component parameters Δa_i, $(\Delta a, a)_i$.

The tolerance of an output parameter is determined by plugging the known tolerances in component parameters into the error equation. Regular components (middles of tolerance fields) are added together algebraically:

$$m(\Delta A / A) = \sum_{i=1}^{n} k_{bi} \cdot m(\Delta a / a_i), \qquad (2.4.10)$$

Therefore, it is possible to compensate for tolerance of individual components.

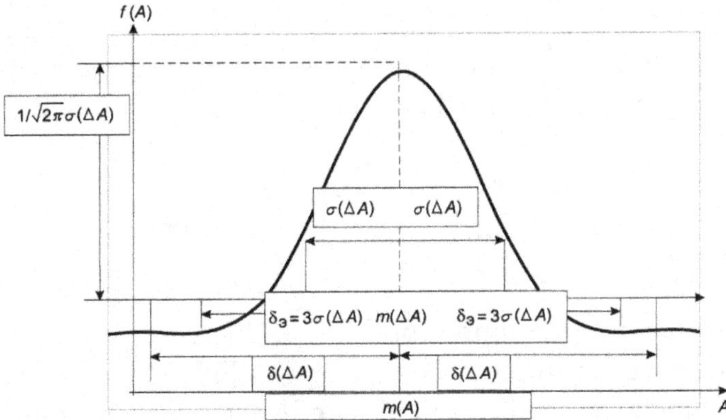

Fig. 2.2 Probability density distribution of parameter deviation

A is the current actual value of the output parameter; Ao is the nominal value of the parameter; $f\Delta A$ is the probability density of parameter deviation; $m(\Delta A)$ is the average value of parameter deviation; $m(A)$ is the average value of the parameter; $\delta(\Delta A)$ is the acceptable parameter deviation; σ is the standard deviation; δo is the operating tolerances.

For random and independent parameters of components, the random portion of tolerance of the output parameter is calculated based on the dispersion theorem for a sum of independent random variables:

$$\sigma(\Delta A / A) = \sqrt{\sum_{i=1}^{n} k^{2}_{bi} \cdot \sigma(\Delta a / a_{i})} \,, \qquad (2.4.11)$$

k_{bi} in both expressions is a coefficient accounting for the influence of error in the parameter of the ith component on the final product output error. When calculating production tolerances, the following is assumed to be known:

$$A = \varphi(a_{1},..., a_{i},..., a_{n}), \qquad (2.4.12)$$

where φ is the symbol of relation within the function; a_i is the parameter of an ith component; n is the number of components within the product.

Equation (2.4.12) is an equation of generalized dimensions of a chain, which, in a general case, would include both electrical and mechanical parameters (dimensions) of the product's components. So, depending on the function of the product (or an assembly), it can be the amplification coefficient, selectivity, amplitude or impulse duration, final length of a part, etc. Subsequent calculations are based on

$$A = \sum_{j=1}^{n_j} \overline{a_j} - \sum_{k=1}^{n_k} \overline{a_k} \,, \qquad (2.4.13)$$

where n_j, n_k are the number of links, an increase in the size of which increases or reduces the dimensions of the final link.

Minimax and probability methods can be used for determining the size chains. Each of these provides for two ways to achieve the desired precision of the final link:

1) Substitution ability: the desired precision is achieved without selecting, adjusting, or alteration of the links to make them fit;

2) Compensation: the desired precision is achieved by introducing a compensating link.

The minimax method to calculate thee nominal dimensions of the final link involves plugging in nominal values $(a_{jo}; a_{ko})$ of link dimensions in (2.4.13):

$$A_0 = \sum_{j=1}^{n_j} \overrightarrow{a}_{j0} - \sum_{k=1}^{n_k} \overleftarrow{a}_{k0} \;., \qquad (2.4.14)$$

The extreme allowable dimensions of the final link that still ensure dimensional compatibility of the product's "links" can be calculated by plugging in the maximum and minimum extreme values of the constituent links:

$$A_{max} = \sum_{j=1}^{n_j} a_{max} - \sum_{k=1}^{n_k} a_{k\,min} , \qquad (2.4.15)$$

$$A_{min} = \sum_{j=1}^{n_j} a_{min} - \sum_{k=1}^{n_k} a_{k\,max} , \qquad (2.4.16)$$

The tolerance is calculated as the difference between its extreme allowable size values A_{max} and A_{min}:

$$\delta(\Delta A) = \left[\sum_{j=1}^{n_j} a_{j\,max} - \sum_{j=1}^{n_j} a_{j\,min}\right] + \left[\sum_{k=1}^{n_k} a_{k\,max} - \sum_{k=1}^{n_k} a_{k\,min}\right] \approx \sum_{i=1}^{n} \delta(\Delta a)_i ,$$

$$(2.4.17)$$

i.e. the tolerance in the final link equals the sum of absolute values of tolerances in the component links. This indicates that in the calculation of dimensions of a chain by the minimax method with a given tolerance in the size of the final link, tolerances for the other components' links can be very strict especially if these links are numerous. Since the distribution of component dimensions within the tolerances is Gaussian (see Fig. 2.2), the probability of an undesirable combination of extreme sizes possible under the minimax approach is very small. Therefore, although the minimax method is very simple, it is uneconomical and can be recommended for the production of custom one-off products or small product series.

The probability method is used for mass production which is essentially very similar to the approach described above. The only difference is that since for mechanical structures the Equation (2.4.5) is linear, the impact coefficients $k_b = 1$ and calculations become simpler. The assumption here is that the dimensions of parts in a batch are randomly distributed within the tolerances in a Gaussian distribution, i.e. most parts have close to average dimensions.

Heat Compatibility

Heat compatibility deals with a technological device or machine's ability to operate under normal temperatures and heat flows in real operating conditions while maintaining the required level of operating quality and without causing any heat impact on other technological devices or machines.

Ensuring heat compatibility is one of the most important tasks in the design process of many types of machinery. A paradox is clearly observable: new advances in microelectronics produce new challenges for ensuring heat compatibility. This is explained by disproportional decreases in the size and electricity consumption of electronics. For example, if the size is reduced five-fold, electricity consumption declines only threefold. This leads to constant increases in the heat loads of electronics per unit of size, which creates the trend of increasing the structural temperature in a system where most components have independent temperatures.

Changes in temperature over time and space (the heat mode) affect components' resistance to interference and performance and undermine the mechanical structural strength.

Overall, the transfer of heat energy Q_i from an isothermal surface with temperature θ_i K to an isothermal surface with temperature θ_j can be described as:

$$\theta_i - \theta_j = K_{ij}^{[T]}Q_i, \; or \; \theta_j - \theta_i = K_{ji}^{[T]}Q_j, \qquad (2.4.18)$$

where $\theta_i - \theta_j, \theta_j - \theta_i$ is the temperature differential; $K_{ij}^{[T]}$ is the ratio coefficient, or the heat coefficient $(K_{ij}^{[T]} = K_{ji}^{[T]})$, and the structure of this coefficient does not depend on heat transfer methods (heat conductivity, convection, radiation) implemented in each specific case.

Calculations are made for three types of heat transfer (conduction, convection and radiation) based on the appropriate table data and the appropriate mathematical models.

Use of classical methods to solve some problems arising in connection with heat compatibility is not especially efficient, for example, for devices with built-in sources of heat, which is typical of devices aboard spacecraft. The Laplace method is widely used to solve problems of non-stationary heat modes.

However, it is difficult to use the Laplace integral transformation to solve problems when the initial data is functions of space coordinates and some multidimensional problems. In these cases, methods of integral transformation based on space coordinates matching the geometric shape of the object being analyzed are used (a parallelpiped shape is used most often).

The heat flows chart (Figure 2.3) provides an insight into the challenges of ensuring heat compatibility of an automatic spacecraft. The external heat flow for communication satellites is defined by the energy flows generated by the Sun.

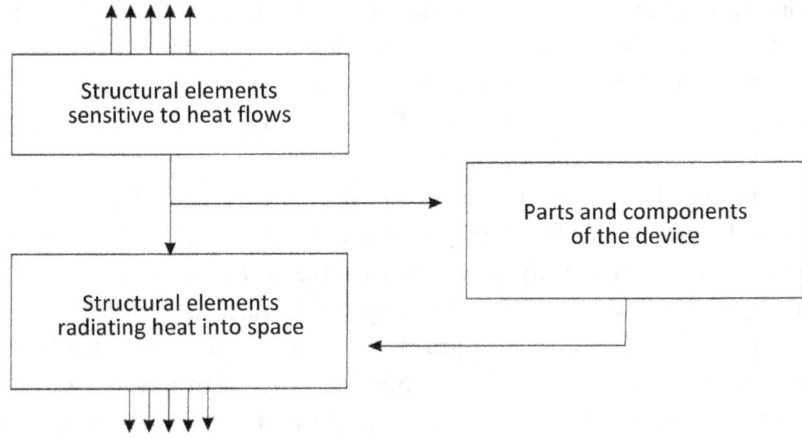

Fig. 2.3 Heat flow chart for a space communication device

The intensity of this flow is proportionate to the value of a_c, which depends on the properties of the surface exposed to the Sun, i.e. on the material and finishing of the surface. To obtain the desired value of a_c, a special coating is applied to the surface of a communication satellite. To reduce the absorption of the Sun's energy, the surface of the spacecraft is protected by heat shields, for example, by a vacuum heat shield, a 5-15 micron thick polyethylene terephthalate (PET) film spray-coated with aluminium.

A complete analysis of the temperatures of devices installed in a communication satellite requires knowledge not only of the temperature of all devices, but also the connection between these temperatures and how they depend on the temperature of the spacecraft's outer surface. This so-called internal problem can be reduced to studying an equation system that determines the distribution of temperatures inside a communication satellite. In simpler cases (e.g. for smaller communication satellites like S-1, S-1M), this equation system can be purely algebraic, while in more complicated cases equations may include partial derivatives.

A complete analysis of temperature regimes of the entire communication satellite would require an equation system comprising an equation for the spacecraft as a whole and equations for all onboard components and systems. This equations system would become too cumbersome even for smaller communication satellites. Therefore, approximate methods are used for analysis and calculations. The most widespread approach involves looking only at established temperature processes for the different operation modes of a communication satellite. The ultimate goal of this approach is to obtain enough data points for temperature regimes to approximate the entire operating heat regime of the spacecraft.

The physical reason for the great complexity of ensuring heat compatibility lies in the fact that all three types of heat transfer come into play between the many components of the spacecraft.

The arrangement of onboard components and assemblies has a very important, even decisive influence on the heat compatibility of a communication satellite. The heat compatibility of adjacent or proximate heat-emitting and heat-sensitive components is achieved through installation of heat shields or putting the components at a greater distance from each other on the structural supports within the spacecraft.

The accuracy of this approximate approach makes the successful design of a communication satellite possible. However, final conclusions about the degree of heat compatibility are based on the results of experimental tests of heat modes.

Electromagnetic Compatibility

Electromagnetic compatibility is the ability of devices generating electromagnetic fields to work together in such a way that radio interference would not exceed a certain permissible level and would not prevent each of the devices from operating normally. The problem of electromagnetic compatibility emerged together with electronics. Electronic devices operating at the same time create interference for each other. In certain conditions, this interference reaches an unacceptable level and can prevent radios and electronic devices, e.g. computers, from functioning. Interference can also be produced by industrial, transportation and household electrical devices, as well as by natural phenomena – lightning and solar flares. (Fig. 2.4).

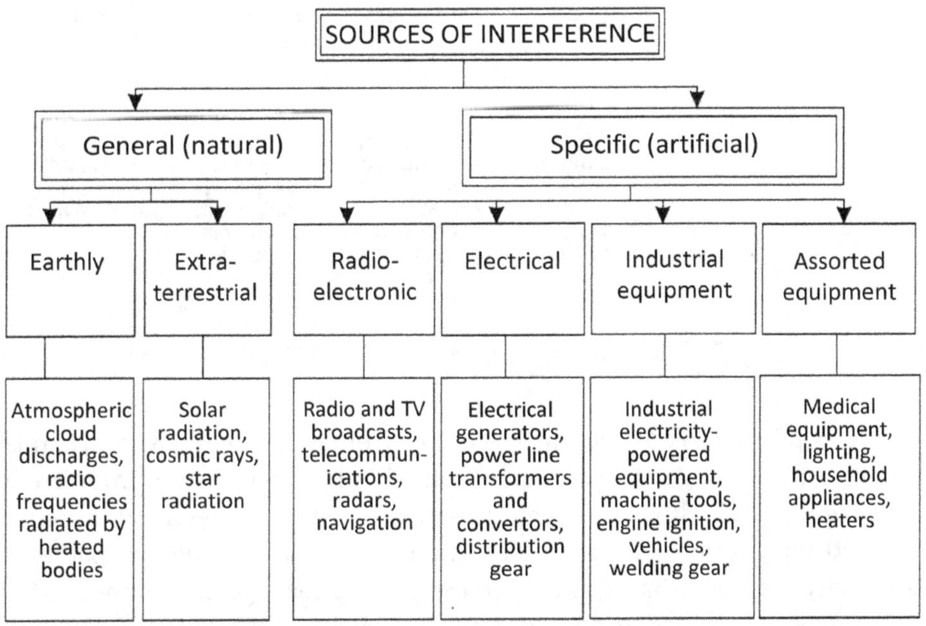

Fig. 2.4 Sources of unintended interference for radio and electronic devices

Specific sources of interference are of the greatest interest and cause the greatest problems. Two challenges arise in this connection:

1) Minimization of the effects of unintentional interference through efficient design of radio electronics;

2) Ensuring the emission of a useful signal in a way that produces the least amount of harmful interference from other sources.

A broad range of objects are susceptible to electromagnetic radiation (also known as interference recipients) (Fig. 2.5). Susceptibility of natural (general) recipients of interference, including human beings, may call for a limit on the total power of radiation by radioelectronics and other sources of radiation, becoming the reason for the specific arrangement of interference sources within smaller devices. The effects of interference are mostly produced through a radiowave receiving device.

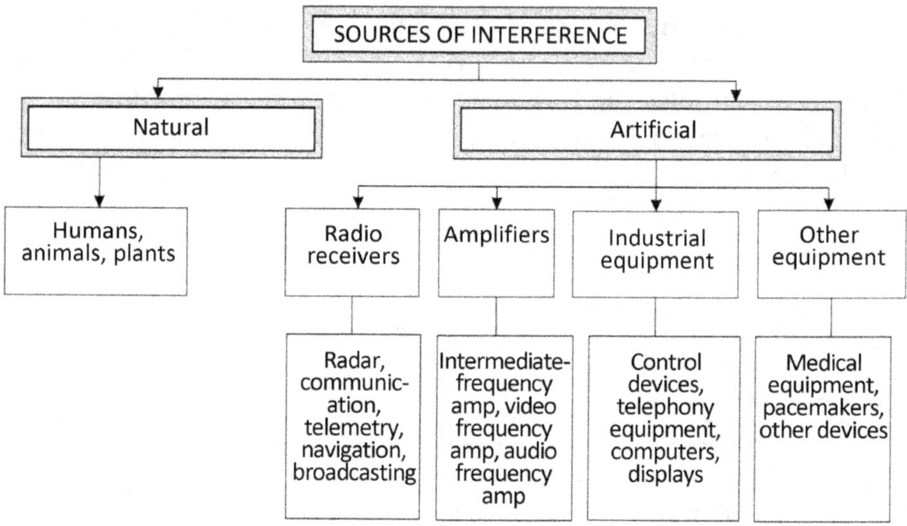

Fig. 2.5 Categories of devices affected by interference

Let us take a look at the physics of electromagnetic compatibility in the case of signal leakage. The source of parasitic leakage causing interference can be connected with the receiving device through an electrical, magnetic or electromagnetic field and can manifest itself through capacity or inductivity. Capacity-based interference-causing leakage can connect to the interference-prone device via a proximate electrical field.

Parasitic "cross-talk" as a type of interference can be created through the electromagnetic field of emission over a great distance (exceeding five times the wavelength) between the source of parasitic interference and the "receiving" device susceptible to interference, where the direct capacity-based and inductive parasitic connections are practically non-existent (transmissions and associated emissions by nearby radio stations, lightning, industrial interference), or through the electric mains. For all instances, fairly effective methods and methodologies for prevention and suppression of parasitic interference were developed over time (shielding, metallization, filtering, changes in electrical chain parameters and the mutual arrangement of electronic device components, the use of magnetic dielectrics and ferrites, the coordination of the types of materials to be used at operating frequencies, installation of spark-reducing gear, etc.).

Suppression of crosstalk is usually limited to eliminating or weakening the parasitic connection between the source and receiver of crosstalk by putting a shield between them, i.e. through limiting the outflow of electromagnetic energy to a specific restricted space by preventing its spread through all possible means. Shielding the electromagnetic field of the emission is achieved through the reflection of electromagnetic waves from the metallic surface of the shield and the fading of waves refracted by a remote shield.

Mathematical analysis of the electromagnetic compatibility of physical fields produced by various devices serves the limited purpose of studying differential equations with partial derivatives of the second degree or higher.

The objectives of calculating electromagnetic compatibility are, strictly speaking, non-linear. However, in order to simplify the search for solutions, many problems can be assumed to be linear at the first approximation, making it possible to use mathematical methods of analyzing linear problems. Solving these problems helps to find solutions to many calculation design challenges, e.g. the challenge of shielding devices and tools and links between them.

A systematic analysis of the challenges of resistance to interference and protection against interference requires taking into account the capabilities of the opponents in a "radioelectronic war," the special features of radio counter measures, radio camouflage, and the efficiency of interference of different types.

Operational Compatibility

Operational compatibility is defined in the GOST 22315-77 Standard as coordinated technological parameters that enable a device or other piece of technology to preserve its features during operation. Operational compatibility is based on a fundamental criterion of reparability (Fig. 2.6).

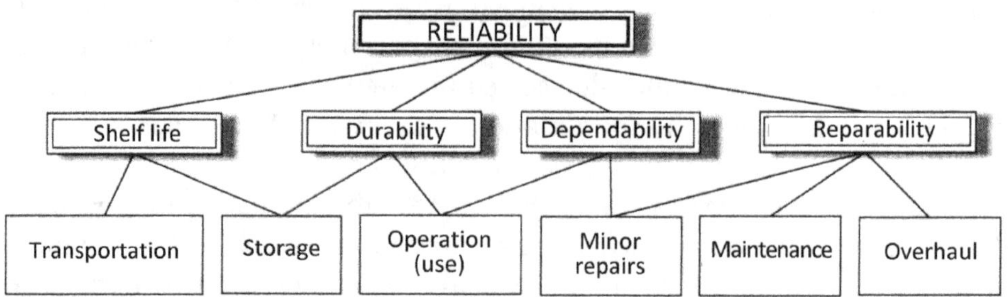

Fig. 2.6 Equipment reliability and lifestyle structure

Severe barriers to ensuring reparability create unproductive losses of time. This problem can be solved in two different ways.

The first way relies on statistics and is based on data about the amount of time required to fix malfunctions resulting from a failure of standard components in devices of different designs. This method is usually used for approximate calculation of the average time of repairs at the design stage. The calculation starts by identifying the overall number of standard components by group. Then the average failure frequency of components of this type is determined:

$$q_i = n_i \lambda_i / \sum_{s=1}^{m} n_s \lambda_s \, , \qquad (2.4.19)$$

where m is the number of component groups; n_i is the number of components in the system; and λ is the frequency of failures.

Using accumulated statistics about the average time of repairs $\overline{T}_i$ for components in the ith group is calculated as:

$$\overline{T} = \sum_{i=1}^{m} q_i \overline{T}_i \, , \qquad (2.4.20)$$

giving us three average expected time of repairs of the device or machine.

Therefore, this method relies on a very simple methodology, but requires gathering a great amount of statistical data. However, this method has limited value first of all because it is only valid for devices and machines which are going to use the same design methods as devices for which $\overline{T}_i$ data has been collected. The introduction of innovative devices and methodologies makes the available old statistics invalid and unapplicable.

The second way is the method of evaluation of operations. It is based on the pattern linking the average value of the random variable with the possible values of this variable and their respective probabilities. We can express the average time of repairs as:

$$\overline{T} = \sum_{j=1}^{N} q_j \overline{T_j}, \qquad (2.4.21)$$

where q_j is the conditional probability of breakdown of the device because of failure of the jth component out of N components; $\overline{T_j}$ is the average time of repair of the device if the jth component has failed.

This method of evaluation of operations requires knowledge of design features of the device being evaluated, and therefore it can only be used after a component prototype has been manufactured.

Information Compatibility

Information compatibility requires creating an information model corresponding to a computer that would match the operator's ability to receive and process the entire flow of encoded information and to operate the machine effectively through its controls. The operator receiving the information should be regarded as a process of forming a perceptional (sensory) image, or a subjective reflection in the human mind of the properties of an object impacting the human being. Formation of a perceptional image is a gradual process of three stages: discovery, discerning and identification. The duration of these stages depends on the complexity of the signal being received. Three types of analyzers are identified depending on the modality of the incoming signal. The visual analyzer is the most important for the operator's activity, followed by the aural and tactile analyzers. Other analyzers are only marginally involved in the operator's actions.

These analyzers help the human being not only to perceive these signals, but also to differentiate between them. To describe this differentiation, the concept of a differentiation threshold has been introduced, which is understood as the smallest possible difference between two stimuli (signals) or between two states of the same stimulus. Experiments have established that the magnitude of the differentiation threshold is proportionate to the original magnitude of the stimulus:

$$dJ / J = k = const \, . \qquad (2.4.22)$$

where J is the original magnitude of the signal (the stimulus); dJ is the value of the differential threshold; k is a constant with a value of 0.01 for a visual analyser, 0.1 for the aural analyzer and 0.3 for the tactile analyzer.

Based on this, we can determine the relationship between the magnitude of the signal and that of the sensory response it is eliciting:

$$S = k \times InJ = C, \qquad (2.4.23)$$

where S is the magnitude of sensory perception; k and C are constants.

The expression (2.4.23) is known as the Weber-Fechner Law, which states that the intensity of perception is directly proportionate to the log of the stimulus intensity. This correspondence is sometimes described as an exponential function.

Quasilinear models of the human operator engaged in sensory tracking have become the most widespread in psychological engineering practice. These models describe a human being's adaptive ability, delayed reactions of the human operator, as well as describing the properties of the human operator's neural and muscular system.

These models provide a fairly accurate description of the law of signal conversion by a human operator:

$$y = H(p)u + n(t) \, , \qquad (2.4.24)$$

where y is a mathematical description of controlling actions by a human operator developed by the operator as a result of intentionally "processing" data u.

The function $n(t)$ adaptively superimposed over the intentional regular activity of the human operator is called the "remnant" function. It is usually assumed to be a random function. The amplitude and properties of the remnant $n(t)$ depend on the properties of the input impulse.

These models can reflect significant variation in the features of sensomotor tracking. So, the tracking error, the remnant $n(t)$ and the transfer function $H(p)$, describing the model of sensomotor activity depend functionally both on the properties of the objects being controlled and on the signal $u(t)$ properties converted by the human operator in the course of sensomotor tracking. From the point of view of ergatic (human-machine) systems, this dependence is represented by a generalized mathematical model.

A combined mathematical function describing the human operator is called a generalized working descriptor. The expression "a stable functional state of the human operator" is used to narrow down the meaning of the general working description. This concept identifies, during a certain time interval τ the state of a human being when he or she is capable of performing the assigned actions Q_h during any sub-interval within time interval τ at fixed values of R_h and c, where Q_h is the operator of functional transformations performed by a human being (h) in information R_h . Naturally, unique psychophysiological qualities of the human operator make the duration of his or her stable functional state a random variable. In many human-machine (ergatic) systems in the realm of technology this random variable is normally distributed. Operators describing this variable reflect system features of the human being's operator activity: appropriate outward aspect, precision, tension, reliability, as well as data complexity. The complexity of the operator's tasks is inversely proportionate to the time it takes to perform them without error within a closed human-machine system (an "ergatic" system).

Energy Compatibility

The analysis of energy compatibility from the perspective of compatibility in human-machine systems presumes that a machine should be created in such a way and with such controls that would ensure harmony between the machine and its human operator in terms of the (muscular) power needed to operate the controls, power consumed, speed, precision and tempo of controlling actions, an optimal load for the human operator's limbs involved in operating the controls, and division of (control) functions among them.

Energy compatibility has to ensure that an operator can securely and comfortably keep any machine in his (her) hands. An operator's decision only makes sense when it is correct and will be acted upon in good time. Implementation of a decision involves inputting the required data in the machine. The human being's "output" channels serve this purpose: the motion (motor) and speech channels. An operator performs a great majority of control actions by movements.

The experience of building and operating human-machine systems indicates that often the preferable solution is to follow the principle of consecutive actions with a quantitative assessment of the arrangement of the controls and indicators on the dashboard.

The following value is assumed to be the measure of poor arrangement of choices in an operating field of n required components out of m possible components when performing each basic operation:

$$h_i = \lg_2 \frac{n - m - b + 1}{m}, \qquad (2.4.25)$$

where b is the number of ways components can be selected in a certain order.

The parameter h_i has the value of 1 when selecting the desired component out of two possible components, and the value of 0 when a subsequent component is selected without any doubt or hesitation. Consequently, the parameter h_i represents the uncertainty of choice of an indicator or control the human operator needs to observe or handle at this stage in the work process. If the human operator performs N actions while at work, the overall disorder of the operating field is

$$h = \frac{1}{N} \sum_{i=1}^{N} h_i, \qquad (2.4.26)$$

The meaning of parameter h is similar to the entropy of a communication source in information theory. It is one of the parameters of the psychological complexity of the human operator's work.

The greater h is, the greater the strain on the human mind and psychological state, especially the human operator's memory and attention. When h rises, the human operator needs better skills and training to cope.

The key movements of an operator can be described by attributes divided into four groups: speed-related (time-related), spacial, strength-related and precision-related.

The spread of repeating actions can be described by the frequency of repetition or the tempo that depends on the size of the controls and the amount of resistance they offer the operator. For pressing movements, the

112

tempo largely depends on the amount of effort that has to be exerted. Spatial characteristics of the operator's movements include the size of the motor field (the area within the operator's reach) and the movement trajectory. The motor field has three distinct reach areas where controls are placed: maximum, acceptable and optimal. The most important and most frequently used controls can be within the areas of optimal and acceptable reach. The speed and accuracy of controlling movements in the maximum reach area are substantially reduced, and fatigue sets in much faster. This is why work is only possible for short periods of time in this area.

Biophysical Compatibility

Biophysical compatibility essentially deals with reaching a rational compromise between the physiological condition and working capacity of a human being on the one hand and the influence of various factors and his (her) environment[124] on the other, while taking into consideration the volume and quality of tasks he (she) has to perform and the duration of the work. The overall influence of the parameters of the internal and external working environment on a human being's physiological condition is shown in Figure 2.7.

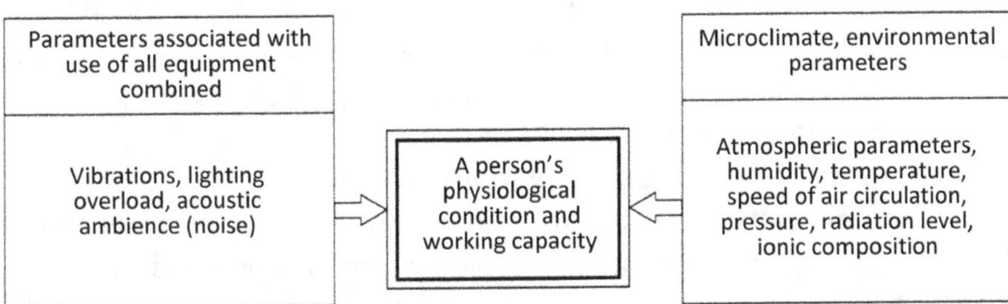

Fig. 2.7 Impact of external parameters on an individual's physiological condition

Speaking further of production processes, the working (production floor) environment is an important component of a workplace, e.g. an operator's workplace; this environment affects the operator's functional state and capacity for work. The working environment also directly affects

---

[124] В.А. Морозов Новые методы управления природопользованием. М.: МГУ, 2009.

the operator's reliability, speed and accuracy. Physical and chemical factors are most important in a working environment. One must take these factors into account when designing a human-machine system, creating the best possible working conditions for the human being. The following discomfort/comfort levels are used in regulation of workplace factors:

• beyond extreme (severe), i.e. hazardous, causing pathological changes in the human body and/or making it impossible for the operator to continue working;

• extreme (severe), reducing the human being's capacity for work and causing functional changes in the human body outside the acceptable range, although not resulting in pathological changes;

• relatively uncomfortable: if applied for a certain extended period of time, may cause unpleasant subjective feelings and functional changes within the acceptable range, while not reducing the required level of capacity for work and not undermining the operator's health;

• comfortable, i.e. ensuring optimal fluctuations in the human being's capacity for work, well-being and preservation of his (her) health.

The work environment can have both a direct and indirect influence on the human being's condition and work quality. Let us consider the examples of the effects of noise and vibration. The direct influence of noise can create interference for voice communication between operators, when they receive acoustic signals, organize voice data input/output to/from a computer, etc. Indirect effects of noise include, among other things, deteriorating attention and concentration (see Fig. 2.8). Noise can reduce the speed and accuracy of sensorimotor reactions, which is especially apparent during complex, minutely coordinated processes.

Vibration causes the human body to oscillate at a certain frequency and amplitude and may interfere with precision operations relying on vision and motion, and undermine concentrated observation and perception of depth and space. Indirect side effects of vibration may include lower resolution and acuteness of vision. Consequently, vibration may cause undesirable effects on types of operator activity that rely heavily on visual analysis.

The examples confirm the importance of taking into consideration both the direct and indirect impact of environmental factors on the condition and work results of the human operator when designing human-machine systems.

Similar changes also take place in the structure of activity. The key parameters of an activity essential for serving the purpose of the activity can be maintained at an adequate level at the expense of compromising some secondary parameters. The key, essential parameters in this case would begin to deteriorate only after the core components of the system are no longer capable of providing the required level of quality because of age or disrepair.

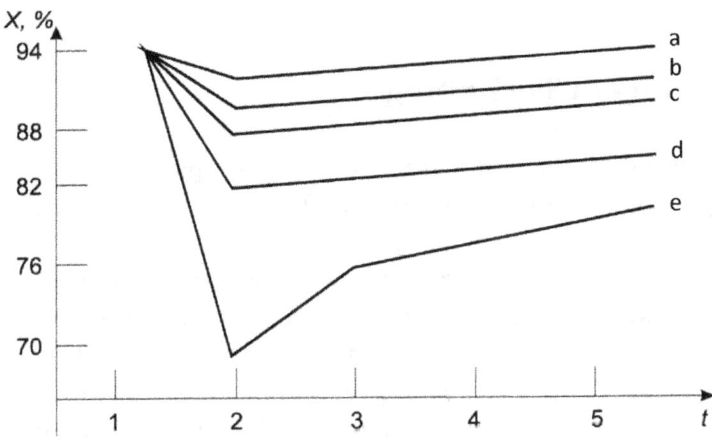

Fig. 2.8 Effects of noise on concentration

1 – Before exposure to noise
2 – Immediately after exposure
3.5 – 30, 60, 120 minutes after exposure
Noise intensity, dB: a – 60, b – 70, c – 80, d – 90, e – 100
X – % of full concentration

This pattern, although somewhat idealized and one-dimensional, is the source of several conclusions of great practical significance. First, to be able to evaluate the impact of the working environment on the condition of a human being, one must know which parts and systems of the body and their associated functions would compensate for and which would stabilize the effects of a given factor affecting that human being. Second, certain engineering and psychological recommendations can be made to compensate for changes in the structure of the activity.

Organization of the working environment depends to a great extent on the effectiveness of technological and other means that ensure maintenance of environmental factors at the desired level. At the same time, one should bear in mind that these means, while supporting some factors at a certain level, may be the source of other, unfavorable conditions in the same environment. For example, air conditioners, while maintaining a desirable microclimate, may emit acoustic noise; lighting systems providing the desired amount of light in the workplace may cause the workfloor to heat up above a comfortable level. One must consider these and similar conditions when attempting to ensure biophysical compatibility while designing and equipping a workplace.

Compatibility of Technology

Methodology, concepts and definitions for compatibility in the field of technology are presented in V.D. Tsvetkov's book on designing technological processes.[125] He formulates the compatibility of technology principle in the following way: technology objects and equipment can be combined in a system if they are compatible in the most important types of links and relationships, i.e. the kind of common functions, common structural and functional properties that enable them to function together as an integrated technological system working to its specifications. This compatibility of technology principle is fairly uniform and applies to technological systems of any type and size.

The compatibility of technology concept can be expressed, in general terms, by a set of several key premises. The defining moment in ensuring compatibility of technology comes at the time of designing a technological manufacturing processes for parts, assemblies and accessories. The design process starts with examining the terms of reference.

The next stage in the design process involves zeroing in on possible solutions for key tasks that would ensure the best possible technological processes for making products at the next level in the hierarchy. The design process π_T is divided into several interconnected levels:

$$L = \{l_i\}; i = 1,...,m, \qquad (2.4.27)$$

characterized by successively increasing the working out in detail j_n of design solutions from one level to the next:

$$\pi_T \rightarrow (\pi^1{}_{jt}, \pi^2{}_{j1},...,\pi^m{}_{j1}), \qquad (2.4.28)$$

The compatibility of technology principle incorporates the experience of

---

[125] В.Д. Цветков Системно-структурное моделирование и автоматизация проектирования технологических процессов. Минск: Наука и техника, 1979.

solving complex design and technology problems, when insufficient information available before the start of the design process causes first-level solutions to be most generic and abstract, with the necessary detail emerging at the subsequent levels. The type and number of levels depend on the complexity of the process being designed. A multi-level process unfolds from the top down, i.e. moves from synthesizing a very general "in principle" to providing design solutions R_{qk} of the required degree of detail at the preceding ℓ-1 level used as additional source data for the design process at the ℓ-$м$ level:

$$y^{l} : \left\{ ИД, R_{i}^{l-1} \right\} \rightarrow \left\{ R_{ij}^{l} \right\}, \qquad (2.4.29)$$

Multilevel deconstruction reduces the design objective to identifying the most effective features of technological processes at the initial, intermediate and final levels which provide the desired precision parameters at the lowest cost of design.

A technological process usually has material, energy and information links to systems in its environment. These links can be controlled in a computerized technological process.

Compatibility of subsystems within a technological system can be achieved in different ways, each of which is associated with a different implementation cost. This speaks to the need to improve the system.

In light of the above, the cost-optimal way to achieve compatibility of technology will be associated with a technological process that ensures cost minimization for a given processing quality, including the cost of special equipment; auxiliary tools, the preparation of installation facilities and other components. Therefore, although the aspects discussed in this section do not cover all the possible aspects of technological compatibility methodology, they provide a general idea of its content.

Cognitive Compatibility

The first time Russian scientists reviewed cognitive compatibility was in a relatively recent book on ergonomics.[126] However, the author did not define the concept of this compatibility type.

---

[126] В.М. Мунипов, В.П. Зинченко Эргономика: человекоориентированное проектирование техники, программных средств и среды. М.: Логос, 2001.

Cognition is a Latinate word that means knowledge or the process of obtaining knowledge. Therefore, cognitive compatibility can be interpreted as a match between a human being's ability to learn and the level of complexity of operating a machine (including, without limitation, a computer). This ability comprises three components: intellectual capability, professional ability and skills, and psychophysiological aptitude. In a similar way, cognitive compatibility has three specific types (see Fig. 2.9).

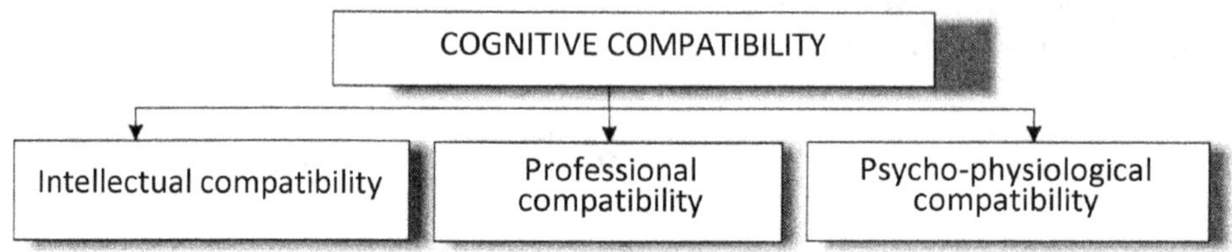

Fig. 2.9 Cognitive compatibility chart for a "human-machine" system

Intellectual compatibility implies a match between a human operator's intellectual ability and the level of tasks he or she has to perform within a human-machine system. Certainly, this compatibility type was studied, and ensured, with no attempt to categorize it as an independent type of compatibility in human-machine systems. The complexity of the intellectual tasks that a human operator faces is defined to a great extent by the uncertainty of source data for decision-making, including uncertainty:

- arising from the great number of objects involved in a situation;
- arising from insufficient, inadequate information because of social, technological and other reasons;
- caused by the excessively high, unaffordable cost of certainty;
- introduced by the decision-maker, etc.

In addition to this classification, sometimes researchers also identify incomplete uncertainty, in which source data is several random variables with known distributions, and (complete) uncertainty, in which the source data is several random variables with unknown distributions. The decision-making procedure and decision quality in different uncertain situations and categories of a human-machine system will be of a different nature, requiring different intellectual capabilities from the human operator.

Intellectual compatibility can be tested through correlation analysis. A control group of human operators is selected for this purpose. Depending on the specific nature of their activity, each of them has a certain parameter x_i assigned, representing success in this activity (for example, the time required to solve a task, accuracy, productivity, etc.). For each of these human operators, parameter y_i is also assigned, describing a certain quality being tested. The degree of correlation between this quality and success of an activity is defined by the correlation coefficient r, which is calculated as:

$$r_{xy} = \frac{1}{N-1} \frac{\sum_{i=1}^{N}(x_i - \bar{x})(y_i - \bar{y})}{\sqrt{Var_x Var_y}}, \qquad (2.4.30)$$

where N is the number of human operators in the control group; Var_x and Var_y are the variances of variables x_i and y_i, respectively; x and y are the average values of those variables.

In some cases, variables x_i and y_i cannot be expressed as numeric values. In this case, they are assigned a specific rank from 1 to N so that the rank correlation coefficient can be calculated:

$$\rho_{xy} = 1 - \frac{6\sum_{i=1}^{N}(x_i - y_i)^2}{N(N^2 - 1)}, \qquad (2.4.31)$$

where x_i and y_i are ranks of variables x and y for i^{th} human operator.

Values of correlation coefficients r_{xy} and p_{xy} above $0.3 \div 0.4$ reflect a significant correlation between the variables being compared.

People with very rudimentary training and an undeveloped skill level can apparently be hired to work as human operators of human-machine systems with the most basic operating algorithms that completely determine the range of tasks they have to perform. However, human-machine systems that require decisions involving probabilities and pushing the boundaries must be operated by highly-trained individuals of great intellectual ability who are capable of creative, heuristic thinking.

Psychophysiological compatibility describes a match between the individual's psychological and physiological capabilities and the requirements for the human operator in a specific job. Psychophysiological attributes of compatibility between a human being and a machine are shown in Figure 2.10.

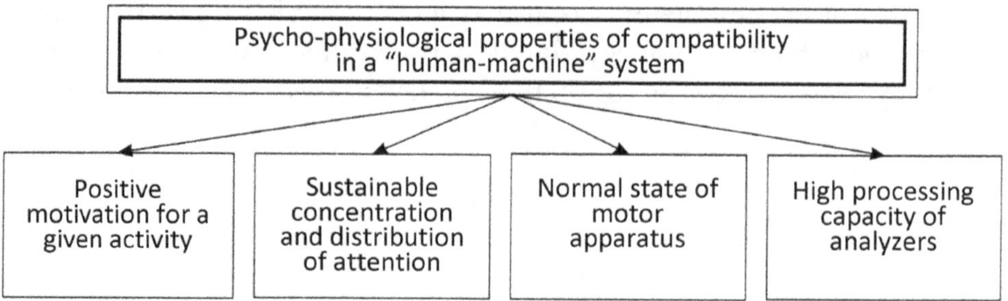

Fig. 2.10 Psycho-physiological compatibility properties chart of a "human-machine" system

This kind of compatibility also entails various psycho physiological requirements (for emotional stability, attention, memory, reaction speed, some specifics of the central nervous system) for the human operator: from very minimal and relaxed, if the human operator works in a comfortable environment, to maximum and very stringent when the human operator has to work in extreme environments or in situations when the environment can deteriorate rapidly and unexpectedly, at which time the human operator's psychological balance and willpower – composure, concentration, etc. – have paramount importance.

Experience of disasters, catastrophes and emergencies shows that a psychologically stable individual with a strong will can not only reduce the impact, but also completely prevent death and destruction (unfortunately, sometimes at the cost of his or her own life). A man with a weak mind and will and compromised physiology may still be capable of performing the required actions perfectly in a normal situation, receiving top appraisals of his or her performance. However, in emergencies, breakdowns and catastrophes, which usually happen without warning, the same individual would be likely to go into shock (a nervous and physical paralysis) and may even make the situation worse. Individuals are usually tested to see if they meet psycho-physiological requirements.

One should also bear in mind that the psychophysiological qualities of individuals develop and change over time as they go through life. This is why targeted training and education can certainly produce a positive impact. However, the degree of this impact can be uneven, because people have limits to the flexibility and changeability of their psychophysiological qualities including perceptory thresholds, capacity of short-term memory, etc.

Professional compatibility envisages a match between an individual's professional skills and education and the type of activity he or she has to perform in a human-machine system and is ensured by its four main components: professional selection, training, advanced improvement of professional skills in the context of specific psychological personality features and the individual's motives and interests, as well as putting together workplace teams (crews, teams and shifts) for working in a group.

The study of human abilities is the foundation for developing methods of professional selection. Abilities in psychology is understood as a complete set of an individual's qualities which are a condition for successfully mastering certain types of activity, perfecting one's skills at those types of activity and achieving excellent results. The question of the origin of abilities lies at the center of the "abilities problem." Psychological studies indicate that an individual's capabilities take shape and develop during life. However, they do not come out of nowhere. The natural foundation and source of abilities are the potential ("the makings"), i.e. some innate properties. The link between abilities and the potential is neither rigid or unambigous. Similar potential can become the foundation for different abilities in different people, and conversely, different potential can lead to the development of similar abilities.

Therefore, cognitive compatibility is one of the most complex compatibility types in a human-machine system, because it deals with the human operator not only as far as his or her operating ability is concerned, but also in all of his or her psychophysiological characteristics. There is room here for relevant research by scholars and specialists representing many different fields.

2.4.3. Compatibility of Treatment Methods in Medicine

In recent years, medicine often resorts to comprehensive treatment. Various physiotherapeutical treatments and remedies in combined use can either reinforce or mitigate each other's effect. This is why it is important to take into account the compatibility phenomenon, including where physical treatment factors are assigned in a certain sequence.

Compatibility or incompatibility of treatments controls combining physiotherapy, hydrotherapy, electrotherapy, balneological and climatic treatments in a certain sequence, with exercise therapy and medication added to the mix.

Principles of combined and concurrent use of physical treatment factors are used in contemporary medicine.

Combined use is currently understood as the sequential administration of two or more treatment factors during a course of treatment. Procedures may be administered in quick succession on the same day, on alternate days, or a course of treatment by one factor can be replaced by another course of treatment.

The principle of concurrent use is the simultaneous administration of two or more treatment factors. Complex physical-chemical and physiological processes lie at the heart of the way in which compound physiotherapy works, with synergies, sensitization and antagonism having especially great significance.

The synergy principle makes it possible to achieve a stronger final effect by including a set of physical factors with a similar effect in the treatment plan, i.e. through the addition of similar reactions from certain physiological systems or the potential effect of various physical factors. Sensitization takes place when one physiotherapy treatment puts the body or some of its systems into a state of heightened sensitivity to the effects of another physical factor.

The antagonism principle most often finds practical applications to mitigate undesirable side-effects of one of the factors: for example, contrast showers and baths help avoid blood vessel atony, venous hyperemeia which can be caused by the action of pure heat.

The principle of amplification of a local reaction can be manifested when factors with predominantly general and local effect are combined. A local reaction becomes stronger if a local procedure is followed up with a procedure producing a general effect.

If a correctly composed plan of physiotherapy treatments ensures that the positive effects of several physical factors pulling in the same direction add up, while the negative effect of some components is reduced, additional effects on body systems and some aspects of the pathological process are introduced, the duration of subsequent effect of treatments administered jointly is increased.

Let us talk about the compatibility and incompatibility of physiotherapy and balneological treatments, which can cause a significant long-term reaction in a patient. Therefore, administering several treatments with a powerful effect on the same day is usually inadvisable. A cumulative effect of multiple powerful additive stimuli can result in various functional disruptions in the nervous, cardiovascular and other essential systems within the human body.[127]

Treatments affecting the same reflexogenic area through which they produce their overall effect on the human body, should not be combined on the same day (the collar and sinocarotid areas, mucous membrane in the nose, and others). Treatments with the opposite effect are usually incompatible, (e.g. heat and cold treatments, soothing and stimulating), except where a contrasting reaction needs to be achieved (e.g. contrast showers or baths). When putting together a combined therapy treatment plan and addressing the practical matters of (in)compatibility of physiotherapy treatments, one must take into account the special aspects of the effect that separate physical factors may have. In medicinal electrophoresis, which is based on reflexive reactions, the following has particular importance: galvanic current produces a high concentration of accumulated medications introduced into the body through other channels in the tissues and organs in the space between the electrodes. This principle is used in so-called intra-tissue, or intra-organ electrophoresis.

The basic principles of compatibility and incompatibility of laser therapy with other kinds of physiotherapy treatments are the same as for other types of light treatment. Heat treatments (mud baths and mud and mineral wax applications), if applied to large or reflexogenic areas of the body are incompatible with hydrotherapy (baths, showers), microwave therapy, UHF treatment in amounts sufficient to make the application area warmer, general d'arsonvalization, light baths, infrared irradiation, erytemic UV irradiation (i.e. strong enough to cause skin reddening), and other full-body physiotherapy procedures. Mud baths and applications are incompatible with any other kinds of heat treatment.

For example, acupuncture is more effective in treating lung and cardiovascular conditions if it is combined with climatic therapy. Inhalation of medicines (aerosol therapy and electric aerosol therapy) can be combined with electric therapy and other physiotherapy treatments on the same day.

As for combining massage therapy with exercise therapy, massage can be administered either before or after exercise and can be combined with all types of physiotherapy, except for UV irradiation of the same area of the body in amounts that cause skin reddening (in erythemic dosages).

---

[127] Совместимость и последовательность применения лечебных физических факторов: Метод. рекомендации / Под ред. А.А. Шатрова. Ялта, 1986.

As for the compatibility and incompatibility of climatic and physiotherapy treatments, it is advisable to use the following both at and outside health resorts: various types of aerotherapy (staying out in the open for an assigned period of time or round-the-clock, sleeping on the beach, air baths), heliotherapy (exposure to sunlight), swimming in the sea or other natural bodies of water: a river, a lake. The following combinations of climatic treatments may be assigned depending on how serious an illness and the overall clinical condition are, and on the stage in the treatment process that determines the admissible additional strain on the human body, and also depending on the season, weather, specific conditions at the resort: aerotherapy (without any other climatic treatments); aerotherapy in conjunction with heliotherapy, heliotherapy and swimming in the sea; aerotherapy and swimming in the sea. Each of the climatic therapy combinations listed here may include machine-assisted physiotherapy (including hydrotherapy and electrotherapy). Doses of the various factors in combined climate-physiotherapy and the amount of exertion during exercise therapy are set on a case-by-case basis depending on the disease and the patient's overall condition.

The brief specific notes on whether certain treatments can or should be combined with others may become the basis for individually-targeted treatment or rehabilitation plans for patients with different conditions. New scientific data on the compatibility and desirable sequence of administering various physical medical factors will be narrowed down and expanded, as in other fields of science and technology.

Automated systems that control the treatment process can be included in control software algorithms to monitor the process and make sure that correct, compatible treatments and procedures are used in the correct sequence, and also to make adjustments to assigned treatments.

Several diagnostic devices are currently used as implementation of these compatibility algorithms and to ensure the correct sequence of application of physical treatment factors and medicines, including Gamma-1. It also makes sense to combine as automatic control boards the tools used to administer balneological treatments which are used in healthcare and prevention care facilities.

These principles of putting together rational treatment plans based on the latest available data on compatibility, incompatibility and the desirable sequence of physiotherapy, balneological and climatic treatments help with more differentiated and better-targeted use of physiotherapy methods (including hydrotherapy and electrotherapy methods), expanding the range of indication and preventing harmful, negative reactions.

Changes in clinical symptoms and the findings of specialized tests (on the system that is the human body in this case) are used to evaluate the effectiveness of treatment.

The differentiated approach helps to expand patient coverage by physiotherapy methods at healthcare institutions, reduce the number of adverse reactions, and, most importantly, reduce the number of days of temporary disability in the course of a year.

CHAPTER 3

COMPATIBILITY AND DEVELOPMENT OF MAN AND SOCIETY

3.1. Compatibility of Bionergy Capabilities and Limitations of Human Beings

Evolution finds many reasons for reconciliation and compatibility. Right now, Earth is home to 25-30 million species, of which biologists have identified and described approximately 1.5 million.[128] Our species, Homo sapiens, therefore represents less than 1/10,000,000 of the planet's biodiversity. The majority (more than 99%) of the species that have ever lived on planet Earth are now extinct. Therefore, humans represent only approximately one-billionth of the biodiversity created on Earth by the evolutionary process.

The problem of the origin of life raises many questions for science to answer and creates considerable discord between scientists and thinkers

---

[128] И. Ясина Человек с человеческими возможностями. М.: Эксмо, 2010.

who assume that life emerged because of an intervention by a higher power (a deity). The latter include many physicists and biologists who disagree with chemists and other biologists.

Chemistry was destined to discuss this scenario (or at least it should have done so). Life is so complex, even from the chemistry perspective, that the probability of recreating its emergence in a laboratory is practically zero. It is important to think in terms of probabilities, i.e. find the arguments that would make it possible to identify the processes that could have conceivably led to the emergence of life from the so-called primordial soup of inanimate organic molecules, processes that would match our understanding of molecules and reactions involving them.

The species of Homo sapiens in essentially its modern shape emerged in Africa some 100,000-150,000 years ago. This is less than 1/20,000 of the time life has existed on Earth. If we convert the time intervals to the more familiar format of days and assume that the entire time life has existed on Earth equals one year, we would have humanity enter the stage at 11:45 pm on December 31. On this scale, we would have existed as a species for only 15 minutes.

If we take the accumulation of scientific knowledge over the past 200 years to be 100%, the first century would contribute only 10% to the total, with the second century accounting for 90%. Not only the overall volume of knowledge, but also the pace of knowledge accumulation is increasing. If we assume that the pace of knowledge accumulation accelerates ten-fold every century, the volume of knowledge would increase 10,000 times by 2100 and 10,000,000 times by 2200 using the year 1800 as the comparison base.

Human beings are a biological species that emerged thanks to other species which were not, strictly speaking, humans themselves.[129] To understand the nature of human beings, we must understand our biological profile and provenance, the history of our humble origin.

Our closest relatives in the animal world are great apes, with chimpanzees the closest of all – in fact, they are closer to Homo sapiens than they are to gorillas. Homo sapiens branched off from chimpanzees approximately 5-7 million years ago in Africa, evolving into Homo Erectus by approximately 1.8 million years BCE.

Humans are substantially different from animals not only in their anatomy, but also, and much more importantly, in their individual and

---

[129] И.А. Неумывашкин Биоэнергетическая сущность человека. М.: Диля, 2012.

social behavior. The most prominent distinguishing futures of human behavior include:

1) symbolic (creative) language;
2) self-awareness and realization of one's mortality;
3) making tools and creating technologies;
4) nuanced expression of emotions;
5) intellect — the ability to think and build arguments;
6) ethics and religion;
7) science, literature and art;
8) laws and political and economic institutions;
9) social organization and collaboration.

People live in organized social groups, just like other primates. However, primates lack the complexity of social organization that people have. Culture is a distinguishing feature of human society. What are the boundaries of human biology? Biological heredity is based on passing genetic data from parents to offspring. Genetic data is encoded in a linear sequence of nucleotides of the DNA ("letters" of the genetic alphabet recorded using the letters G, A, T and C). Every human being has two sets of 23 chromosomes, one from each of his or her parents. The total number of DNA[130] letters in each chromosome set is approximately 3 billion. To record the DNA sequence of one genome – the entire hereditary information of an organism – one would need approximately 3,000 books of the same size as the Bible.

The first significant step toward understanding the principles of decoding genetic information was made in 1941, when George W. Beadle and Edward L. Tatum demonstrated that genes control the synthesis of enzymes – catalysts that regulate chemical reactions in all living organisms. At the same time, chemical reactions within an organism should be organized, and the organism should be able to switch specific genes on and off. Francois Jacob and Jacques Monod discovered in 1961 the first control system for the gene responsible for producing the enzyme to break down sugars in Escbericbia coli bacteria. Many different methods of gene control in bacteria and other microorganisms have since been discovered.

The next important step is to find a solution to the differentiation problem. A human body comprises approximately one trillion cells of

---

[130] Gerard, R. Change Your DNA, Change Your Life! Binghamton: Oughten House Foundation Inc., 2000.

approximately 200 different types, and all are produced by the sequential division of a fertilized egg, a single large cell 0.1 mm in diameter. The first several divisions serve only to increase the mass of the main cell. Subsequent divisions produce folds and differences in the mass of cells, ultimately creating different tissues and organs. The full set of genes doubles after each cell division.

The data regulating differentiation of cells and organs is contained in DNA strings, but only in the molecule's short segments. What sequences do these controlling elements represent, where do they lie and how does one decode them? Mammals have controlling strings operating at a higher level than control mechanisms triggering and disabling individual genes. These higher-level strings act on entire gene groups rather than individual genes. Structural details of this control mechanism,[131] interaction between various control mechanisms and many other issues have yet to be explored to understand how a human being becomes who he or she is. The DNA controlling elements will be sequenced, but this would be only a small step towards understanding all 3,000,000,000 nucleotide pairs comprising the human genome.

The benefits that humanity should expect from understanding the processes of ontogenetic decoding are immense. This knowledge should provide crucial insights into the aging process and enable scientists to understand how to treat complex genetic diseases, including cancer – an illness that for now kills people who successfully resist other conditions. Cancer is an ontogenetic decoding anomaly. Cells divide (multiply) even though the well-being of the entire body requires that they should stop dividing. Individual genes have been identified (oncogenes) that trigger the onset of specific kinds of cancer. However, oncogenes need to be compatible with other genes in the body, as well as with a cell's internal and external environment, to trigger cancerous processes.

Aging is also a (built-in) error or incompatibility in ontogenetic decoding processes: cells can no longer perform functions wired in their genetic code, or are no longer capable of dividing to replace the dead cells.

Diseases with clear, well understood causes – tuberculosis, syphilis, measles and many "childhood" diseases – can nowadays be cured successfully at a moderate cost, achieving excellent results.

---

[131] А.С. Татарчук Современные возможности предварительного исследования. М., 2011.

The human brain is the most complex and most developed organ in the body. It consists of more than 3 billion neurons, each of which is linked to other neurons by axons and dendrites. From an evolutionary perspective, an animal's brain is an important adaptation instrument enabling the body to accumulate and process data about environmental conditions and then find ways to adapt to them. This ability is developed to the extreme in human beings, while the hypertrophied human brain makes abstract thinking, language and technology possible. These tools have enabled humanity to take adaptability to a new collective level: the level of adaptation to culture and compatibility of development of the human community.

As the human brain grows more complex, biological revolution reaches beyond its "natural" level, transforming into a new kind of evolution:[132] evolution by adaptation through technological influence on the environment. The body adapts to the environment though natural selection by changing its genetic structure over generations, to meet the demands of the environment. People alone have developed the ability to adapt to hostile surroundings by transforming their immediate environment to match their genetic predispositions. Making clothes and building shelter gave people an opportunity to venture beyond the warm tropical zone of the Old World, to which they were best adapted naturally, and populate almost the entire planet. In a similar manner, people did not sit around waiting to grow wings or gills; they conquered the ocean and the sky with artificial devices. Our brain (the "residence" of the human mind) has made us the most successful extant species.

The human genome does not have enough DNA molecules to describe the trillions of connections appearing in the human brain between neurons. Consequently, the genetic code has to be organized as a hierarchical control system, as described earlier,[133] to send the control signals from one level to lower levels using a network of channels and process compatibility. In fact, the development of the human brain is one of the most intriguing aspects of a human being's development.

The Human Genome Project which is currently under way, mostly outside Russia, has not, on the whole, brought us closer to knowing ourselves or understanding where we are headed.

---

[132] McConkey, E. How the Human Genome Works. Sudbury, MA: Jones & Bartlett Learning, 2004.
[133] А. Марков Эволюция человека. М.: АСТ: Астрель, 2011.

Decoding the human genome will be only the first step towards understanding the genetic structure of human beings. A human being is not a genetic machine. Our mammalian features, abilities and behavior determined by genes match the environment according to patterns which are intricate and unpredictable in all details — these patterns contain our unique identity. For human beings, the environment acquires another dimension, and this dimension becomes dominant. A key distinguishing feature of a human being is culture, which can be understood as a combination of the human being's actions which are not biologically predetermined. Culture incorporates societal and political institutions, modes of action, religious and ethical traditions, language, common sense and scientific knowledge, art and literature – in other words, all creations of the human mind. Culture is undergoing an evolution of its own, which is built over the organic evolution and has become the key form of human evolution in the past several millennia. Cultural evolution has become possible because of cultural memory, an exclusively human method of adaptation to the environment and of transferring the skills of such adaptation down the generations.

Humanity has two types of heredity: biological and cultural, sometimes also called organic and super-organic, or endosomatic and exosomatic. The biological heredity of human beings is no different from the heredity of animals and other organisms breeding through intercourse, as noted above. Cultural heredity, on the other hand, is based on the transfer of information through education, which does not depend on biological heredity in principle. Culture is learned through education, example and imitation, through print literature, radio, TV, cinema, works of art and other communication media. An individual receives culture from his parents, other family members, significant others and friends, from his entire entourage.

Inheriting culture gives people something unavailable to other living organisms: a way to accumulate and transfer experience down the generations using the "social memory" (a concept proposed by Spanish philosopher Jose Ortega-y-Gasset). People, unlike all other animals, have created culture precisely because they can pass on their combined, generalized experience from one generation to the next.

Cultural heritage makes cultural evolution possible, i.e. the evolution of knowledge, social institutions, ethics, and other components unavailable to other living organism – i.e. adaptation through culture. Cultural adaptation takes priority over biological adaptation for human beings, because the former is much faster and can be directed in a specific way. A new scientific discovery or advance in technology can be shared with the whole of humanity, at least potentially, within a time shorter than one generation. Furthermore, if the need arises, culture can stimulate the compatibility of necessary changes to achieve its goal. Biological compatibility depends on the uncertain chance of a favorable mutation, as well as on the time and place of this mutation. It takes several hundreds of generations for a more compatible mutation to triumph over others.

Changes in the genes affecting specific anatomical features will also result in changes in other human features.[134] This cascade of chance often unfolds over extremely long periods of time and is in most cases unobvious. Genes can tell us little about literature, art, science and technology, ethics and political institutions. They will also be very unlikely to tell us much about a person's character traits. It is far too early to promise that decoding the DNA sequence in the human genome would help us better to understand the human being, all the more so because the human brain is not fully utilized.

Based on John Templeton's assumption of exponential growth in the amount of knowledge,[135] implying a 10-fold increase in the speed of accumulation of knowledge every century and if the amount of knowledge expanded by a factor of 10 between 1800 and 1900, in the century between 1900 and 2000, the rate of knowledge accumulation accelerated 10-fold, and will accelerate 100-fold between 2000 and 2100, and 1,000-fold in the years 2100-2200 over the 19th century. The amount of knowledge between the years 1800 and 2200 should therefore increase 10 times 10 times 100 times 1000-fold, or 10-millionfold, expanding by a factor of 100 billion by 2300 compared to the amount of knowledge humanity had two centuries ago. These numbers may appear amazing, but they are based on a reasonable assumption of a 10-fold acceleration in the speed of knowledge accumulation over every century. In any case, these numbers indicate how little we know at present, and should be reason for humility and hope for the future, forecasting how much we have yet to learn in the years and centuries ahead. But can the human brain absorb this amount of data and derive some benefit from it?

---

[134] И.П. Неумывакин Биоэнергетическая сущность человека. М.: Диля, 2012.
[135] Templeton, JM. Worldwide Laws of Life. Radnor, PA: Templeton Foundation Press, 1998.

We have mentioned earlier that the human brain contains 30 billion neurons.[136] The network of neurons and connections between them is unimaginably intricate and has infinite capabilities. We can calculate the total number of these links through simple multiplication which would yield an "astronomical" number. In fact, it will be many times greater than the number of atoms in the Universe, a number with 75 zeroes. The Universe would not have enough string to thread along all these links, if each of them had been a kilometer long. Let us try to imagine the network of links between each neuron and a thousand other neurons, and we will get only an approximate idea of the brain's complexity. The next step would be to understand the connection paths between neurons which are not linked directly. There are a thousand million million different shortest possible paths from A (via A–B–C–D–E–F) to F-level neurons (where F is any neuron removed by five steps from neuron A), and an infinitely greater number of longer, roundabout ways to reach F-level neurons.

The point of this exercise in arithmetics is simple: the number of communication channels a human being uses in his life is ridiculously small compared to the available capacity. According to Edison, an individual uses less than a millionth of a percentage point of his brain capacity during his entire life. We do not know how to use this untapped capacity, but we will find a way to do this, because the knowledge of humanity will expand thousands- and millions-fold over the next several centuries. One of the ways to use the brain capacity is the distributed computing model that makes it possible to increase the power of computers connected in a network.

Another step towards assimilation of new knowledge by humanity would be through a search for an effective way to connect (through communication signals, rather than physically) the brains of different people, thousands and millions of different people's brains. This is where we may have crossed the line between simple speculation about the future and science fiction.

Indeed, we know very little about the natural world, almost nothing compared to what we have yet to learn. When we talk about the energy compatibility of man, we turn to wave medicine, a new field.

Our genetics apparatus has an infinite number of languages. This property can be used to study damage of the multi-dimensional structure of

---

[136] McConkey, E. How the Human Genome Works. Sudbury, MA: Jones & Bartlett Learning, 2004.

the human being.

This can be done by using the contact between the consciousness and the subconscious through the chromosomes using speech and the radiesthesic method. Since consciousness is essentially a matrix of words, and the genome has a wave information transfer channel between the word and speech-like constructs recorded in the genome, one can influence certain control functions of the consciousness.

Contemporary medical science has thoroughly explored the structure of the brain and the nervous system as well as internal organs in the human body. To find out what state they are in, doctors use special testing devices and direct the patient to be examined by CAT scans, X-rays, ultrasound or other diagnostic methods. A human being has the capacity for wave medicine within himself.[137] The human being with well-developed internal vision can, all by himself, see the state of internal organs in another person through directional clairvoyance. Controlled, directional clairvoyance makes it possible to enter any cell in any internal organ in a human body, adjust the DNA helix, heal any rifts, delete the record of illness and record information about health and harmonious development in its place.[138] And a man suffering from illness will begin to recover. Unfortunately, few people in Russia have the ability, skills, or knowledge to do this. But if there are such, it means that they have within themselves the framework for perceiving various wave frequencies and producing influence at different frequencies from different sources within themselves.

If diagnostics by clairvoyance is unavailable, the root causes of a person's incompatible condition (illness) can be identified by the "bioradar" method using the appropriate radiesthesic charts. "Bioradar" is very effective in practically all people, whose health has not been undermined by subjecting them to negative programs (a hereditary family curse, jinxing, hexes or similar), the excessive presence of toxins in the body, someone with a clear aura without aural inclusions.

Information about the causes of a person's diseases can be obtained from the information fields of the person's consciousness and from those of his genetic relatives. Our body is a unified complex, intricately organized system, and any division into separate systems is purely arbitrary and is based on function, with several multifunctional elements of the body

---

[137] В.П. Павлов Волновая форма человека: исцеление с помощью мыслеформ. Пенза: Золотое сечение, 2009.

[138] Т.А. Ордынская Волновая терапия. М.: Эксмо, 2008.

explored repeatedly by the corresponding systems. Every physiological system has a biocomputer of its own (BCO) containing the program for running the system's functions. Every cell comprises seven layers — a material (physical) one and six wave layers (an ethereal layer and five fine layers). Wave traces at the molecular level were identified during DNA molecule experiments at the wave genetics lab.

Illuminating DNA molecules with a laser beam revealed that not only were the molecules dispersing the laser beam, but also empty space where the molecules had just been. In addition, it was discovered that real chromosomes and their phantoms had very similar dispersion spectra. The conclusion was reached that chromosomes leave a wave trace in the process of their Brownian motion, and that trace is picked up by the measurements. The trace can be preserved for a very long time. A DNA molecule as a whole creates certain wave matrices which define the development of a biological object. In other words, a DNA molecule has a wave (energy) double. Every organ and the body as a whole have similar doubles.

The combination of all ethereal layers of cells, tissues and organs create the ethereal body, which is not simply an arithmetic sum of the layers but rather a system with properties, i.e. new system-wide parameters: a volume, a frequency range, data content, polarization, a structure, a form, synchronization and rotation velocity.

The same is true of all the fine bodies. Every individual body has a peripheral control biocomputer (PBC) of its own, which is subordinated to the central biocomputer (CBC). Therefore, the multidimensional structure of a human being is a combination of a physical, an ethereal (intermediate) and five fine bodies controlled by a hierarchical chain of peripheral biocomputers, which are controlled by the CBC through special "software."

When a person states a request for desired information, certain parts in the chromosomes of paleocortex neurons respond to the sound of every letter in the request, becoming agitated. At this time, the chromosomes begin to radiate, emitting fine fields of consciousness in the form of sequential codes. This sequence of codes guides the search for the required information in the person's consciousness, in the chromosomes of his physical body cells, in the space of his self (soul) and in the fields of Earthly and Cosmic consciousness. The information is processed there, with the results being sent back to the individual's paleocortex neurons, which sent the request as a sequence of codes. After receiving the processed results of the query, these neurons begin to create a series of electric impulses with an amplitude of around 0.8 Volts, sending it to a hand holding a pendulum string. The hand starts making micromovements by the sensor (the pendulum) with an increasing amplitude towards the sector where the root cause of the illness lies. Feedback takes place through the person's eyes

The precision of bioradar measurements is very high. Edwin McConkey does not provide in his book a methodology for the recovery of an individual's capability for obtaining information by using his bioradar, and one has to turn for this information to what an individual's consciousness is and what development levels it has from the perspectives of philosophy and integrative yoga (Satpren, Sri Aurobindo No. 15).

The only type of consciousness we are aware of is the mental process: I think, therefore I am. We place ourselves at the center of the universe and acknowledge the existence of consciousness only in those who share our lifestyle and our perception, our world outlook. This is so-called mental consciousness. Mental consciousness is a purely human "frequency band," falling far short of covering the whole possible range of consciousness, just as human eyesight cannot perceive all shades of the color spectrum, and the human ear is inadequate for the full range of sound frequencies. In a similar way, there are planes of consciousness above and below the human plane; a regular, common man has no contact with these planes and sees them as devoid of consciousness. As we move toward compatibility of cognition, toward perceiving the soul in ourselves and in various objects, we realize that consciousness is present in a plant, in a piece of metal, in an atom, in electricity – in any physical object. Furthermore, consciousness in many "inanimate" forms is in fact more intense, more lively, and quicker, if rather less than obvious for mental perception.

Some the very sensitive people can, under certain circumstances, feel certain concentration centers, power nodes within themselves at different levels; with each of these centers with a vibration type, or vibration frequency, of its own. For example, you could sense the great vibration of a revelation; you could also experience heavier, more unpleasant vibrations of anger or fear, as vibrations pulsate at different levels and with different intensity. We have a set of vibration nodes compatible within one body, or consciousness centers, each of which has only one unique vibration type.

The mind is only one of these centers, only one vibration type,[139] only one form of consciousness, although it tries to take the primary position.

---

[139] Teltscher, F. Biorythmustheorie. Quoted from the Russian edition: Тельчер Ф. Теория биоритмов (трех биоритмов). Инстург, 1997.

The Seven Centers (Figure 3.1) lie in four zones (which Hindus call chakras).

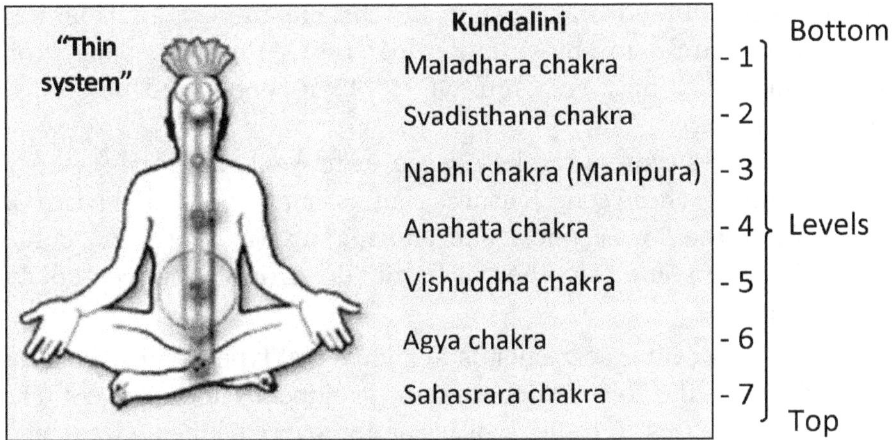

Fig. 3.1 Chakra diagram

The Superconscious, with the only center slightly above the crown of the head (the Sahasrara chakra), which controls and guides our reasoning mind and corresponds with higher mental areas – with a mind experiencing an epiphany, an intuitive mind, a supermental mind, etc.

The Mind, which has two centers: one between the eyebrows, which is in charge of the will and changes in our mental activity (it is also the center of fine vision, the "third eye," described in some yoga traditions (the Ajna chakra); and another one at the throat level, which controls all forms of mental expression (the Vishuddha chakra).

The Vital, which has three centers: the first one, at the heart level, controls our emotional life, including love, hate and other emotions (the Anahata chakra); the second one, at the navel level, controls our power impulses: the drive to rule, to possess, to conquer, as well as our ambition and similar drives (the Manipura chakra); the third center, the lower vitality center is embedded between the navel and the sexual center near the mesenterium; this center controls the lowers vibrations: jealousy, envy, lust, greed, anger (the Swadhisthana chakra).

The Physical and Subconscious, with a center at the base of the spinal column: this center controls our physical being and sexual impulses; it is also open to the impulses coming from the lower subconscious regions (the Mukadhara chakra).

In their normal state, these centers are dormant, or closed, or they have very weak flow running through them required for limited existence of the personality. In fact, a human being is walled in within himself, he cannot communicate with the world directly, and this communication is limited to a very narrow circle; in any case, he does not see other people or other objects, but rather only sees himself in other people and objects, only himself everywhere.

Consciousness centers can be opened using yoga, spiritual methods or thought forms.[140] These consciousness centers can be opened in succession, starting from the lower ones, and moving up (methods for inducing Kundalini energy), and the other way around – from higher centers going down (Figure 3.1).

Every energy center corresponds to a universal type of consciousness or energy: opening the lower vital centers, or subconscious centers, at the beginning exposes us to the risk of becoming overwhelmed, swamped not only by our own petty personal problems but also the streams of universal mud, because we automatically come into contact with the disorder and dirt of the world.

A descending force helps us avoid this threat. We deal with the lower centers only after our being has become strong in the higher lights of the superconscious. After fully opening the centers of consciousness, a person indeed begins to see objects,[141] beings, the whole world and ourselves just as they and we are, as the person already perceives pure vibrations at every level in every object and every being, which nothing can conceal any more, rather than seeing merely the outward attributes, ambiguous, unreliable words and gestures — all these attempts at mimicry by a person walled in within himself, or the misleading outward aspect of objects.

In the following sections of this book we will discuss the ladder of human needs and the institutes of governmental and international regulation of the development of society, which are in accord with the organic structure (of energy levels) of human consciousness, its perceptions and interactions of the "physical" space on Earth.

It is known that everything is in constant motion; possibly, everything comes to us from a mind wider than ours, a universal, vital, broad mind. Our little "husk," our puny "front" of physical shape is apparently surrounded, supported, intersected and set in motion by a whole hierarchy

---

[140] К.В. Титов Чакральные коммуникации. СПб.: Афина, 2007.
[141] Т.Н. Березина Резервные возможности человека. М.: Когико-Центр, 2000.

of "worlds,"[142] which was well-known to ancient thinkers: "Without effort, one world moves within another."[143] Sri Aurobindo calls this hierarchy "a ladder of consciousness planes," which are ranged in sequence from pure spirit to matter, and each of them is connected to one of our centers.

Let us assume that consciousness is present everywhere in the Universe, at any level, and has central nodes within us. One cannot find consciousness "off the shelf," prefabricated and ready to use — it is something that needs to be lit, like a fire.

If consciousness is power, the opposite also holds true: power is consciousness, all power is conscious. Let us assume that when we establish contact with the "flow" of consciousness – power in itself, we can connect to any plane of the universal reality, to any point, and perceive the consciousness at that point, and even influence it — for the "flow" of consciousness is the same everywhere; only vibration types are different.

Let us assume that it is present in plants and thoughts of the human mind, in the luminous superconscious and in an animal's instincts, in a piece of metal and in our deepest meditations. Unless a piece of wood had consciousness, no yogi would have ever been able to cause it to move through the power of concentration, because contact between them would have been quite impossible. If even a single point in the Universe had been devoid of consciousness, the entire Universe would be without it, because existence must be a unity. Einstein's mass-energy equivalence equation is truly a great discovery, because it tells us that Matter and Energy are interchangeable: $E = mc^2$, that is, Matter is condensed Energy, or, more precisely, Consciousness is Energy.

Oriental sages say that everything around us is Consciousness, because everything is Existence, or Spirit. The history of our earthly evolution is nothing but the slow conversion of Power into Consciousness, or, in figurative terms, Consciousness immersed in its Power, slowly remembering itself.

When a person with a certain set of abilities begins to become aware of his inner consciousness, he can do various things with it, either send it, as a flow of power, to a certain destination, or create a circle or wall of consciousness around himself, or direct a thought in such a way that it will enter somebody else's head, etc.

---

[142] Верищагин Д.С. Параллельные миры восприятия. СПб.: Афина, 2009.

[143] Ригведа (Книга гимнов). Избранные гимны. Пер. с санскр. М., 1972. П. 24.5.

3.2. Compatibility of Human Needs with Societal Values

A need has two components, or two sides: objective and subjective. The objective aspect of a need is defined by properties of the outside world and the human body, while the subjective side of a need is determined by the human being, who perceives and understands the objective reality that exists independent of his will. At the same time, the need would depend to some extent on the world view and system of values, etc. of this particular human being. The presence of this subjective component means that in the same situation different people have different needs. In this connection, it makes sense to view a need as "a unity, a tightly-knit combination of objective predilection, affinity and a subjective urge."[144]

We could describe the state of a person based on the contradiction between the available and the necessary (or something that the human being perceives as necessary) as *Need,* which urges him into action to eliminate this contradiction,[145] this incompatibility.

Realization of this desire for a need has a deep underlying connection to the world outlook on the system of values. In a commonly accepted definition, "world outlook" is a system of a human being's views with regard to the world at large and the human being's place in this world. In every society and social stratum, its unique world outlook serves as the basis of a value system. In turn, value is the meaning of objects and phenomena to a human being and society, an evaluation of phenomena and events from the perspective of good and evil, usefulness or harm, beauty or ugliness, the acceptable or the taboo, fair or unfair, etc. Knowledge about the world reveals the objectives laws of nature and society, while an evaluation of certain events establishes their value for the human being and defines our attitude towards them.

The system of values itself is built as a result of complex interactions of family upbringing (and its core element – moral education), economics, politics, cultural tradition, religion, science, art and the whole varied range of social processes.

---

[144] В.В. Фетискин Потребности. Деятельность. Личность: Социально-философское исследование. М.: РГАЗУ, 2001. P. 8.

[145] Н.Н. Михайлов Социализм и разумные потребности личности. М.: Политиздат, 1982. P. 30.

There are several different classifications of human needs, including biological, which are approximately identical for human beings and animals, as well as social needs, which arise from the foundation of key features distinguishing the human and human society from nature, i.e. labor and thought. It is common to make a distinction between individual and social, material and spiritual needs.

The most fundamental world-view foundation of the theory of needs is the general philosophical concept of man and his place in the world.

So what is the philosophical concept of man?

Man, or the human being, is a product of infinite development of the material world. Four main qualitatively different forms of matter arose in the known Universe: physical, chemical, biological and social.

Development of matter has followed a clearly defined path from the lower to the higher orders of organizations. Thus, the physical form of matter emerged before other forms (as a result of the Big Bang). The chemical form of matter is more advanced than the physical form (as atoms combine into molecules and interact now at a more sophisticated level), but less so than biological and social forms of matter.

Two consistent patterns were in effect during the process of development of matter: the higher forms of matter were becoming increasingly complex in their content while also growing increasingly scarce, as they took up less space than lower forms of matter. The main criterion making it possible to tell the higher from the lower is that the higher forms retain the full basic content of the lower forms, while adding new, more complex content to this foundation.

Society, which exists and operates according to its own social laws, takes up much less space than does living matter. This objective law of the decreasing prevalence of higher forms of matter compared to lower forms clarifies the relative quantity of different forms, making it possible to depict the overall realm of matter as a cone (Figure 3.2).

The great leaps in the development of civilization in recent millennia have almost no impact on the physical organization of the human being.

After discovering labor, man created the material process, making it possible to realize the hidden capabilities of nature. Society has begun to develop through simpler forms of matter. This brings us the world of artificial, humanized objects: the "second nature," "technosphere," "anthroposhere," "noosphere." This mechanism of society's development can be depicted as reciprocal feedback with other forms of matter (see Figure 3.2).

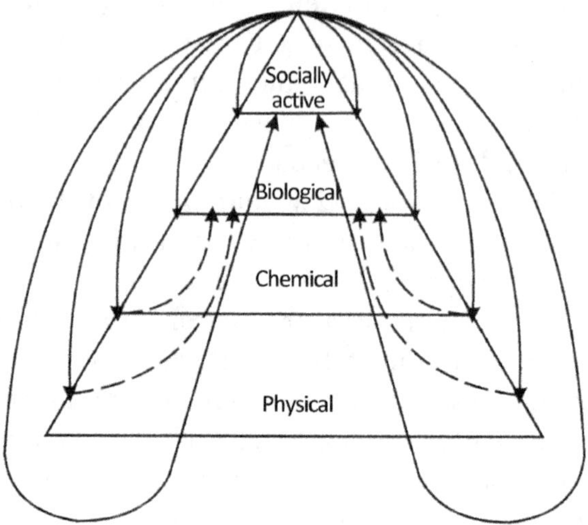

Fig. 3.2 Hierarchy of key forms of matter in development

Society's "onward and upward" development happens because it looks back, rebuilding simpler forms of matter, both those known at this time and those that will be discovered in the future. This developmental direction is very well expressed in the incompatible, paradoxical aphorism: "Going up a ladder leading downward."

Human needs are divided into biological and social. Biological needs include the need for food, clothing, shelter, procreation, having a natural environment that matches the specific features of the body, and ensuring normal conditions for life and the operation of the body.

Social needs are more complex than biological ones, because they belong in a qualitatively more advanced method of existence or way of living. They are built ultimately on a foundation of labor and abstract thinking. These needs can develop indefinitely, because human needs are perceived and therefore can to some extent be subjected to conscious, targeted modification, construction, and control. Every social need has a biological component, and requires expenditure of physical (biological) energy to be satisfied.

Some contemporary scientists divide needs into three groups: material, social and spiritual. However, all social needs can be included in the realm of material or spiritual needs. Our judgment is based on the fact that needs are divided into material and social according to one criterion, while division into social and biological needs follows a different principle.

We can identify two layers: relatively simple biological needs and more complex material social needs. Material biological needs include the need for food, clothing, shelter, a healthy, beneficial environment, physical health and physical safety, as well as the need for procreation.

Material social needs (the social is more than a matter of thinking, according to Hegel) include some very tangible material activity involving objects of the world outside. They include labor and the labor-based process of material production. If the needs for food and shelter are the main biological material needs of man, the main social material need is the need for labor.

Spiritual needs should logically include the needs for knowledge, different frames of mind, strong emotions and impressions, the need for cognition, education, upbringing, and the need to know the meaning of life. They can also be classified based on forms of social consciousness, dividing them into moral (ethic), legal, political, aesthetic, religious or atheistic needs, or the need to have a world view.

Spiritual needs include some relatively simple ones, existing on the level of everyday consciousness, and more complex needs that can be satisfied with theoretical and artistic consciousness.

The need for cognition, i.e. the yearning of man to know objective phenomena, properties and fundamental patterns of reality, is derived from material needs for successful work, which cannot exist, let alone grow, without accumulation of knowledge about the world. At the same time, the need for cognition may become relatively independent, turning into the ultimate goal in itself, making its connection to material needs more tenuous, less direct and more veiled. In religion, actual knowledge about the world is intertwined with a belief in the supernatural, i.e. ideas which are proclaimed as the truth without any proof, merely based on tradition. Scientific and artistic cognition have to be categorized as the most advanced forms of cognition.

While scientific cognition is aimed at revealing objective laws of nature and society, the explanation and prediction of changes in phenomena being studied, artistic cognition is a special aesthetic internalization of reality in an artistic, image-driven form. It may be implemented via art and includes an evaluation of events as beautiful or ugly, base or noble, tragic or comic.

The need for education is essentially the need for a process of absorbing systematic knowledge, abilities and skills. It is one of the primary human needs, as it has become the necessary condition for preparation for work and communication. Essentially, it is both a more specific and a more complex form of the need for cognition.

The need for moral education essentially deals with a targeted influence on man to prepare him for dispensing the entire great variety of social functions (labor, communication, cognition and others).

The most complex spiritual need is the need for life to have a meaning. It manifests itself in shaping the world view – a system of a man's ideas and views of the world at large and his own place in it. There are several main concepts of the meaning of human existence, which many people reach at some point of their lives. At the same time, the concept of the meaning of life directly depends on how man's abilities were developed and how his needs for cognition, education and moral education were satisfied. Various social unities, movements and organizations have tried, from times immemorial, to influence the inner world of man, to shape a kind of world view and understanding of the meaning of life that matched the ideology of these movements and organizations. A broad range of techniques are used to achieve this kind of influence on shaping spiritual needs: carefully dosed information and disinformation, the emotional impact of the arts, a sense of camaraderie and solidarity, propaganda in the mass media, and, finally, a simple material interest in receiving certain benefits. Spiritual needs – which are in a way summarized and united in the need for a meaning of life – to a great extent define the behavior of man. This is why both society as a whole and certain elements and associations, organizations and groups within it, are constantly trying to influence them in their own interests.

It is a fairly common opinion that lack of religious needs equals narrow-minded base materialism, a complete lack of interest in spirituality or art (rather than a simple lack of interest in religion), and at the same time society has developed a great number of valuable non-religious spiritual needs, such as the need for scientific and artistic activity and creativity.

A person's needs are shaped both by natural unique features of the personality and the influence of the social environment.

At various times, society had the need to use a broad range of people's natural potential and abilities.

One of the main trends in developing relations between the human being and society is the individualization of personality. Economic development and the increasing complexity of production processes have required increasingly trained, competent and independent workers. This results in the gradual development of a personal style of production activity and an associated individual style of consumption.

Human communities have always included differences, and therefore contradictions, between the needs of individuals, groups of people and society as a whole. Special mechanisms were developed over time to regulate interactions between society and the individual (and achieve a coordinated compatible interaction), primarily morality and law.

Therefore, when we meet the social needs of a community, we also meet the individual needs of people in this community.

Society or social groups take longer to realize their needs than do individuals (and this process is more complicated). Often, a small group of people or a government agency is the first to perceive a societal need, then attracting everybody's attention to it and striving to ensure it is recognized and satisfied across the whole society. Today, we are in the process of perceiving and recognizing the need for solutions to the environmental problems of civilization or the need for the exploration of outer space. In more democratic societies the emphasis shifts to fuller satisfaction of citizens' needs and is an important priority of government policy.

Alongside the division into biological and social, material and spiritual, individual and social, human needs may also be divided into routine and creative. The former (routine) needs consist in consuming, using already manufactured objects and services by established methods, while creative needs are the need to create new material and spiritual values or to understand better, analyze and process what has been created or learned.

From a philosophical perspective, they can be described as needs for functioning and needs for development, or consumer and creative needs. Abraham H. Maslow divides all needs into deficiency needs (including the basic essential needs) and growth needs (the needs for personal creative development). The possession mode drives a person to consumerism, to satisfying only routine needs, while the existential mode encourages people to satisfy more complex creative needs associated not with the simple support of physical existence and entertainment, but rather with personal improvement and the progress of society as a whole, with revealing the person's creative ability.[146]

Both routine and creative needs exist and are satisfied in society. A certain compatible balance is established between them, or an oscillating balance.

---

[146] Fromm, E. Psychoanalysis and Religion. The Art of Loving. To Have or to Be? Quoted from the Russian edition: Фромм Э. Психоанализ и религия. Искусство любить. Иметь или быть? Киев: Ника-Центр, 1998.

Speaking of needs, we should not forget another kind of manifestation of human personality – ability.

Ability is an individual property of a personality which is a condition for successful accomplishment of a certain type of activity. The capability to create these conditions necessary for the human being, and satisfy his needs, takes ability. Therefore, needs and ability coexist and mutually determine each other: needs create a demand for the demonstration and development of ability, while ability enables a person to satisfy needs and stimulates the generation of new abilities, ensuring their compatible perfection: self-development.

The development of human abilities in itself is one of the deeper, existential needs of civilization, i.e., a personality begins to be established not from abilities even, but rather from potential (anatomic and physiological features of an organism which are the foundation for the development of abilities).

As S.L. Rubinstein (1889–1960) said, "the distance is very great between the potential and ability; the entire path of personality development lies between the one and the other."[147]

Apparently, society still neither is able nor wants to develop human abilities at the very age when it can be done most effectively.

A man with an inclination for a certain type of activity because of his potential, is usually irresistibly drawn to this type of activity.

Spiritual abilities, just like material abilities, include a guiding spiritual component and a subordinated material component. The spiritual aspect of spiritual ability is psychological processes of analysis and generalization (i.e. synthesis, drawing generalized conclusions) and a system of thought operations — a logical output, counting, etc.

The interaction between abilities and needs is associated with one of the deepest contradictions in the human personality which has become more acute in the era of mass manufacturing when the producer is interested primarily in maximizing profit, when life according to possession or the existential principle creates in people different need systems, driving them toward different consumption models. A system of contradictions of the modern personality emerges.[148] Production of life amenities, which allows human ability to shine, is viewed as something secondary and is taken for

---

[147] С.Л. Рубинштейн Основы общей психологии: В 2 т. Т. 2. М.: Педагогика, 1989.
[148] Fromm, E. Psychoanalysis and Religion. The Art of Loving. To Have or to Be? Quoted from the Russian edition: Фромм Э. Психоанализ и религия. Искусство любить. Иметь или быть? Киев: Ника-Центр, 1998.

granted. This orientation impoverishes the personality and weakens the whole social system.

Ways to oppose this one-sidedness (make it incompatible) are designed through government regulation and legal restrictions on excessively destructive types of activity (enriching oneself by illegally seizing property, drug trafficking, depredation of the environment, etc.), through morality and tradition, family moral education and upbringing, through activity of public association and movements.

There is a different world beyond personal enrichment. At this point in our history, a humanistic value system is proclaimed in modern developed society. Truth, kindness (goodness) and beauty are the main fundamental values of life and culture.

Value concepts produce a powerful impact on the world of needs. The mechanism of this impact can be reduced to the following five key components:

1) Shaping needs on the basis of values;

2) Needs are divided into reasonable and unreasonable based on the idea of values;

3) The value system establishes the order (the hierarchy) of satisfying needs, ranking them by importance;

4) The value system becomes the foundation for developing ways to satisfy those needs;

5) Activity to purposefully create and change needs is also built on the basis of a man's value system.

Sociology and psychology have a scientific tradition of investigating needs, although this system has yet to be developed in depth and in detail. The concepts of needs created by American psychologist Abraham Maslow, Polish psychologist Kazimierz Obuchowski and Russian theatrical director and psychologist P.M. Yershov are the best known and often recognized as the best.[149]

Therefore, psychologists usually divide needs into primary, or essential, and secondary, or non-essential, the satisfaction of which is not a necessary condition for physical existence of the human body. From a philosophical, world-view perspective, needs can be divided first of all into material and spiritual. Material needs are further divided into relatively simple biological

---

[149] See, for instance: A. Maslow. Motivation and Personality. 3rd Edition, 1997; К. Обуховский Галактика потребностей. Психология влечений человека. СПб.: Речь, 2003; П.М. Ершов Потребности человека. М.: Мысль, 1990.

needs and more complex social needs. All spiritual needs are social. Spiritual needs include moral, legal, aesthetic and religious needs for learning, education, moral education and the meaning of life. We can also identify social needs in creative scientific and artistic work, in the need for spiritual development of the human being. The integrated, generalized need of society at all stages of its development is that for the preservation and development of social life. This need is present in an individual as well as in society as a whole. From an individual's perspective, all needs can be divided into personal, group and societal. There are creative as well as routine needs. All these types of needs are identified on different grounds and it is hard to combine them into a single logically coherent, interrelated system.

The best known attempt to systematize needs is Maslow's hierarchy of needs. He placed fundamental needs in a five-step pyramid, starting from basic, essential needs without satisfying which a human body cannot physically exist, and ending with the most complex – social – needs. Here is this famous classification:

1) physiological needs;
2) safety needs;
3) need to be loved, need to belong;
4) need for respect;
5) need for self-actualization.

Maslow believes that the needs of each subsequently higher step become relevant to a man only after he has adequately satisfied the needs on the previous step. After satisfying the essential physiological needs (the need for food, clothes, shelter), the human being starts paying attention to the need for security, then he begins to feel the need for love, and after that need is satisfied, the need for respect comes to the fore and becomes relevant, and, finally, the need for self-actualization. Maslow emphasizes that higher-level needs can become so important for a human being that the preceding, more fundamental needs fade into relative insignificance for him. At the same time, no flight of creative fancy can liberate an individual from the need to eat, keep hydrated, breathe, etc.

Meeting fundamental, basic needs at all five stages directly depends on the social system in place, the prevailing political views and cultural traditions (unlike Karl Marx, Maslow does not consider the economic foundation separately). "There are certain conditions which are immediate prerequisites for the basic need satisfactions [...] Such conditions as freedom to speak, freedom to do what one wishes so long as no harm is done to others, freedom to express one's self, freedom to investigate and seek for information, freedom to defend one's self, justice, fairness, honesty, orderliness in the group are examples of such preconditions for basic need satisfactions."[150] We note that the values and conditions listed by Maslow were understood in different ways throughout history and became established in this detailed form only in modern Western civilization.

The five-step hierarchy does not comprise all possible basic needs. One of the conditions for meeting all the basic needs is the ability to learn and the need to learn. Maslow identifies another hierarchy outside his main one – a parallel hierarchy of cognition needs, including "the desire to know" and the "desire to understand." "Even after we know, we are impelled to know more and more minutely and microscopically on the one hand, and on the other, more and more extensively in the direction of a world philosophy, religion, etc. [...] This process has been called by some the search for "meaning." We shall then postulate a desire to understand, to systematize, to organize, to analyze, to look for relations and meanings, to create a system of values."[151] The need to learn about and understand the world, as well as aesthetic needs, does not constitute a separate step in the main hierarchy, permeating instead every step of the hierarchy.

Some authors modify Maslow's hierarchy of needs, adapting it to the goods and services market. They identify the following types of consumer needs:

1) physiological needs;
2) the need for safety and health;
3) the need for love and friendship;
4) the need for financial resources and stability;
5) the need for satisfaction;
6) the need for social image;
7) the need to have, to possess;
8) the need to give;
9) the need for information;
10) the need for variety.[152]

---

[150] Maslow, A. Motivation and Personality. 3rd Edition. 1997.
[151] Ibid.
[152] Blackwell, R.D., Miniard, P.W., Engel, J.F. Consumer Behaviour. 10th Edition. SW College Pub., 2005.

3.3. Compatibility and Hierarchy of Social Institutions

3.3.1. Institutions as a Compatibility Format Within Society. Their Classification

The idea of unity of human society and natural existence is but a logical development of the thought of unity of man and nature. Society, despite all its unique features, still represents such universal qualities of existence as its discrete nature, its structured character, its changeability and dynamism. As philosophers, starting from Auguste Comte, the founding father of social science, began to recognize this unity, they started to identify two key aspects in social life: its static nature and its dynamics.

The static snapshot of society has come to be understood as the established structure of society, its components, elements and connections between them. Dynamics are generally meant to be the processes of operation, movement and change. In the real life of society, these two factors are never separate.

At first, society is analyzed "at rest," in a static condition, as a snapshot at a given moment, as a combination of elements and parts, as a certain structure, and then, on the basis of these initial concepts, the details of society's movement and development – its dynamics – are also explored.

Modern philosophy starts from the idea that the world around us is divided, discrete, but also united and continuous at the same time. It consists of separate parts, objects, and also includes all the diverse properties of these objects which express the specifics of connections and relations between these objects.

Like any natural structure, the structure of society includes not only individual elements, parts – individual people and separate groups of people, but also their qualities and relations, which enable us to differentiate between some social objects and others. There is no, there can be no society without certain groups, or unities of people, just as there can be no society without individuals, acting as indivisible "social atoms," "the basic bricks" of social existence. Man acquired his key general properties as a collective being. This is why man and society have always been and always will be linked inseparably like two sides of the same coin. And yet, man and society are two different phenomena, far from identical to each other. Just as a living organism has properties that none of its constituent cells has, society not only is bigger than a single individual, but also is more complex than a simple sum of all its constituent individuals. Every social unity is therefore not only a combination of individual qualities of the people comprising it, but also a set of certain properties of its own, which none of its constituent individuals has, and which give this unity its special, unique character.

Therefore, the social structure of society is an inseparable unity of two key components: 1) a combination of individuals, people and their associations, and 2) a combination of interactions, links, relations between people and social groups. Links and interrelations between people are invisible, ethereal, non-material in nature. This is why the meaning of these invisible links and relations in social life did not become immediately apparent. Their significance was felt by people intuitively for a long time, which is evidenced by the fact that one of the most significant social institutions, which arose from the spiritual link between people, is denoted by the term "religion" (from the Latin religare "relation, connection").

There are many prejudices in evaluating their role. The most common of them are:

- extreme individualism (or anarchism);
- militant collectivism, with its most dangerous manifestation in fascism.

From the point of view of extreme individualism, or social nihilism, only individuals exist, and there are no social connections, relations, and therefore, no society. According to proponents of militant collectivism, social phenomena reflected by concepts like "society" and "state" not only do exist, but also represent a higher value than individuals comprising the society, that there is only society, society alone, and nothing but society. Both approaches are incompatible with society as a complete concept.

The social system comprises, as its subsystems, the material, spiritual and other aspects of life, each of which comes with its own components. Thus, the spiritual area of life incorporates religion, science, art, law, morality, etc. All these varied aspects of society are connected, welded together by a variety of relations, interactions, which turn the combination of individual components in social structure into a unity, just as close connections between cells create a living organism.

A relationship is understood as a certain link, an interaction between parts and elements of society. Relationships are the sort of an invisible cementing material that brings together people into society, making a whole monolith from it.

Stable, permanent, recurring relations and interactions between people gradually lead to the establishment of stable groups within society, or institutions, which in turn engage in relationships of some kind between themselves.[153] The richness and diversity of social relationships are signs of a well-developed democratic society improving the compatibility between man and society and between society and man. And conversely, uniformity, poor state of development, or paucity are signs of a totalitarian, undemocratic society, in which the personality is lost and incompatibility arises – the links connecting man and society and society and man are broken.

Descriptions of the body social in modern philosophy note that the social system is substantially different from natural systems. The following are the main of these distinctions:

1) A multiplicity of elements, subsystems, levels, their functions, connections and relations in a society;

2) Different qualities of inhomogeneous social elements, which, in addition to various material phenomena, also include rich, full-color ideal, spiritual manifestations. This is why a complex approach is especially fruitful in the study of society: an approach using the methods of both humanities and natural science, as demonstrated by Vladimir Vernadsky's biosphere concept and Lev Gumilev's passionarian concept of history and culture, as well as many others;

3) The unique nature of the key component of a social system: the human being, who has extensive creative ability, freedom of choice of behavior, which makes development of society very uncertain, and, consequently, quite unpredictable. Substantiating this thought is one of the central themes in modern philosophy.

As philosophic thought identified the extreme complexity and variety of social life, researchers started trying harder to find a certain common foundation, a common denominator for all the variety and multiplicity. In this desire, philosophers merely followed scientists from other fields, in each of which a certain common fundamental smallest constituent "brick" was discovered: elementary particles in physics, atoms in chemistry, living cells in biology, responses to irritants in psychology, and so on.

---

[153] В.А. Морозов Развитие общественных институтов // Маркетинг. 2012. № 2. С. 3–20.

Many scientists and thinkers (A. Comte, M. Weber, T. Parsons et al.) saw the foundation of society in social action, which was defined as human behavior directed at another person. Even though social activity has a great fundamental, system-forming significance, it is not the exhaustive, ultimate foundation of human existence which "cannot be further divided." There are at least two main reasons for this.

First, social activity arises from and is defined by the various material and spiritual needs, interests, motives and core values that form its foundation. US sociologist A. Maslow (1908–70) proposed a special pyramid of human needs that included fundamental needs of safety and satisfaction of physiological needs (the need for food, shelter, etc.), with the remaining three levels being secondary and including the needs for communication, respect from others, and for creative expression and self-actualization (we have discussed this at greater detail in an earlier section).

Second, we must also take into account that human activity can be destructive as well as constructive for society. As an unexpected result, it can produce a whole world of things incompatible with the human beings who created them or even produce social interactions and institutions, political and ideological phenomena that are outright hostile to humans. Any description of social life would be sorely lacking if it did not include these incompatible, destructive consequences of human activity.

We can also identify and review especially another essential aspect of social life: the combination of connections, dependencies among people. They can be explored for major spheres of human life and activity such as religious, scientific, artistic, economic, political and other types of activity; both relationships within these spheres and between them can be subjected to analysis.

Society can also be analyzed from the perspective of diverse organizations, agencies, institutions operating within it, established to ensure its stability and closer interaction between different social strata. This aspect of social structure also incorporates a large number of social organizations and establishments, including different kinds of business and economic organizations, companies, firms, as well as educational, scientific, healthcare organizations, central and local governments and government agencies, i.e. the entire complex network of political, economic and cultural organizations that meet the various human needs.

The structure of social activity comprises a number of people, things and symbols, but that is not enough to create social action or social life as a whole, unless these individual components are connected and interact with one another. This is precisely why stable connections between people, things and symbols, repeated many times over, gradually taking shape on the levels of individual action, social groups and society as a whole, and have paramount importance for people's social life together.

Therefore, there are four elements of any human activity: people, physical things, symbols and links connecting them. The necessity for their continuous reproduction generates the main types of social activity, creating a fundamental structure in the multi-aspect social system. Consequently, the four main types of basic social action are matched by four types, spheres or areas of social activity: material, spiritual, regulatory or managerial, and service activity, sometimes also called humanitarian or social in the narrow sense. All of them, by meeting the necessary conditions of any human activity, at the same time lay the groundwork for the life and operation of society as a whole. Self-sufficiency is the ability of a system to create and reproduce all the necessary conditions for its existence and operation through its own activity, producing everything required for life together within society. Self-sufficiency is the key difference between society and its components. None of the types of social activity listed above can operate on its own, and not a single social group taken in isolation can survive on its own or provide everything it needs from within its ranks. This is a characteristic feature of society as a whole and society alone, as a product of joint activity by people who can, through their own efforts create all the conditions necessary for their existence.

The human community is a system of real relationships between civilizations, nations and ethnic groups, relationships people enter in the course of their daily activity. As a rule, they do not interact with one another in random or arbitrary ways. There is acertain orderliness about their interactions. Sociologists, for example, describe this orderliness – the intertwined relationships between people in repeating, stable patterns – as the social structure. It manifests itself through a system of social positions and distribution of people across this system.

The structure of community creates the impression that life is well-organized and stable, because it presumes the existence of constant, organized, non-random linkages between members of the group or society. The idea of "structure" is closely associated with status, role, social groups, institutions and various societies. It is absolutely essential for humanity to be able to order, regulate and fix certain relationships of social import, making them mandatory for community members. Institutions are the basic elements, the building blocks of social life regulation.

Institutions are traditional stable forms of organization of communal activity and relationships and interactions between people that have taken shape over the ages and perform functions of great significance for society. When we talk about the institution of family, the institution of education, the institution of the army, the institution of religion, and so on, in all cases we are talking about stable types and forms of social activity, connections, and relationships, through which social life is organized, and which ensures the stability of connections and relationships.

The key purpose of institutions is to ensure the fulfillment of important needs of life.

Herbert Spencer was among the first to notice the problem of the institutionalization of society and to stimulate interest in institutions in sociology. In his social organism theory of human society which is based on a structural analogy between society and an organism, he distinguishes three key types of institutions: reproductive, kinship (marriage and family); distributive (or economic); and regulating (religion, or political systems). This classification is based on identifying key functions that all institutions have.

Institutions are formed on the basis of connections, interactions and relations between specific individuals, social groups, strata and other communities. But they, like other systems, cannot be connected to a sum of these individuals, communities and interactions. Institutions are at a level above individuals, they have a system quality all their own. Consequently, an institution is an independent social organization with its own development logic. From this perspective, institutions can be defined as organized systems with a stable structure, integrated element and somewhat flexible functions. Institutions are capable of fulfilling their intended function through organizing, standardizing and formalizing public activity, public connections and relationships. This process of organizing, standardizing and formalizing is called institutionalization, which is nothing but the process of creating an institution.

The emergence of a need that requires joint organized action and the conditions necessary to satisfy that need are a precondition for creating an institution. Man is a social animal, and human beings attempt to satisfy their needs by acting together.

An important point in the institutionalization process is the emergence of values, standards and behavior rules in the course of spontaneous social interaction, through a process of trial and error. In the course of social practice people make their choices, picking acceptable specimens and appealing communication and behavioral stereotypes out of several, which turn into standardized custom through a process of repetition and evaluation. A necessary step on the way towards institutionalization is the "solidification," i.e. the codification of these patterns as mandatory norms based at first on public opinion, and then on the strength of a formal function by authorities (e.g. through government agencies). This becomes the basis for developing a system of various requirements and permissions. Therefore, institutionalization is first and foremost a process of defining and codifying socioeconomic and technological values, standards, behavior patterns, statuses and roles, building them into a system that can operate towards satisfying various needs.

Institutions are a system that guarantees similar behaviors by people, reconciles their actions, channels their certain urges and desires into certain paths, establishing ways to satisfy their needs, resolves conflicts arising in the normal course of day-to-day life, ensuring its stability and good balance which are essential for compatible joint development. In order for institutions to be effective, they have to become part of an individual's inner world, be implemented in the form of social roles and statuses. Internalization by individuals of all sociocultural elements, and building a system of an individual's needs, core values and expectations is another essential component of institutionalization.

One of the key elements of institutionalization is the creation of an organizational format for the institution. On the outside, an institution is a combination of individuals, organizations or offices equipped with certain material means and tools and performing a certain socioeconomic or similar function. Every institution has a purpose to its operations, specific functions designed to fulfill this purpose and a set of social positions and roles typical of this institution. Based on all of the above, an institution can be defined as an organized unity of people performing certain functions of social import that ensure joint fulfillment of the purpose on the basis of institution members' performance of their roles determined by social values, standards and behavioral patterns.

Western structuralist sociologist P. Blau based his classification of existing institutions on values these institutions represent in their standard-setting structure:

• Integrative institutions which perpetuate particular values, support social solidarity and maintain the order and identity of the social structure, i.e. their primary purpose is to support solidarity and existing particular values in society;

- Distributing institutions represent and implement universal values, which are a means of keeping intact social contracts designed to produce and distribute the necessary social benefits, investments and various rewards;
- Organizing institutions use values to achieve their goals, they serve the purpose of perpetuating authority and organization required to mobilize the resources and coordinate collective efforts aimed at achieving social goals.

Integrative institutions must meet the need for secrecy, while distributing ones have to meet the need for adaptation and organizational institutes must meet the need for integration and achieving the ultimate goal. Depending on the area of operation and functions performed, Western sociologists divide social institutions into three types: relational, regulatory and integrative. Relational institutions define society's role structure according to a number of different criteria: from age and gender to profession and ability. Regulatory institutions define the acceptable boundaries of individual behavior relative to a standard of action in effect in a society as well as punitive sanctions for any attempts to cross these boundaries (including all types of social control mechanisms). Integrative institutions are associated with social roles responsible for ensuring the interests of the social community as a whole.

Sociology dictionaries define five key sets of social institutions:

1) economic institutions serving the purpose of production and distribution of goods and services;

2) political institutions regulating the dispensation of power and access to power;

3) stratification institutions which define the disposition of actors and resources;

4) institutions of kinship associated with marriage, family and socialization of younger people;

5) cultural institutions associated with religious, scientific and artistic activity.

Russian sociologists also offer multiple classifications of social institutions. For example, A.A. and K.A. Radugins[154] identify six types of social institutions:

1) economic and social; 2) political; 3) sociocultural and educational; 4) standard-setting and guiding; 5) standard-setting and sanctioning

---

[154] А.А. Радугин, К.А. Радугин Социология: курс лекций. М.: Центр, 1999.

(permitting); 6) ceremonial, symbolic and conventional based on specific situations.

A.P. Limarenko[155] divides social institutions into the following categories from the perspective of the content of their functions:

1) economic (banks, exchanges, corporations, consumer and service-oriented companies, etc.); 2) political (the state with its central and local government and government agencies, political parties, social associations, foundations, etc.); 3) educational and cultural institutions (school, family, theater and others); 4) social institutions (in the narrow sense of "social"): social services and special care, various self-governing organizations, voluntary societies, clubs, associations).

These groups of social strata institutions can serve as the controls, the direction levers for developing and building a new society. But in whose hands are these controls? Most likely these controls are in the hands of the powers that be, the authorities, the government, for the most part. And yet, people with new ideas often go to public organizations outside the government. And, strangely enough, these ideas may be taken into consideration and even used as guidance or, occasionally, acted upon. However, this is only a "drop in the ocean" of social upheavals. It is only when there rises a tidal wave of socioeconomic suffering in a significant part of society that the authorities and relevant institutions have to search for compatibility of universal coexistence. And they seem to find it, for a while. On the whole, working conditions are established to produce economic (material) benefits, without bringing a commensurate jump in work satisfaction or an emotional uplift that can bring a man real happiness and joy (as opposed to fleeting "pleasures"). The most important thing for societal development, apart from the individual safety of citizens (including their independence from bureaucracy), is the establishment of conditions conducive to individual initiative by citizens in all areas of life. However, it has become clear by now that neither socialism nor the "free market economy" (which went hand-in-hand with the proclaimed "freedom of nations") can give people this. Therefore, to achieve a deeper compatibility within the new community of people, when a healthy economy is not achieved exclusively at the expense of leaving other economies ailing, a huge number of draft models and experiments will be required to develop and preserve in each human being the motivation to improve oneself and

---

[155] А.П. Лимаренко Методологические основы социологии: социология как наука. Минск, 1992.

bring society as much benefit as he can. For this, social institutions must offer, for example, a more attractive consumption model (what is better for the human being and not harmful for the environment) – more attractive from a biological and sociocultural perspective, based on selective-production programs. This will prod into action another group of economic and legal institutions which will strive to introduce legislative restrictions on manufacturers' right to generate profit and set the allowable standards of maximum profit from goods (as well as directing production towards certain types of goods). Gaps will appear between demand and supply in certain product groups, alleviated by government institutions, with the possible result of a new economic system which is closer to people, more "individualized." Active involvement of professional and consumer associations in this process will speed it up (by "promoting" consumer boycotts).

Development of society depends to a great extent on tactical compatibility of actions by organizational institutions capable of transferring part of their control powers to regional governments (regional management) at an appropriate moment, e.g. by decentralizing giant industrial multinationals in order to replace their bureaucratic approach to management with one that is more humanistic. It is a well-known fact that the bureaucratic spirit is incompatible with the principle of active personal involvement in one's work. It is important for management methods to be focused on people and the situation at hand, rather than on strictly following rules and written instructions. Operation of institutions of this kind at the intergovernmental level involves a much higher level of responsibility because they are dealing with universal values of humanity. An example of this would be rich countries giving up on the idea of economic and political influence, i.e. ceasing to extend their principles to nations in Asia and Africa with their own ethnic culture. This incompatibility would have led to irreconcilable clashes because of the widening gap between the rich and the poor. As discussed earlier (see Section 1.2), the institutions of culture, religion and science have a level of compatibility that enables them to provide expert advice to national governments and politicians, as well as training citizens in need of new knowledge, etc.

The middle class comprises a very large stratum of society today, and the middle class has neither economic nor political power, assumes no responsibility and makes no concentrated effort to think about the future of society. The incompatibility in this situation is that, after gaining a taste of joy and happiness of this life, the middle class – the majority of the population in the Western world – derives no satisfaction from its prosperity.

This implies that the institutions of society need an energy discharge to motivate at least this significant part of the world's population – the driving engine of humanity – for intellectual and spiritual growth. What kind of a charge would it take for these institutions to come through?

The author proposes a step-by-step review of the meso-level composition of institutions. It makes sense to differentiate the initial content of product and economic institutions into two levels (in terms of differentiation by the end product). Manufacturing, consumer-oriented and service companies, together with inter-sector and construction companies, are the first, product-centered, material level, meeting people's natural needs. Organizations offering a financial, economic end product (banks, financial services groups, exchanges or similar) comprise the second material level, more universal, covering, in monetary terms, access to more advanced human needs, although this level is not a key criterion for successfully passing the subsequent development stages (of the human being and society).

Compatibility of institutions is defined as both establishing groups of institutions and ordering them in a hierarchy of institutions by their affiliation. Compatibility is defined by both coordination of views and common action and established order and a well-adjusted organized state of institutions.

Let us look in greater detail at the compatibility and order of the following levels – social and political, where institutions "dictate" the direction and mode of product-proprietary operations; and financial and economic institutional levels, based on the hierarchy of human needs.

3.3.2. Hierarchy and Compatibility of Social Institutions

We propose to start an exploration of this topic with an overview of the social institutions of society. "Orderliness" and "organization" have been recognized for centuries as one of the most significant attributes of social reality. Thomas Hobbes in the 17th century defined "the primary purpose of social theory" as "conceptualizing the social order and its possibility, or social action."[156]

As for institutionalizing order as a consequence of compatibility of a standards and rules system, the following oppositions fundamental for social science are the most significant: "individual versus society," "subjectivism versus objectivism." A structuralist approach to explaining institutionalization of order is essentially a holistic understanding of social reality, i.e. the primacy of "society" (or, rather, social structures) over an individual. A society as a structured order exists "objectively", and social structures are mandatory, are imposed on an individual.

Talcott Parsons defines institutions as "prescriptive, normative models defining what is seen as a 'proper,' legal and expected course of action and interaction in a given society."[157] At the same time, "institutions are closely connected, and, at the very least, grow out of a value system shared by members of the society. They are a moral phenomenon in the strict sense."[158]

Institutionalization of normative order in society therefore presumes its legitimization, and the cultural system of society – higher-level compatibility of social institutions – performs this function. "The main functional requirement for relationships between society and the cultural system is legitimization of a society's prescribed standard order," because only "the reference to culture lends significance and legitimacy to standards and rules."[159]

Society is a combination of people united within it, original and cultural collective groups, interacting and exchanging services with one another. All these collective groups form society on the strength of their existence under a common authority that enforces its control over a territory delineated by borders, supporting and imposing a more-or-less common culture. These factors convert a combination of relatively specialized original corporate and cultural collective teams into a society.[160]

---

[156] Cited by: Goran Therborn Being part of a culture, place within a structure and human activity: explanation in sociology and social science // THESIS. 1994. Issue. 4. P. 9.

[157] Parsons, T. The Structure of Social Action. 2nd Edition. Free Press, 1969. Quoted from the Russian edition: Парсонс Т. О структуре социального действия. М.: Академический проект, 2000.

[158] Parsons, T. Prolegomena to a Theory of Social Institutions // American Sociological Review. 1990. Vol. 55. № 3. P. 320.

[159] Parsons, T. The Concept of Society: Components and Their Interrelationships // THESIS. 1993. Issue. 2. P. 102 of the Russian edition.

[160] Shils, E. Society and Societies: a Macrosociological approach. Quoted from the

It is culture (values) that is responsible for introducing structure into role interactions, integrating the various roles into a single system, and thereby solving the problem of order, including in other territories of power.

Institutional compatibility of standards and rules is an equilibrium – a state in which, at a given combination of players' strengths and a "given set of contractual relationships ... none of the players believes he can benefit from expending resources to restructure the agreements already in place."[161]

Institutions are closely connected and interrelated, and often a change in one institution requires changes in others, too (in the so-called "adhesive effect"). All of this significantly increases the quality of the established institutional order, reflected in the famous path dependency concept.[162]

The quality of institutional compatibility depends on many factors and ranges from monopolization of all benefits by rules or their agents to a democratic state based on the rule of law. If the motivation is economic, compatibility would have only an exterior shell, because higher-level political, cultural and ideological institution levels, which are above economic institutions, degenerate. As a consequence, society suffers from the number of economic solutions, and has weak, if any, prospects for developing in deeper, fundamental ways. Rules and standards are frequently understood as institutions. First, as P.V. Panov notes in his book Institutions, Identities, Practices,[163] on which this section is based, the social order is institutionalized within the framework of a certain social group. Furthermore, rules presume a collective realization of meaning of the corresponding social interaction. Second, rules and standards become detached from specific actors and are reassigned to positions (statuses); the meanings also become "detached" from individuals and take on a collective meaning. Third, social constructivism is based on the assumption that collective realization of meaning does not "exist" in its own right, and rules

---

Russian edition: Шилз Э. Общество и общества: макросоциологический подход // Американская социология: Перспективы, проблемы, методы. М.: Прогресс, 1972).

[161] North, D. Institutions, Institutional Change and Operation of the Economy. Quoted from the Russian edition: Норт Д. Институты, институциональные изменения и функционирование экономики. М.: Фонд экономической книги «Начала», 1997. PP. 111–112.

[162] For more on path dependency in political studies, see: P. Pierson Increasing Returns, Path Dependency, and the Study of Politics // American Political Science Review. 2000.Vol. 94. № 2.

[163] П.В. Панов Институты, идентичности, практики: теоретическая модель политического порядка. М.: РОССПЭН, 2011. P. 39–56.

and standards, including collective realization of their meaning "exist" only in interactions, because they are reproduced in interactive practices.

Social interactions constantly result in social construction of new rules. Interactions in "new situations" do not take place on a completely "clean slate." On the contrary, the actors tend to interpret "new interactions" based on their ideas that became formed on the basis of their previous experience, although these pre-existing concepts change under the influence of "new situations."[164]

The institutional level of culture in this book is understood as a "web of meanings," a "conduit of meanings people use to interpret their life experience and direct their actions."[165] This conceptualization, proposed by Clifford Geertz, serves as a very good match for the social constructivist approach. Paul DiMaggio, for example, defines culture in a similar way: "We understand culture as cognitions, values, norms and expressive symbols shared by people." Culture is a "well-ordered system of meanings shared by a group."[166]

Cultural institutions, including those ranging from religion of tribes and ethnic groups to ideological culture that unites us all, give members of social groups a common knowledge (shared knowledge), which enables them to "make sense" of reality around them, "assign meaning" to things in the material world and social phenomena, including "understanding" the social actions of their counterparties. Culture also includes cognitive blueprints, i.e. mental models which serve to perceive and interpret the world around us (categorizations, typizations, binary oppositions of the "good versus evil," "clean versus dirty" type), as well as producing typical social interactions. Cognitive models taking every one of us to the intellectual and (scientific) spiritual level (which enables us to be artistic, create, make discoveries in every field of knowledge), are usually so deeply embedded in our consciousness that they are usually taken for granted, as something about which there can be no doubt, and are "reproduced" in social interactions without thinking, without reflection, or at least, without articulating, as is the case with Anthony Giddens's "practical consciousness."[167]

---

[164] В.А. Морозов Развитие общественных институтов // Маркетинг. 2012. № 2. P. 3–20.

[165] П.В. Панов Ibid, P. 39–56.

[166] DiMaggio, P. Culture and Economy. Quoted from the Russian edition: // Западная экономическая социология. М.: РОССПЭН, 2004. P. 471, 484.

[167] Giddens, A. The Constitution of Society. Cambridge: Polity, 1984. Quoted from the

Institutionalization of social order includes a combination of processes of compatible quality: emerging rules of interaction at different levels of institutions, i.e. legitimization within cultural layers, internalization of cognitive layers, creating organizations to support the social level's order.

At the same time, institutions, as L. Offe writes, "establish an order which can always be potentially contested."[168] Some members of a social group for some reason or other question the established order and try to change it as best they can. Consequently, the order includes not only reproduction of rules and collective meanings, but also their constructive denial – as compatibility of non-local renewal.

A literature analysis helps to identify at least four different conceptualizations of institutions: 1) cognitive concept; 2) institutions as organizations; 3) institutions as rules and standards; 4) institutions as social practices. In addition, some conceptualizations frequently try to cover various aspects, offering a "broad" view of institutions (see table 3.1).

Table 3.1 Institutional columns and conduits [*]

Conduits	Columns		
	Regulatory	Normative	Cognitive
Cultures	Rules, laws	Values, expectations	Categories, typifications
Social Structures	Governance systems, power systems	Regimes, authority systems	Structural isomorphism, identities
Routines	Protocols, standard procedures	Conformity, meeting obligations	Adherence to behavioral programs and scripts

[*] *Scott W.R.* Institutions and Organizations. Thousand Oaks: Sage Publications, 1995. P. 52.

Russian edition: Гидденс Э. Устроение общества. М., 2005. PP. 45–46.

[168] Offe, K. Designing Institutions in East European Transitions // The Theory of Institutional Design / Ed. by R. Goodin. Cambridge: Cambridge University Press, 1996. P. 204.

Below are four different ways of looking at institutions, four different conceptualizations:

1) The cognitive concept of institutions as a "thought stereotype." The definition of institutions as standard-setting structures generating evaluations has given way to interpretation of institutions as cognitive constructs (categories, typizations, scenarios), which form constituent meanings that serve as a basis of action;[169]

2) Institutions as organizations — one of the biggest points of contention in the institutional discourse. It might make sense to differentiate between institutionals as rules of the game as opposed to institutions as organizations, as actors;

3) Institutions as constituting rules and standards that exist only in interactions and to the extent that they are reproduced in the practices of interaction. They have a constituting meaning, rather than regulatory, as in the theory of rational choice, or prescriptive, as in structuralism;

4) Institutions as practices, i.e. certain behavioral patterns enabling people to have certain expectations with regard to each other's behavior and incorporating interests and value systems as well.[170] Investigation of the social level of compatibility reveals that the rules and resources defined as a structure are only a virtual order, a sample of social relations. It exists as structural properties of social systems. Consequently, institutions are not reflected in rules as much as rules are reflected in institutions: "Types of rules are included in the process of reproduction of institutional practices, i.e. practices deeply embedded in space and time."[171] Every institution focuses its attention on a single aspect.

Institutionalization of social order assumes acknowledgement of social norms as cultural specimens, although it does not include culture and its components among social institutions, as they belong to a different institutional level of societal compatibility.

Sergey V. Patrushev proposes the following definition of institutions for political science (for the political level of social compatibility): "An institution in political science can be understood, in general terms, as:

1) a political establishment — a set of formal and informal principles, norms, rules defining and regulating human activity in the political realm,

---

[169] DiMaggio P. Culture and Economy P. 489 (page cited by the Russian edition).
[170] Lane J.E., Ersson S. The New Institutional Politics: Performance and Outcomes. L.–N.Y.: Routledge, 2000. P. 4.
[171] Панов П.В. Ibidem.

2) a political establishment or organization – a unity of people organized in a certain way, a certain political structure, 3) a stable type of political behavior expressed as a certain system of collective actions, a procedure, a mechanism."[172]

Lev D. Gudkov and Boris V. Dubin take a similar position: "A social institution is a stable social interaction based on certain values and standards or certain roles which arises around a certain cultural value, is codified and regulated by law."[173] Every institutional structure or order is developed, supported or changed through the process of ongoing interactions, negotiations, and a struggle among those involved in this process.[174]

Moving from social organization and order up to political organization and order, we note that politics is understood here as a group activity that has to do with the organization and operation of agencies representing the government's public power. Writing of the juxtaposition of the "political" and the "social," Hannah Arendt, among other things, says that the "social" for classical Greek thinkers was something "mundane, associated with joint activity aiming to satisfy purely material needs, because these needs for human life are clearly the same as for other forms of organic life."[175] The political is a fundamentally different type of activity that involves communication among citizens, who are free from material concerns, aiming to achieve common good. It was considerations of common good, rather than material interests, that was the driving force for citizens of a polis, a city-state of antiquity. It was no accident that Aristotle contrasted both households (oikos), small units in which people engage in production of material goods, and ethnos, barbarian societies like those of the Celts and Persians, incapable of producing common good and therefore apolitical, with the polis, a political group.

---

[172] Патрушев С.В. Институционализм в политической науке: Этапы, течения, идеи, проблемы// Институциональная политология: Современный институционализм и политическая трансформация России / Под ред. С.В. Патрушева. М.: ИС РАН, 2006. С.10.

[173] Гудков Л.Д., Дубин Б.В. Институциональные дефициты как проблема постсоветского общества // Мониторинг общественного мнения: экономические и социальные перемены. 2003. № 3 (65). P. 41.

[174] Eisenstadt, S., Roninger, L. Patrons, Clients, and Friends: Interpersonal Relations and the Structure of Trust in Society. Cambridge; N.Y.: Cambridge University Press, 1984. P. 25.

[175] Arendt, H. Vita activa, or On Active Life. Quoted from the Russian edition: Арендт Х. Vita activa, или О деятельной жизни. СПб.: Алетейя, 2000, P. 84.

If we take the polis as a foundation of our ideas of politics, the nature of political compatibility is clearly completely different from that of social compatibility. The political order is institutionalized because citizens are driven by ideas of common good, and therefore political institutions help to shape a higher level of compatibility within a community.

Issues of societal and territorial globalization appropriately belong on the supra-governmental (supra-political), i.e. the religious and theological level of society's institutional compatibility, which unites states and territories adhering to a certain religion with their compatible laws. At the other extreme is pure particularism, the "rules" of personal interactions, and any social order by definition assumes depersonalization of rules, i.e. a certain degree of universality.

The Center reigns supreme over the periphery and permeates it – or at least attempts to, and, to some extent, succeeds. Society becomes more closely integrated — from the Center to the periphery — in its persuasions and actions.[176]

There are always social groups (the mafia, certain ethnic communities, etc.) which are not integrated into mainstream society; there is always someone who does not recognize universal principles, does not share the idea of a nation as a political societal group of equal free citizens, and is driven purely by his own private interests rather than the principle of the common good in his political interactions.

As A. Shedler notes, "communities without conflict have no need for political action."[177]

In this way, political compatibility unites social compatibility in certain social groups.

It follows from the above that institutionalization of political compatibility assumes the emergence of a power center capable of generating shared behavioral models and systems of cultural meanings which are common for the whole heterogeneous macrocollective, and thus linking together social compatibility in separate social groups.

The political level of compatibility within society generates a nationwide, state-wide ideology, with roots coming from the religious beliefs of dominant peoples, ethnicities and ethnic groups in the territory of the state. The fact that there is only one center makes it possible for it to

---

[176] Shils, E. Society and Societies: a Macrosociological approach. P. 349–350.
[177] The End of Politics? Explorations into Modern Antipolitics / Ed. by A. Scedler. N.Y.: St. Martin's Press, 1997. P. 6.

reproduce "unified" behavior models and a sufficiently complete perception of social reality. In addition, political compatibility is reproduced, as it were, over social compatibility of a lower meso-level, because universalist political practices are fairly clearly differentiated from institutional practices, which are reproduced in separate social groups.

Orderly political organization in this work is understood not as a certain "objectively existing" structure, but rather as a social construct, a result of social interactions, which lead, alongside the institutionalization of social order at the microlevel (in separate social groups), to institutionalization of the order at the macro level, in complex/compound groups, in which heterogeneous, open social groups find themselves interlinked and interdependent. Political compatibility is both the result of and a condition for social order, because it connects social order within separate social groups.

Achieving political compatibility, as with achieving any compatibility is a multidimensional process. Political compatibility does not eliminate social compatibility at the meso-level, but rather takes shape alongside social compatibility. In other words, "alongside" the rules and norms, cultural meanings, organizations, which are reproduced in practices of separate social groups, where political rules and norms, cultural meanings and organizations, reproduced in interactions of the meso-level environment, are institutionalized. Institutionalization of political compatibility presumes the existence of a center capable of generating shared behavior patterns and systems of cultural meanings for this extremely heterogeneous macro-collective, thereby linking social order in separate social groups.

Because political compatibility is institutionalized in heterogeneous groups, it cannot be conflict-free, and connection of social orders emerging from separate social groups presumes the existence of a center or centers capable of generating common, shared behavioral patterns and cultural meanings. This centricity, therefore, is a source of incompatibility, a permanent fundamental political conflict, and the subject of ongoing struggle or incompatibility of existing views and actions, which we cover in the subsequent sections of this book.

Speaking of higher levels of compatibility, one has to look at the worldview (ideology) of social and political units within a community, giving it a cultural dimension of political magnitude: compatibility, similar to social compatibility, revealing the nature and the role of identity for each compatibility level.

In order to identify the worldview, culture is understood as a combination of collective meanings shared by members of a social group, peoples or ethnicities, converted to a shared faith. When separating the levels of compatibility spheres in the life and operation of people, we note that a higher level – political order – is both a condition of social orders and an idea of reality as "a whole," a condition for collective understanding of its component parts by separate social groups.

The processes of collective differentiation, classification and categorization are essential for building collective perceptions of the division of the world into social groups (peoples and ethnicities). We will identify five aspects of identity: identity as a phenomenon of collective self-perception (and "selfness"), as an aspect of individuality, as a result of social interactions, as a foundation for social action, and as a product of competing discourses. These meanings clearly complement one another. When looking at the phenomenon of identity from different aspects, in this case the first aspect is particularly important: "Identity understood as a specifically collective phenomenon means a fundamental consequential self-perception (and selfness) of members of a group or a category. When talking of social compatibility, one can also note that "the social order" is reduced to a collective classification achieved by adding the classifying judgments and those being classified, through which the agents classify, categorize the world and themselves."[178]

The meaning of the worldview is precisely that it arranges, organizes and links, in a way, the various meanings of the identification matrix in a more or less non-contradictory, compatible way. It sets a coordinates system of sorts, in which social reality becomes relatively whole and understandable. Consequently, a political identity is the kind of identity that can have an ordering, organizing meaning within the structure of an information matrix. This identity provides an angle at which "the world as a whole" is collectively understood, as are political interactions on the macro level, reaching beyond the boundaries of a single social group. The political identity is linked to a central cultural system.

The political identity is that which is actualized through political interactions, just as other identities are actualized through social, economic, religious and theological interactions.

A worldview is not a harmony cast in stone; on the contrary, it is always

---

[178] Bourdieu, P. Peractical Reason: On the Theory of Action: Stanford University Press, 1996. Quoted from Russian edition: М.: Институт экспериментальной социологии; СПб.: Алетейя, 2001. P. 268.

subjected to doubt. To a certain extent, any meso-level social group has to deal with rivalry between competing ideas of social reality "as a whole" (known as the fight for worldview). Collective identities are built on the basis of "differentiation," and three interrelated components can be identified in the process of social construction:

1) the definition of "we"/"us"; 2) the definition of "them" (others); 3) the definition of boundaries between "us" and "them."[179] Any worldview identifying collective identities as "organizing" (political), should also define this, i.e. give it content of some kind. This happens through accenting different meanings, and a certain degree of discord and incompatibility is always found here. As a result, social strata appear within a single worldview, which have different opinions on "secondary" issues (secondary in the context of this worldview). For example, we can consider Catholics, Orthodox Christians and Protestants as "secondary" religious identities within the Christian worldview, or Shiites and Sunnis as secondary within the Islamic worldview, or liberals, conservatives, socialists as "secondary" political identities at the political level.

Identities, including political identities, define the place of man within social reality. It is precisely when interactions, rules and norms are collectively understood and internalized by members of a certain heterogeneous group as meaningful for interrelations on the macro level that they acquire a general meaning. And the group itself becomes politically compatible in the process.

In this sense, political order is first and foremost a symbolic order within which there may be social incompatibility; most probably, it is always there in its latent form. Conflicts or competition may arise between groups like these. These social conflicts can easily escalate into conflicts between opposing thinking systems, in which each of them would assert itself, at best discrediting and, in the worst-case scenario, eliminate the conflicting knowledge system.[180]

---

[179] Баньковская С.П. Другой как элементарное понятие социальной онтологии // Социологическое обозрение. 2007. № 1 С. 75–86; Климова С.Г. Критерии определения групп «мы» и «они» // Социологические исследования. 2002. № 6. С. 83–95.

[180] Berger, P., Luckmann T. The Social Construction of Reality: A Treatise in the Sociology of Knowledge. New York: Anchor Books, 1966. Quoted from the Russian edition: Бергер П., Лукман Т. Социальное конструирование реальности: Трактат по социологии знания. М.: Медиум, 1995. PP. 140 – 141.

Any social and political order is fraught with conflict in the cultural dimension. The political level of compatibility should guarantee moral and cultural alignment of social life, setting the boundaries of meanings shared by all citizens despite their differences.

In the modern situation, we observe a certain sense of being lost, which has to do with the "end of the world as we know it," with it slipping away from us, etc. It can be overcome and definitely will be overcome through politics and people's religious convictions about the wholeness and unity of the world and their worship of the single God (a higher mind). Compatibility at the social level is achieved by actual uniformity. Uniformity can be explained by interests, i.e. by the rational goal-orientation of behavior of isolated individuals with identical expectations, by their morals and ways, and simply by their habits. People reproduce corresponding behavior models voluntarily, because they are seen as significant for an individual's behavior, i.e. mandatory for him, or serve as an example worthy of emulation.

From social, political, and religious and theological perspectives, only internal compatibility can be guaranteed, namely: 1) purely through feelings — by emotional loyalty; 2) rationally, through values — by belief in the absolute value of order as a manifestation of the highest-order immutable values (moral, aesthetic, others); 3) in religious terms — by the belief that preservation of the existing order is a sine qua non of the common good and salvation.

This has to do precisely with the cultural and world-view dimension of the existing order, which lies above and guarantees a peaceful coexistence. Internalized rules and norms are not entirely unlike customs, but are not identical to them. People's behavior here does not happen "by itself," but is instead guided by maxims – general social and cultural norms.

The level of social compatibility can be characterized by a spectrum from admonition (expressing a "wish") to coercion, which would describe social orders based on the idea that following the rules benefits the interacting actors (whose actions are determined by their interests). At the same time, there are social customs based on voluntary adherence to customs.

Where multiple ethnic groups are living together, a legitimate social order would be based on internalization of rules (only internal guarantees of legitimacy) as well as a combination of internal and external guarantees of legitimacy. Legitimate coercion-based social arrangements are in place (providing only external guarantees of legitimacy). In fact, the same is also true for higher levels of compatibility, including at political, religious and theological, and cultural and world-view levels, which we place into a hierarchy in this book. Furthermore, the spectrum from "simple wish to mandatory/coercive" is also typical of lower compatibility levels: the level of products and technologies and the financial and economic level.

We note that varieties of rules of different types present a significant problem. This prompted scientists to develop a "grammar of institutions," designed to make a distinction between different types of rules with a "mathematical precision." An institutional "grammar" paradigm can have five different aspects at the most:

1) A — attributes;

2) D — "the ethical modality component" — permission, obligation or prohibition (may, must, must not);

3) I – the objective;

4) C — conditions — different variables (where, when, to what degree);

5) O (or else) — sanctions imposed for failing to perform a requirement. Norms have been introduced to achieve social compatibility — rules connecting the elements together and providing for punishment (sanctions) for violations.

It is important to identify three idealized typical (basic, fundamental) types of social groups (for subsequent exploration of compatibility of groups and organizations), they are associations, communities and organized social groups. Social identity comes to the fore in describing the types of social groups as communities. The phenomenon of community is closely associated with and is based on the cultural dimension of social orders. Communities can be defined as social groups in which interactions are based on internalization by the group members of rules and norms collectively understood within the group. Associations, conversely, are social groups, interactions within which are based on matching instrumental interests. The key difference of an organized social group from other "basic" varieties of social groups has to do with the fact that an organized group produces a specific type of activity, not only oriented towards order, but also designed to enforce order. An organized social group, first, enforces control over behavior of group members (by monitoring them) and, second, imposes sanctions against violators of social norms (see Table 3.2).

Table 3.2 Compatibility of actions within social groups

Type of social groups	Type of social action		NORMS / RULES
	Non-instrumental	Instrumental	
Organized social groups with designated governing bodies	Law		NORMS
Organized social groups (self-organized)	Conventions		
Unorganized social groups	Internalized social norms	Interests base	RULES
	Customs		
	Communities	Associations	

In the case of organized sociopolitical and other groups with dedicated governing (power) bodies a phenomenon arises which is best described as organizational hierarchy. Hierarchy is defined as a form, among other things, of social differentiation and stratification (into castes, classes, different statuses, or other dimensions), in which individuals, groups or organizations are categorized and arranged from the top down. A hierarchy makes it possible to find a starting point for joint, and, most importantly, compatible start of voluntary action. Apparently, T. Parsons did not describe community as a system as a "societal community," by accident, emphasizing that "in order to survive and develop, a societal community must follow a common cultural orientation shared as a whole (although not necessarily uniformly and unanimously) by its members as a foundation of their cultural identity."[181]

Political compatibility links social compatibility in various social groups and presumes a struggle for "centricity", i.e. for the ability to create common behavior models and cultural meanings to uphold religious and

---

[181] Parsons, T. The Concept of Society: Components and Their Interactions – quoted from the Russian edition: Парсонс Т. Понятие общества: компоненты и их взаимоотношения // THESIS. 1993. # 2.

theological and cultural and world-view (global) compatibility. The world picture itself, on the one hand, creates concepts of the world shared by the whole organized community, and on the other hand is constantly contested and subjected to different interpretations. Consequently, political compatibility presumes that the political community is an "organized community" capable of generating shared behavior patterns and systems of cultural meanings (for the global culture), as well as guaranteeing their legitimacy. This helps to create (achieve) compatibility of mutual development of all social groups found in the territory considered for research.

The "centricity" mode may be typical of religious and theological as well as political organizations in all the meanings stated above. When creating special bodies of power, they usually become the focal points of "center formation," because the bodies of power, in addition to coercion, try to legitimize the established order and create a minimal, but strong compatibility level.

Social, political, and (multi-level) religious order, first of all, cannot be based on coincidence of instrumental interests, and, second, is always based, to an extent, on identities and collective ideas rooted in the shared culture, which create "loyalty," "attachment," etc. (and therefore a "political community" is not a normative, standardized ideal, but rather a completely empirical phenomenon and a manifestation of multilevel compatibility at the same time); third, it is never based on cultural affinity alone, while society is never a community in a pure sense of the word, because an admission of multi-level compatibility is always guaranteed through certain (non-violent) coercion effected by organizations at each level.

Samuel P. Huntington wrote that in a complete absence of social and theological conflict, political institutions of forced compromise are not needed; and they are impossible in a complete absence of social harmony. Two groups that see each other as bitter, irreconcilable enemies cannot build a foundation for their joint community until their mutual perception changes.[182]

The multilevel propensity for conflict manifests itself through several aspects: first, as a struggle for control over bodies (instruments) of power; second, a political organization at any level engages in forcing others to follow rules and standards, which always causes protests and resistance of

---

[182] Huntington, S. Political Order in Changing Societies. Quoted from the Russian edition: М.: Прогресс-Традиция, 2004. P. 29.

participants; third, this organization is established to address and resolve other public problems, produce common benefits, mobilize and distribute resources. All these matters are essentially contentious, causing arguments, conflicts and discord. Fourth, any organization assumes the existence of an organizational hierarchy. Any hierarchy is called into question and contested by those who have only a marginal position within the hierarchy. Unilateral activity by leaders of one religion in a multinational and multi-confessional state causes indignation from other religious denominations, creating religious conflict; political parties and social strata operate in similar ways.

Compatibility that defines a certain, for example, political order, represents reproduction of institutional political practices. These practices simultaneously both reproduce consent and resolve incompatibilities (conflicts) typical of politics. This propensity for conflict should not be seen as a deviation or a threat, a danger; on the contrary, it is standard for political compatibility. First, the political order, which requires minimal compatibility, is a fundamental source of conflict. The political order assumes that there is a center capable of generating general behavior models and cultural meanings, which serves as a trigger for the struggle for "centricity." Second, the struggle for centricity becomes a trigger for incompatibility, as a clash of different ideas of how the world is arranged. Third, the existence of special power bodies becomes a trigger for incompatibility and conflict, as they create a struggle for control over them (through politics).

Any sociopolitical order is based on rejecting other possibilities; it always expresses a combination of relations of power.

The state of compatibility is a certain "snapshot" order, it is not a rigid state, but rather a process that "exists" within interaction practices and is never "complete." In particular, the centricity conflict results in constant change in the configuration of centers and social groups, putting them into the state of political collective groups, and vice versa. Political compatibility and the order established by it are based on a certain agreement with regard to itself and, at the same time, on some disagreement, conflict or struggle over itself. In its very nature, order presupposes changes within itself, it is based on these changes and is reproduced in a struggle over its own foundations, so it would be a mistake to contrast order with change.

The structural conflict can be viewed in the context of a general methodology of compatibility of development. A non-constructive conflict is a process that leads to the emergence of a constructive conflict and subsequent creative development of the parties involved.

The social institution compatibility issues reviewed above make it possible to make an assumption about the composition of institution groups, shaping the levels of compatibility of society operation. Based on the hierarchy of human needs, the rough hierarchy of social institution levels would look as follows, descending from higher-level institutions at level 5 to fundamental institutions at level 1 inclusive:

5. Cultural and world view;
4. Religious and theological;
3. Political;
2. Social;
1. Financial and economic.

We will attempt to expand the number of these levels in the following discussion.

3.4. Organizations – Processors of Compatible Environments for Societal Development

3.4.1. Environment Compatibility Levels as Development Factors for Organizations Within Society

The development and success of an organization are usually and substantially determined by external influences. An organization as an open system depends on deliveries of resources and materials, and energy; it also depends on personnel, and, certainly, on consumers. The external environment can be described as a combination of factors affecting its operations, including consumers, the competition, government agencies, suppliers, financial institutions, sources of labor, as well as technological and scientific progress (a scientific and intellectual sphere of the environment and some individuals), culture (including global processes, theological and national developments), the state of the broader society (including political and social events and developments) and natural phenomena.

Because the external environment can affect an organization through different impacts, they are divided into direct and indirect factors, and the entire environment can be subdivided into direct and indirect impacts.

Consumers are individuals who are interested or can be interested in products and services produced by an organization. Peter F. Drucker believed that the only true purpose of any business is creating its consumers, which ultimately defines how much production resources an organization needs. If an organization has its own consumer, then even if it faces fierce competition (and is adversely affected by aggressively negative financial, economic, social, political, theological and general cultural factors), if there is still a minimal possibility of covering costs, the conditions can be considered as minimally viable, and they would be recognized as compatible with the organization's business operations at a given point in time.[183]

In order for general development compatibility processes (at different levels) to be effective, a business organization needs to make products that are in demand with consumers. Hence, the customer matches the products manufactured. If the customer (the consumer) is intelligent, makes a point of complying completely with all the social and national (ethnic) moral and ethical standards (in effect where he is), enjoys good physical, spiritual and mental health, and is psychologically balanced, the goods offered to this person should target ("match") these qualities. If there is no match (no compatibility), the goods would have deviations and faults, creating a mismatch with the set of requirements; i.e. the goods would have defects (technological, biological, functional, social, pricing, aesthetic, "moral," etc.), reflecting incompatibility (a mismatch) between external requirements (imposed by the environment) and the organization's production capabilities.

Consumers should include the population, industrial consumers, intermediaries, and the government as an economic agent, as well as all constituent entities of the entire multilevel external environment. All these components of the external environment, including the competition, are "forcing" the organization constantly to refresh and improve its product, first in quantitative terms, and then through qualitative change (revamping the product). For this, the (business) organization should rank suppliers by price, quality and terms of delivery. Precisely these trends of compatibility in shaping an organization's output can influence the overall sales that are

---

[183] В.А. Морозов Предприятие и внешняя среда: уровни взаимодействия // Российское предпринимательство. 2012. № 8 (206).

instrumental to the company's success. If a company's products are selling, its potential increases (in terms of applicable factors) — including economic, social, sociopolitical (of the territory where the business organization is based), ethnic/national (what ethnic/national group or religious denomination the organization most identifies with), cultural and world view (because every member of the team, as with the organization as a whole, is striving to achieve the best results required in the relevant areas of operation) and scientific (intellectual) and spiritual (defining creation of new products making the life of society better).

So why are these factors arranged in this particular order? As we look at human needs, we go back to the famous Maslow hierarchy of needs, which puts physiological needs at the foundation, adding next the need for safety (safety in general terms, in the context of the market economy, few understand this as financial and economic security capable of protecting an organization from various impacts that come with a certain "cost component"; paying that cost would protect a member of an organization or the organization itself from a certain negative influence and risks). After that, we look at needs for belonging to a social group and the need for love. This raises us from the financial and economic level to the social level, reflecting everything and all of the organization's environment, its members, and its members' families. By paying compensation to its members for their work, an organization satisfies both a lower-level need (financial and economic) and a need of a higher order: a social need. In other words, the level of the organization (its status, profitability, the range of problems and interests it can address) makes it part of a certain "social group" (in figurative terms), also automatically making its members part of the same social group. Social groups (as with organizations themselves) are united by territory and by industry, forming certain constituent societal layers, taking us a step up to look at the next, political level of compatibility between a company and its environment.

The next level in the hierarchy of needs is the need for respect. All people in modern society need stable, well-substantiated and relatively high self-esteem. This always depends on recognition and respect by the people around oneself. The political level has both a national/territorial and ideological flavor uniting the various social groups into a nation, a state.

As we can see, we need from the hierarchy of human needs the key component of needs – the need for love – leading the human being (an individual, organization member) to happiness (or manifested through the organization's success — development of its production potential). In this connection, we need to consider this point: we have a multitude of national and ethnic groups, different peoples, which are affiliated with a certain faith. After all, only the pillars of age-old national culture can make a man a more organic part of his environment, make him happy in his work and daily life.

And here we move on to considering the next step in human needs – the need for the meaning of life and self-actualization. The need of an organization member and the organization itself for a deeper understanding of their existence and activity, their operation, is the most meaningful and far-reaching, comprehensive need. In this connection, we should look at it from two perspectives where it belongs to the upper levels of compatible interaction with the external environment. This is important for both the organization and its members, because under conditions of natural globalization (increasing compatibility of concepts and realities of daily life) of society, we consider the satisfaction of needs for the meaning of life and self-actualization in two institutional layers of compatibility: 1) the more general cultural and world-outlook layers (as a merger of all national, ethnic and religious denominational cultures); 2) a more personal level for every one of us — the cognition (intellectual) and spiritual level (the level of the need for self-actualization), which focuses on the main actor in all events — the human being. Abraham Maslow wrote that the satisfaction of fundamental needs by itself does not give us the same level of meaning and guiding points in life.[184] In turn, Albert Camus described the question about the meaning of life as the most immediate of all questions facing man.[185]

We can describe the first compatibility level, which we just reviewed very briefly above as a product-proprietary level because the entire environment of an organization (of every business organization in a nation's economy) consists of similar organizations dealing with creation, manufacture, sale and service (or products and goods, including technology products and structures and buildings, including recycling them at the end of their life). It includes a great mass of organizations producing material products and everything that surrounds man in non-virtual terms.

The institutional environment of indirect influence is understood as factors that may not produce a direct and immediate action (influence) on the organization's operations, but still can definitely affect its viability in the

---

[184] Maslow, A. Motivation and Personality. Quoted from the Russian edition: Мотивация и личность. 3-е изд. СПб.: Питер, 2003. P. 24.
[185] Camus, A. The Myth of Sisyphus. Quoted from the Russian edition: Миф о сизифе. Эссе об абсурде. М.: Радуга, 1990. P. 31.

long term. This includes the overall state of the economy as a whole, scientific and technological progress, sociocultural, political, and other changes that rank higher by measures of strategic influence.

The second level is the financial and economic level of compatibility in society. Factors of the financial and economic institutional environment must be constantly evaluated, because the state of the economy affects the firm's goals and ways to achieve them. These include, among a great variety of general and local factors: inflation rates, the international balance of payments, levels of employment, interest rates on business lending, etc. Each of these factors can be either a threat or a new opportunity for an organization. Thus, US Dollar exchange rate fluctuations vis-à-vis other currencies can generate large monetary gains or losses.

The third factor affecting the development and success of an organization — the social compatibility level of the external environment — includes public organizations that directly influence companies' operations. This influence has become especially strong in recent decades. The influence of trade unions (or similar organizations) is well-known: these organizations stand up for workers' rights, establishing a balance of relations between an organization's owners and its hired employees. Consumer rights groups and organizations (including those representing the interests of specific social strata, including social minorities) and environmental organizations advocating healthy life for the population and environmental conservation also have seen an increase in their influence.

The government, which represents the political level of compatibility (the fourth factor), influences organizations (whose missions put them at different layers of compatibility with the external environment) through legal regulation of their operations. The number and complexity of laws directly regulating business have increased sharply.

Changes are taking place in various accounting forms of businesses and other organizations; tax and customs regulations are also changing. The state of current law is complex and in flux, and often there is a degree of uncertainty involved. Uncertainty about the current influence of government authorities on the private business sector arises from the fact that the requirements of some organizations come into conflict with those of others, and at the same time, many organizations have government agencies behind them, enforcing the requirements as mandatory. Stability in society is most important for organizations' business — especially for the product and proprietary (1) and financial and economic (2) organizational compatibility layers, as well as for the social order above (3) (see the preceding section for details). The inflow of investment and other resources to specific regions depends on this. The attitude of authorities to the business sector is manifested through setting various breaks and benefits (preferences) or taxes (and charges), which either encourage business development in a certain region, or squeeze it out, creating incompatible conditions for various ranges of similar organizations. Lobbying methods are also used before various government agencies and organizations for the benefit of specific industrial groups, which also has an effect on the democratization of business processes as a whole.

When organizing the operations of a business organization, one has to take into account the theological and cultural environment (the Level 5 factor) in which they exist and operate. This is mostly about the prevailing life values and religious traditions in the area of operation (values and traditions of peoples, ethnic groups and civilizations on Earth). This becomes the basis for a behavior standard, which is sometimes called the "cultural code." For example, the principal distinction between US and Japanese standards is well known. In the former case, the standard is based on an "individualistic" approach to the organization, while in the latter case the approach is more akin to that within a traditional family. Therefore, a strong focus on career growth and changing jobs on a regular basis is regarded as normal in one case (a man is expected to change jobs once every several years in the US), while in the other a man often works in one organization all his life, regarding his superior as a father figure he must obey.

Up to eight different civilizations currently exist on Earth, comprising the majority of the planet's population. However, we all live together, our numbers are increasing all the time, affecting the compatibility in our relationships in terms of quality. Therefore, we need a holistic, integrated understanding of the world around us. Through this perception of communal living everyone, while retaining his national (ethnic) unique features, must also follow his own traditions at the same time. Compatibility of a general development of cultures is very important, and it works through an integrated, unified cultural and world-view perception of the existence of society as an integrated, whole community.

The sixth level, the cultural and world-view level is in this way the denominator of unity and a great variety of cultures in their combined development as they overcome the domination of individual uncoordinated interests.

While previously it was a generally accepted belief that the international milieu should be the bailiwick exclusively of export-oriented organizations (including those in the product/proprietary layer), now changes in the international community affect companies of different types in different industries operating at practically all levels. The modern world is the scene of a strong trend towards globalization of the market for manufactured products of different kinds. This means that national borders are becoming more transparent, more tenuous for business, multinationals are on the ascendant, and the influence of international economic, social and political organizations rises. Factors encouraging development of international business include: lower costs of doing business in some countries, the desire to avoid trade restrictions within certain countries, as well as investment opportunities and production capabilities of countries other than an organization's home country. One must also take into account that Russia, too, has acceded to the WTO.

The pinnacle of development compatibility (self-actualization in the hierarchy of human needs) in an individual, in organization members, and in the organization itself, as a form of human community, and in a more general sense, is the progress towards improvement (and ultimately towards perfection), self-renewal, self-enrichment by knowledge, skills, spiritual growth, and unity with nature and attaining a deeper understanding of the universe. We call this uppermost (seventh) level of environment compatibility for anyone and everyone the scientific and intellectual level (the level of cognition and spirituality), which offers a way of qualitative renewal, the development of the entire community through everyone and through every individual member.

The seventh compatibility level, acting as a factor of the external environment and affecting the development of business organizations defines the possibility of not only bringing production efficiency to a qualitatively new level, but also refreshing, renewing the organization itself because of the intellectual and spiritual development of its members, and, consequently, increasing the efficiency of ways to satisfy new needs (as well as creating new ways to do that). In order to enable an organization to be competitive,[186] it is necessary to collect, store and distribute large volumes of information about innovations emerging in the organization's field of operations. Completely novel technologies for processing information resources and data have emerged in recent years: computer and laser

---

[186] В.А. Морозов Формирование конкурентных преимуществ отрасли // Маркетинг. 2011. № 5.

technologies, robotechnics, satellite communications, bio- and nanotechnology, etc. Researchers talk about the high speed of technological change, and this trend continues.

We believe there exists a compatible connection between environmental factors (and therefore methods of influence), which ensures that a change in one environmental factor (level) entails changes in the strength and endurance of influence by another factor. A variety of factors exist in the context of a certain hierarchy of their qualitative mutual influences and their significance for operation of organizations and their members.

The external environment has a high degree of changeability (volatility, or fluidity), which at a certain period of time creates highly compatible[187] (well coordinated) conditions for the development of organizations, or, conversely, barely compatible or incompatible (completely contradictory) conditions of operation, which can lead to breakdown and disintegration of the organization within a very short time. This makes it essential to control diverse kinds of information, ensuring the precision of ongoing processes at levels of compatibility of the external environment — factors affecting organizations' activities and operations. Experts in the field have introduced the term "chaotic change" to describe this.

Speaking of key types of socioeconomic systems, we consider the issues of compatibility and compatible influence taking into consideration system type (1) the external environment (institutions) and system type (2) the object of our inquiry (the organization). We consider the above in this way because the description of objects (organizations) has limited distribution in space, whereas this type of system has no distribution in time (on the time axis). In order to demonstrate these limitations for objects (organizations, as a system type), we have presented the types of key groups of organizations by their association with compatibility levels of the external environment the way we see it (this association).

We provide a way to visualize the relative positions of organization groups — uniform directions included in the external environment's compatibility levels described above (see Table 3.3).[188]

---

[187] As a reminder, we understand compatibility as the voluntary interaction of parties to achieve their goals which do not conflict with the goals of their partners.

[188] В.А. Морозов Предприятие и внешняя среда: уровни взаимодействия // Российское предпринимательство. 2012. № 8 (206).

	Levels of external environment	Composition of basic functional organizations
1	Product and material	Joint-stock companies (with liability of different types) in manufacturing, trade and service industry. Start-ups focused on implementation of R&D. Individual private enterprise. WTO. Associations to manage environmental projects spanning several sectors. Business incubators, R&D-intensive multinationals, corporate universities
2	Financial, economic	Banks, exchanges, investment organizations, IMF, economic and financial organizations (ministries/offices) and the like
3	Social	Social groups (voluntary, national, territorial, special-purpose, professional, youth, women's and men's organizations), social strata (classes, castes) and similar
4	Political	Political organizations, parties. Government organizations (regional, municipal). Inter-governmental military and law enforcement organizations
5	Religious and theological	Institutions of major religions, including sects, separate friaries, orders, worship organizations of peoples and ethnic groups. Atheist organizations. Inter-denominational organizations and similar
6	Cultural, relating to world view	Organizations: cultural and historical; arts. Organizations that educate and look after health (health care). Voluntary associations and societies aiming to integrate different cultures
7	Scientific (cognizant)-spiritual	Global and national (government-run) research institutions and labs, research universities and centers, colleges, private personal research

Table 3.3 Multilevel external environment and objects through which it operates

It is important to consider details of specific interactions of an organization with its environment in a single context that depends on the goals of compatible development and, consequently, on the goals of mutual influence. If we look at factor compatibility in the implementation of a specific project, its participants would face limited distribution in both space and time. If the participants are of the process system type, there are no spatial limits; the only limits are temporal.

In our case, to consider specifically the operations of business organizations, their environment and the organizations themselves are viewed as objects (an object system type), which are limited in space, but have no temporal limits.

Every business organization that belongs to a certain category of organizations of the levels discussed here must have a clear understanding of and "feel" for the external environment as a set of multifaceted and multifunctional objects (organizations) and processes; a combination of various projects that unfold within overlapping micro- and meso-environments. This would enable it actually to perceive the ongoing developments. This classification of system levels and types would enable a business organization to perceive its goals in a harmonious manner and see its own priorities it incorporates in its end-product. This defines an important quality of organizations – their ability to interact with the external environment in a compatible manner (a necessary condition for an organization's "lucky stars"), ensuring an organization's longevity.

We can cite something His Holiness the Patriarch of Moscow and All Rus' Kirill said to corroborate our description of Level 7 (see Table 3.3): "one certainly cannot build everything on scientific achievements, but if the nation produces quality intellectual product, exchange of this product for other benefits is a matter that is, first of all, fair, and, second, very useful, because he who produces intellectual product is always ahead."[189]

---

[189] Церковь призывает к единству. Святейший Патриарх Кирилл. Минск: Белорусская Православная церковь, 2010.

3.4.2. Compatibility of Organization Management Styles and Structures

Processes are constantly taking place in every organization (these processes were described above in detail), leading to the creation of a certain number of new solutions, which, in turn, result in the making of new high-quality decisions. These decisions determine the new development trajectories for the business organization and its subsystems. These subsystems, which act together to shape and propel the whole business organization forward, may run into certain contradictions associated with making completely new decisions about development – decisions at an entirely new level of sophistication. There are top managers in charge of every subsystem (or two closely related subsystems): people who have power and play a specific role for which they are personally responsible. At the same time, they are just people with their own preferences for using certain management styles.

Every process results in quantitative and qualitative changes. These changes create issues, and unresolved issues cause problems, i.e. contradictions that are resolved by ongoing or more long-term coordination of operations by the organization's subsystems, to move forward with the least possible loss and achieve new overall organization development goals.

We can consider the decisions being made as conditions for compatible development of the business organization, i.e. development compatibility may be of a specific variety, combining compatible organizational and managerial decisions with decisions based on the personal style – human decisions – of managers responsible for operation of the business organization's subsystems described above (see the preceding section).

Our discussion will be based on ideas developed by Ichak K. Adizes about four types of managerial roles ("prototypical styles")[190] and their interactions within an organization. The first role (I) is the Producer, who enables an organization to operate efficiently only in the short term, because the products/services (referred to as "products" below) in demand change over time. The second role (II) is that of an administrator, who guarantees the execution of correct actions at the required point in time, ensuring that an organization's processes are productive in the short term. The third role (III) — that of an entrepreneur – makes the organization he

---

[190] Adizes, I.K. Mastering Change. Quoted from the Russian edition: Адизес И.К. Управляя изменениями М.: Питер, 2011.

is affiliated with proactive.[191] This positioning makes it possible to handle customers' future requirements, which ensures the organization's efficiency in the long term. The fourth role (IV) – that of an Integrator – turns an organization's mechanical culture, under which employees and consumers act in isolation of one another, into an organic one, in which people feel connected to one another because they recognize that they have common values and interests.

To ensure the successful operation and harmonious development of an organization, all four managerial roles (management styles) are required, whether in a single manager as a person, or at the level of the whole organization or its division or department. And this is how Ichak K. Adizes describes completely dominant, exaggerated management styles, where each is incompatible with the others:

1) The "Lone Ranger." They are poorly trained, generally unprepared, and lack initiative. They never have free time. They do not delegate their work to anyone else because they believe nobody can do it better than them. According to them, the only way to solve problems is to work more, without any discussions and arguments. They confuse quantity with quality. They put function (what needs to be done) above all, ignoring form everywhere. More is always better to them, their work is always management by crisis.

2) The "Bureaucrat," another faulty management style, focusing on "how" rather than "what." Management is done strictly "by the book," by a set of rules and aims only to make the Bureaucrat's organization productive. Everything is documented; stifling instructions are to be followed to the letter in everything. Over the years, the rule books get thicker and thicker. The more deviations there are, the more new rules get introduced. When the organization goes under, it will do this on time and according to regulations. For him, it is all about details.

3) The "Arsonist" is focused on the future to the exclusion of everything else and is constantly preparing his organization for change. He sees the big picture and has zero interest in details or interpersonal relationships or climate within the organization, because only something new ever matters, and he takes risks. This is essentially management by creating crises. Subordinates cannot follow the leader

---

[191] "Proactive" means "meeting two conditions": (1) envisaging the future, mapping out a scenario of needs development and conditions of organizational development and growth, (2) creative (capable of eliminating gaps in factual information – a deficit of facts).

because they do not understand what is expected of them on a daily basis.

4) The "Super Follower" works "for someone." He is primarily focused on people and their interactions. He never expresses his own thoughts clearly because he wants to know what others think first. He does not lead people because he simply follows the followers.

Let us provide a compatible analogy of correspondence of (top managers') roles and styles (of specific people) in organization management:

I — the Producer — "the Lone Ranger";

II — the Administrator — the Bureaucrat;

III — the Entrepreneur — "the Arsonist"; IV — the Integrator — "the Super Follower."

We have discussed exaggerated cases of an organization managed only in one style, without any admixture of the other styles. If all four styles are equally absent, when none of them can be adapted to new conditions, a fifth style emerges – a style of inaction and empty talk. Things are going really well all the time, if you ask a manager working in this "style."

When new organizations are created, suboptimal combinations of management styles are possible; this also applies to limited liability organizations (which are the most common type of business organization in Russia). This happens quite often, because we may behave one way in everyday life and be somewhat different at work. This is why two "resources" can meet, pool their skills or assets and start a business of some kind. However, once they have to make managerial decisions, profound conflicts may arise because of differences in style. If we compare an entrepreneur (III) with an administrator (II), we immediately discover a complete contradiction in this matter, as the former thinks quickly and focuses primarily on the overall result, while the latter thinks slowly, is possible too structured and detail-oriented.

The situation is broadly similar when an integrator (IV) joins forces with a producer (I): the former is less structured and takes his time to make decisions, focusing on the common interest of all parties, while the latter does not like to consider things for a long time, sees the most obvious part of the picture at a given moment in time rather than the whole picture. Compatibility for these combinations of founding partners and managers works approximately like this: if they assume executive powers themselves, each of them takes the function that is most natural to his liking, which is obvious from the above discussion. An organization has many different services (departments), including some that are essentially entrepreneurial — sales, production and technology, design, planning and analysis, logistics and support, business administration, and others, and the less the founding partners have to interact in their daily work, and the more independence (including financial independence) they have from each other, the more effective their union is going to be. The important thing is where they can add more value to the common cause – to their business. Periodic financial results will tell if the business partnership is working.

Ichak K. Adizes explains this incompatibility of management styles by personal perception by the founding partners-managers of the concepts of what there is, what there should be, and what they want. Producers and administrators are down-to-earth materialists who understand very well the concept of what there is. The picture is a little more complex with other styles: integrators may confuse "there is" with "there should be," while entrepreneurs take it one step further: for them, the concepts of both "there is" and "I want" are equally "real" and "material."

When we consider top managers' styles, we should focus on compatibility of roles (I–IV): no one discussed above can be equally strong in all of the above-mentioned areas (styles) at the same time. And yet, deficiency in any one area (style) causes a fairly predictable organizational disease. Depending on which managerial role is lacking, an organization may become inefficient and non-productive at different periods of time. Taken in isolation and taken purely, each of the four styles mentioned above would be incompatible when paired with another style, according to I.K. Adizes' research. The names he gave these styles sound like an allegory: I is the mind, II is the body, III are emotions, IV is the spirit. In other words, they must be present in an organization just as they are present in a man, but each has its own goals and time of operation as well as the point when it should pass the relay baton to another style (we discussed the energy components of man in Section 3.1).

The human life and changes in it sustain an internal conflict in the human being — an incompatibility of decision-making roles serves the purpose of continuing the movement through life. We pay more attention to emotions, body, spirit or mind depending on what comes to the fore, what becomes more important to the detriment of other aspects (see Section 3.1 for more on this). Incompatibility increases and the number and frequency of changes rise, which our participants would find it harder to balance.[192]

---

[192] В.А. Морозов Совместимость стилей (ролей) управления организацией //

Harmony processes become unsettled, metabolism (catabolism) processes become greater, as we wrote earlier. All people are different in society. Some are driven primarily by spirit, while others rely mostly on their minds. The latter are devoid of emotions and have practically no spirituality. A third kind of people are constantly concerned with their bodies, eating healthily and working out. As for those who are strong of spirit and move (IV) towards higher forms, they attain love. It is common knowledge that love of others starts from love of oneself, therefore, we need participants with all styles from I through IV inclusively to be involved. This further implies the necessity of taking care of the needs of other people in society (or a community). The sense of integration (the spirit) is responsible for regulating, balancing, and, most importantly, harmonization (of processes) and synchronization of components (I–IV) of an organization and the whole of society (which corresponds to compatibility levels). Evolutionary processes are important in this context, which make it possible consciously to enforce self-discipline both in the organization and within social groups as well as in society (community).

The more integrated a system is, the less the society requires administration (in the form of political, social, legal laws and regulations). At the same time, the more the administrative and judicial interference (II) in our personal or family life, the less the integrative (IV) processes and self-regulation; family ties grow increasingly weaker, and the family may even disintegrate. Based on these considerations, the outlines emerge of compatibility of management styles and levels of the compatibility of societal needs, which are based on human needs. That is, the first and second compatibility levels (product-proprietary and financial/economic levels) figuratively match the producer's role (I), the third and fourth (social and political) levels pertain to the administrator's role (II), the third role, catering to future needs and long-term efficiency, belongs in both the political and, to some extent, in the fifth – theological and religious level. An integrator's role is the broadest in society and includes the fifth, sixth (cultural and world view) and seventh (cognitive (scientific) and spiritual) levels.

However, an organization, just like the society, needs not a single all-powerful genius of many gifts, but rather a team of specialists and employees with complementary skills (just like a society comprising different national (ethnic) groups and peoples), mutually complementing

---

one another and sharing a feeling of common differences. If all the components of society or an organization were simply different, they would become vulnerable, because they would be serving mutually exclusive goals. Strength comes from a unity of differences, complementary like fingers on one hand. However, in society, where control and trust are much harder to achieve, each hand pulls towards itself to solve its own material, economic problems and things associated with them, that is, everything that has to do with the first three materials level, creating deep contradictions which can deteriorate into non-constructive conflicts, condemning society to incompatibility of progress as an integrated group, and most importantly, denying it full-fledged compatible development (covering compatibility levels from first through seventh inclusive).

Variety of experience ensures strength, because, when the diverse experience of different people is combined, it tends to offset the weaknesses of one person in certain areas with another's strengths in the same areas. Many people realize that no single culture and no religion is perfect, which implies the need for a complementary team and a complementary society. Conflict is a blood sibling of all change. When we attempt to sweep conflict "under the carpet," it often means that we merely put off its resolution (often to our own grief). Only development suffers from this — which would be a result of finding an agreement of change with conflict. An example of this on political (4th) and consequently on economic (2nd) and social (3rd) levels was the creation of an artificial class society in the USSR. Accumulation of unresolved conflicts eventually made development grind to a halt, and everything had to be started from scratch as a result. A unity, a whole arising from contradictions and disagreements in any case will be better than accumulated, overlooked differences. A society based on democratic principles, mutual respect and trust makes it possible to resolve conflicts constructively (making them synergistic conflicts) and build up the pace of change at each level of compatibility. In a similar way, an organization needs colleagues who respect the opinion of others, and it is often useful to be a colleague for oneself. An Oriental adage says that the wise one is he who treats a stranger as a teacher. Without mutual respect, disagreements do not bring any benefits to anyone, only suffering.

Quality managerial decision-making is very important to an organization. If multiple meetings still reach a certain mutually acceptable compromise, this would imply lack of mutual respect in the business organization. In a similar way, interaction among people is important in society, which requires changes, at a certain rate, on all compatibility levels.

The expression "loss of tempo" (as in "loss of direction") is evidently very true.

Therefore, it appears that compatibility of business organization management is the start and progress of the next development stage. Therefore, we can logically describe compatibility of management styles for an organization as the following preliminary expression:

$$\text{Compatibility of management styles} = \frac{\sum_{i=1}^{4} N_i \times K_i^{ex}}{N \times (1 - K_{cc})}$$

where N_i is the level of influence of the ith management style;

$$N = \sum_{i=1}^{4} N_i$$

is the general influence (the organization's management environment);

K_i^{ex}

is the requirements of the environment for the organization's management style;

K_{cc}

is the possible constructive conflict within the organization.

The constructive conflict K_{cc} comprises both synergistic and symbiotic meaning.

For an organization, an organizational structure is important that will define the division and distribution of authority, compensation, and most importantly, of power. This distribution defines the differences of personal interests. Different management styles determine the content of communications between managers. If we start from changing the decision-making process, redistribute the power, influence and authority (as discussed above), and additionally, review the compensation system, one could say that serious structural change has been achieved. You will notice how employees change overnight, see changes in their working style and general behavior, starting from very basic procedures – their ways to approach solutions for problems and decision-making itself. We have talked about trust and respect, which should be put at the beginning of all structural change. These two components of compatibility shape the organizational culture both within an organization and in all social groups (with a caveat: trust, but verify). The Spanish have a saying: "We do not take offense, but we do not forget, either," which is important to both sides in any dispute so that they will not repeat the same mistakes. This is the essence of growing the responsibility of group members.

The organizational culture established in a business organization, the culture that it took so much effort and trouble to build, is exposed to attacks from the outside environment, if the society around the organization (its environment) is mired in national (ethnic), religious, corruption and criminal conflicts. Russia is known for its huge resources and reserves, but we still lag far behind the Japanese and European communication cultures (in terms of connections and interaction at all levels of compatibility). This is why it is so hard for our society to achieve success, because our internal links were destroyed after the Soviet ideology disappeared (and now fragmentation and internal strife prevail, as the connections are getting slowly rebuilt and reinforced). This is why certain management styles are so important for this country after the demise of the Socialist dictatorship — especially the first (producer) and the third (entrepreneur) management styles which can be very useful in the production and economic, and, most importantly, in the social and cultural realm. The political realm is mostly based upon the social realm, but culture comes from deep within the nation's and the state's history, which was "washed out" almost incessantly over the past century, as the country lost tens of millions of lives of "legionnaires" in all types of culture, including the Russian Orthodox Church and Russian science. After this experience, Russia, our country, does not need an elitist culture, or any expansion of the second (administrator) management style which focuses on control and bureaucracy of laws and administrative regulations; it is essential for Russia to rebuild the fourth (integrator) style (with help from people capable of uniting others on a high ideological and spiritual level).

Because society consists, for the most part, of organizations of different types, pursuing different purposes, matters of self-organization (based on trust and respect) generate a large amount of compatibility relationship energy in business organizations. It is a well known that unless society receives an inflow of energy from the outside, it tends towards chaos, according to the entropy theory, just like any other system. This is why the compatibility energy generated within our community is so important. A good manager (a well-known scientist and designer, active member of a leading political party or simply a family member) is appreciated for who he is, rather than for what he knows and remembers. People like this are usually harmonious, they live by the method of contemplation (by their thought process), rather than by the method of emulation or based on their own trial-and-error experience. They are well-adjusted, balanced and capable of seeing the behavior – management styles we are discussing in this section. Therefore, they are ready for change and for improving themselves and members of their organization (society) for their joint development. The nation, the country must raise and train people like these at all compatibility levels, putting them into positions of leadership in various spheres, because they can answer the question "how should we be?" while people who answer the question: "how do we do this?" should be put under their guidance. This has to do with the fact that the question "how should we be?" has a spiritual foundation, while the question "How do we do this?" is based on a material foundation. Given the hierarchy of compatibility, the question of rank (order) takes care of itself (becomes moot, irrelevant). The American progress of a country is based on a social and material foundation, so it should not be hard to determine where the prospects of compatible development of society are better: in Japan or in the US.

Let us now discuss organization management bodies and compatibility — in what is essentially Part II of the Section. An organization presumes a combination of people's efforts towards common goals, where actions by employees must be coordinated. The work of every one of them must be coordinated with the work of other employees by the organization's common overall goal. The organization's structure is usually what is recorded in the organization chart and personnel schedule, but they almost never match the actual management system of the organization. Henry Mintzberg believes that "the organizational structure can be defined as a simple combination of ways by which the work process is first divided into separate work tasks, and then actions are coordinated to perform those tasks."[193] It follows therefore that once the external environment or the organization's goals and tasks change, its structure is no longer compatible with its strategy and tactics of preparing and implementing solutions. A more compatible structure must be designed on the basis of new workflows and required connections between the organization's components and external parts. These flows are non-linear.

The more compatible a structure is, the more it should harmonize with the situation both within the organization and in its external environment.

---

[193] Mintzberg, H. Structure in Fives: Designing Effective Organizations: Prentice Hall, 1992.

The growing complexity of an organization leads to an increase in the number of managers, bosses and bosses' managers. A hierarchic line of intermediate powers is created between the operations core and the strategic top. The existence of managers becomes the impetus towards an administrative division of production and managerial labor. As the structure becomes more complex, standardization also increases. As business analysts appear, and direct control is replaced by standardization, direct control becomes substituted for mutual regulation, i.e. coordination of connections and compatible interactions, creating horizontal management flows across the steps of vertical power of the business organization's management.

Simple entrepreneurial structures do not require analytical units to ensure managerial compatibility, as direct control is enough to ensure whatever weak division of labor there is and coordination. The strategic top becomes a key element of the overall structure, which tends towards simplicity and dynamism.

Coordination in a mechanistic bureaucratic structure depends on standardization of operating work processes. In this structure, analysts become its key components. It is typical of simple and stable environments. The entrepreneurial function is very limited at the strategic top. When the external environment is stagnant, this type of managerial structure achieves high compatibility.

The structure of professional bureaucracy, as Henry Mintzberg describes it, depends on the coordination and standardization of employee skills. Employees work relatively independently of their colleagues, but in close cooperation with their customers. Coordination among operations employees is achieved through standardization of knowledge and skills. This type of organizational structure emphasizes the power of competence, whereas a mechanistic bureaucracy produces its own standards. Strategy is usually put together by individual employees within the organization. Analysts themselves cannot be regulated. Professionals resist rationalization of their skills, as this would turn them into programmable robots, destroying the foundations of their autonomy and lead the structure to become more of a mechanistic bureaucracy. Structural inflexibility is also negative from the perspective of adaptation to the production of new goods and services. Continued operational compatibility of a structure like this with its environment will depend on drastic reforms. When this does not work, to achieve "velvet reform," changes are insinuated in the form of changing employee profiles, as well as teaching the skills and providing incentives to upgrade these skills (this is a lengthy process).

An innovative organizational structure (adhocracy) is a structure with the least formalization of behavior, and its key mechanism is mutual adjustment. Dynamism of compatibility is there from the beginning, i.e. conditions exist for quickly establishing interconnections and for performing "mutual" (mutually complementary) actions required to perform new tasks. This structure has the least respect for classic management principles, especially for team unity. In this case, the law of unity in variety of equal participants applies to the overall scenario of action. Employees integrate their efforts in cross-functional teams, each of which is created around a specific innovation project. This kind of structure has many managers, including functional, integration and project managers. Project teams are small to ensure better compatibility among their members, and managers become full-scale working members of these groups responsible for ensuring coordination (compatibility at work) between them. In turn, these units are divided into operating and administrative. The former innovate and find solutions to problems together with the market (customers), while the latter also interact with project teams, but their goals are different and include obtaining services for themselves – e.g. design of new tools and processes.

Evaluation of compatibility in the work of existing structures described above for static and dynamic environments may be positive for each of them, as each has its time and place. Skillful use of structures can help organizations achieve full compatibility in their work with minimal losses in interactions of the business organization's subsystems. A large organization can use organizational, economic and financial tools to combine all types of structures at the same time. This, apparently, can be described in the field of management as compatibility of management forms. It is based on key elements that support each other or are substituted for each other, which are: a key coordination mechanism, a key part of the organization, specialization of work tasks, training, formalization of behaviors, grouping, size of operating units, and planning and control systems.

There can be "strong" and "weak," as well balanced matrix structures (organic structures). A "weak matrix" is similar to a functional (hierarchical) structure, while a "strong matrix" is similar to a project (organic) structure.

A "balanced matrix" is at the same time equivalent to the principle of multiple reporting lines and can work permanently when employees have two managers with equal powers. Balance between two organized alternatives is important for compatible management. These kind of managerial structures are important for multifunctional companies. They quickly overcome internal barriers within the organization without detriment to functional specializations, which is positive for corporate culture and employee motivation. All of this increases overall compatibility of the seven subsystems of a business organization (which we discussed above).

Incompatibility in this case may increase because of imprecise distribution of rights and duties among the elements of a structured entity, which triggers power struggles. Problems arise with efficient utilization of employees going forward, as well as problems with effective control at various levels of management (overheads begin to rise); higher skill levels are required (implying lengthy training for employees), as is a corporate culture. Long-term efficient operation of a system like this is incompatible with periods of socioeconomic crises.

We will attempt to describe the compatibility of the management structure (C_{MS}) as a combination of its organic component (O_C) arising from flexibility and organic unity and its mechanical component (M_C), which comprises precision and technological excellence:

$$C_{MS} = O_C \,/\, M_C = (\text{Flexibility} + \text{Organic unity})/(\text{Precision} + \text{Technological excellence}) = 1.$$

The compatibility of management structures will increase when every one of them meets the specific needs of a specific organization.

3.5. Processes, Structure and Model of Compatible Development of Society

Society is presented as a unity of people joined together in a variety of social formats: business organizations, institutions, foundations and foundation-type organizations, associations, which are ranked by their purpose and divided into groups according to levels of their needs. These levels were described in a hierarchical order in the previous sections (see Table 3.3).

Society is a macrosystem. "Like breeds like." In the context of compatibility, this means that everything that comprises society – all the modifications – essentially, its incarnations, are defined through their compatibility. However, the Universe has a large number of different homo sapiens varieties, which explains the existence of different civilizations, which develop consistently and in coordination according to the laws of the universe. We consider society as a multi-level spatial system,[194] and environment (1) that includes numerous objects with a broad range of different functions (2) with processes (3) going on within and among them. These processes are meaningful because they take place on the basis of targeted projects created (4) by objects – projects of different size and timeframe. The four types of systems listed above can be described in terms of the four key processes reflecting operation of a system (including subsystems and their components in a certain environment).

The internal unity of a system (a society) is ensured by harmonization (1), which defines the coordination of subsystems' operation (compatibility levels)[195] and their development. The second process type is evolution (2), which defines changes in macro environmental properties[196] based on the mechanism of self-organization of objects comprising the macro environment. The third process — reproduction (3) is oriented towards replacement of key resources and preserving a system's properties while protecting reproduction (replacement) at lower levels of compatibility. The fourth process reflecting operation within an environment is metabolism (4).

Let us start the review of these processes from the final one. Metabolism is originally a Greek word that means transformation or change. Processes of this kind enable various systems to grow while preserving their structure and responding to impacts coming from the environment. If processes are downward-bound (directed towards simplification of systems), they are described as a "catabolism stage" (M2 in Figure 3.3). We will state the reservation at the outset that catabolism disregards the gradual ladder of seven levels because the vector of development and integration is reversed, as the structure folds instead of developing.

---

[194] В.А. Морозов Экоуправление развития (территории, сектора экономики, человек). М.: Креативная экономика, 2008.

[195] The first level (meso system) is the level of products and property, followed by the financial and economic level (2), the social level (3), the political level (4), the theological level (5), the level of culture and ideology (world outlook) (6), and the spiritual and cognition (scientific) level.

[196] The macro environment is understood as society as a whole, while the objects (organizations) comprise the microenvironment.

Compatibility levels are viewed as meso-systems of the environment (the macro system). Every meso-system essentially creates and disseminates its combined product for which it is intended.

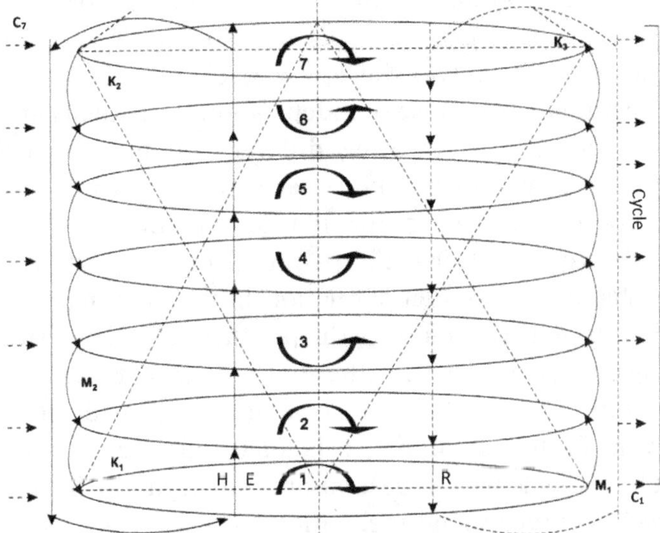

Fig. 3.3 Life of society — Compatible multi-level and multi-functional macro system

K_1 is a material cone (within Cycle 1); K_2 is the non-material (cognitive-spiritual) cone of the cycle; K_3 is a material cone (of Cycle 2).

S_{1-7} are incoming/outgoing signals (processes) of the external environment.

H stands for harmonizing (including morphogenic) processes that create and reinforce a compatible environment.

E stands for evolutionary processes that ensure self-organization of the mesosystem by level (clockwise), and involutionary processes (counterclockwise).

R stands for reproductive processes which provide temporary insurance (protection) for the lowest proximate levels.

M_2 signifies downward catabolic (metabolic) processes, which destroy integrative clusters within cycle development (counterclockwise across levels, just like involutionary processes).

M_1 stands for upward anabolic (metabolic) processes, which shape products of each level.

The main purpose of levels within the structure:

7 — accumulation of integrative knowledge;

6 — globalization (and analysis) of values common to all humanity; 5 — grouping of religious values;

4 — combining ideological behavioural formats; 3 — development of social institutions;

2 — development of financial and economic institutions;

1 — use of material manufacturing facilities.

The first compatibility level comprises objects that create products essential for keeping a man alive and operating (food, clothing, technology and tools, living quarters, etc.).

The second meso-system is the financial and economic level, which is responsible for supporting life and basic operating needs (the inter-relations and interactions on the lower level) and defines the variety of human interactions (both those of independent individuals and members of various organizations) by creating different kinds of securities (with a system for buying and using those securities) which are equivalents of underlying products or assets of the first (lowest) level.

The third level (the third meso-system) of compatibility is the social level, which shapes the product of relationships of a human being and social groups around him, because this is the product of type determination of the human being's engagement with these groups (according to the format of his membership in them). Why do social groups provide context? Because every single one of the human beings belongs functionally and is attached to a certain job, a residence, to recreation, participation in indulging in his hobby, as well as other social inclinations and desires. This level, just like others, comprises a variety of objects with their different properties and special features, expressing the unique nature of connections and interrelations. While human society is part of nature, it has a more complex system and organization than natural systems.

The fourth level (the fourth meso-system) is that of politics (the political level). It produces a synthetic product – a national common good, generates a nationwide ideology that ensures reproduction of common behavioral patterns and a relatively complete perception of social reality based on common cultural meanings and a system of cultural definitions.

The fifth level of compatibility is the theological level, which preserves and refreshes value systems and features of these value systems (every system is closely associated with a specific religion) that help a human being find his place in the world by combining his personal interests with those of society. The systems of norms, culture codes, cultural meanings and prescriptions are designed to promote the interests of society where "people need to take care of their soul, their spirit more than of their bodies."[197] Only the Renaissance humanistic ideology and scientific worldview of the 16th and 17th centuries was able to take its explanation of human nature (and

---

[197] Демокрит. Материалисты Древней Греции / Под ред. М.А. Дынника. М.: Изд. полит. лит., 1955. С. 160.

the origins of human compatibility) further.

The sixth level of compatibility as a meso-system is the cultural and worldview level, which generates holistic, uniting human values, taking into consideration the nationality, ethnicity and religious affiliation of a human being viewed as a well-rounded individual. The product of this level is spiritual globalization, integration of all five lower layers – compatibility levels, unified within each level, which only stands on the threshold of active integrative events (objects that serve as the content of each level have been discussed above).

The next and final (seventh) level is focused on comprehensive scientific cognition to understand the universe and society, to develop man's ability to think. (The global spirit "which is more than just a Hegelian concept" has an ineradicable drive for gaining knowledge of, and achieving harmony with, oneself.) The product of Level Seven is the understanding and forecasting of the future path of society's development while reducing conflict and contradictions within itself (starting from lower levels) through universal harmonious development.

Each of the levels (meso-systems) listed above participates, by producing its own product, in adjacent production processes which, for the most part, belong at higher and lower levels. Using more biochemical terms, anabolism (see Figure 3.3, M1, which is an upward-directed variety of metabolism, trending to making things more advanced and more complex) serves, in the context of the first level – the level of products and proprietary things – as an indicator of financial and economic state (stabilization, growth, weakening) of the next higher level. The state of levels one and two is the necessary condition for implementation of social mechanisms of providing for citizens who belong to various social strata, groups, and organizations.

This is essentially the necessary condition of the prosperity of citizens that gives a human being an opportunity to realize his potential at higher consumer categories (levels). The third meso-system looks at the state of consolidation and dominance of social groups and territories to determine the political platform for their centralization and regulation. The results of state ideology and material benefits adjust the operational vector of Level Five, the theological level. The culture code, shared historic values that define the variety and unity of people also determine (format) the degree of unity in a society (6). The state of globalization, integration and unity of society focuses and concentrates its abilities for speeding up cognition and using the environment in a humanistic and intellectual manner to promote its own unified development. The results of cognition, fundamental discoveries and corroboration of truths that define the development of new multifunctional processes take shape as renewed, nano-modern or more functional intellectual products, applied discoveries in different fields of scientific and humanistic progress, generation of personal, material and intellectual benefits for each human being and for society as a whole.

The second process we look at is evolutionary. When describing a given macro system from the perspective of evolutionary processes, we have to say that changes in the parameters of meso-systems are based on their self-organization mechanism. A volatile external environment makes performing the basic functions at different levels more difficult. This requires adaptation of structural components of meso-systems, i.e. restoration (refurbishment) of the required values of these functions. We introduced two superimposed cones in Section 1.2 (with the lower one representing material systems, and the upper one non-material ones), created by the action of centripetal forces.

The composition of key organizations described in the previous section for each level creates their own combined product. The product may be regarded as high-quality and complete if all participants in the processes at every level are working together, in a well-coordinated manner. Absence of contradiction and non-constructive conflicts and lack of stagnation make it possible to create a product for each level, defining the operation of self-organization mechanisms.

This identifies these processes as most effective (characterized by activity and drive for adaptation), and interaction between organizations at each level in this case makes it possible to identify a common direction vector of movement. Figure 3.3 shows this vector as arbitrary on the vertical axis: the dextrorotation (clockwise) is shown with arrows E1, E2, E5, E7; while the levorotation (involutionary counter-clockwise rotation) is shown with arrows I3, I4, I6.

Dextrorotation of levels is reminiscent of a rising helix, with cycles of forming paired cones. It is necessary to note that as physical conditions (the lower levels) become right, there is an increased probability of active mental progress (beneficial condition of the mind at subsequent, higher levels) for proper cognition of spiritual values.

The reproduction processes in Figure 3.3 are shown with arrows R1–R7. As we look at these processes through which upper levels affect the lower ones, we discover that the first and second levels are characterized by support from above of the production activities and cooperation of all formats of the product and property level. In turn, at the third and second levels, social institutions benefit themselves from achieving stability and solid productive operation of the financial and economic sector in the course of its development. Government authority, represented primarily by political institutions (4–3), strives, through the mechanisms of pressure and indirect trust, to maintain mutual respect and coordination between social groups and organizations. The theological and religious meso-system (5–4) based on history and culture, moral standards and traditions of spiritual behavior, claims its foundations in the international territories of nations and ethnicities that created this religious denomination, uniting these political forces into a community. Globalization of human values in the modern world (6–5), which is only starting to manifest itself, is oriented towards the preservation and evolution of cultural diversity, the experience of which it can use to build the concept of humanistic development of society.

Arrows H1-H7 in Figure 3.3 denote the harmonization processes which make it possible to achieve solidarity, an orderly, neat proportion and agreement in actions at all levels (meso-systems) of the environment (the macrosystem) in the proper order, i.e. moving from lower to higher levels. Speaking of social processes, we have morphogenic (creative, shaping) processes here that define the fundamental innovations and the state of society, and the higher up the compatibility levels we get, the more deterministic their role becomes.

In this case, the product/proprietary meso-system (1) provides a varied multifunctional "nutritional medium" – an environment for its assessment by society and individuals and for all manner of cooperation at the first level through harmonization of financial and economic mechanisms of processing this "environment." The economic meso-system (2) through its general coverage of organizations and individuals and systems of evaluation of the social sphere, ensures the safety of its operation, interaction and contradiction-free development. The social (3) institutional megasystem strives to humanize the fruit of operation of the government and political meso-system (including laws and normative legal acts, moral and behavioral social standards, administrative and monetary solutions and requirements), making every citizen of the country aware of them. Mostly political (4) – for now – state ideologies, regardless of the interests of each individual state (for example, the Russian Orthodox Church and the Roman Catholic Church), implement their solutions to unite groups of states into various communities united by identical or similar religious beliefs (cultural traditions, national/ethnic moral standards, historical values, etc.). The meso-systems of religious culture (5) thanks to accumulated value systems and their evaluations, are based, each in its own way, on truths shaping a uniform understanding of the world and unity (love and respect) of human relationships.

The institutional meso-system of general human values (6) harmoniously defines the direction of progress and the place of the "field of knowledge," letting the human being, based on his elevated spiritual state, create the thought forms of the next order of knowledge, harmonizing (matching) them within new material knowledge (7) for the benefit of society. Practical understanding of new knowledge, tests and experiments with new products at the very least serve to improve significantly the quality (functionality, reliability, affordability, aesthetic appeal, etc.) of the product(s) itself (themselves), and most importantly create absolutely new intellectual products, which open up new spectra of opportunities (compatibility) and new need levels. In this manner, the cycle repeats itself harmoniously.

In order to understand the ongoing processes holistically, let us consider the systematic analysis of processes at a (business) organization, which helps to shape and fill with meaning all levels (meso-systems) within the environment (the macro system). G.B. Kleiner's Enterprise Strategy[198] discusses the structure of key subsystems of a business organization in detail, as well as the business organization's external environment, which is structured in a similar manner. As G.B. Kleiner points out, this arrangement of subsystems corresponds to a "certain order of stages in the innovation internalization process" and corresponds to the Nonaka-Takeuchi theory of "organizational knowledge creation."[199] The superimposed structures are shown in Table 3.4.

---

[198] Г.Б. Клейнер Стратегия предприятия. М.: Дело, 2008. PP. 178 - 185.
[199] В.Л. Макаров, Г.Б. Клейнер Микроэкономика знаний. М.: Экономика, 2007.

Layer #	Key subsystems of a business organization	Structural breakdown of the organization's external environment
7	Historical subsystem	Historical experience of a given country
6	Imitative subsystem	Historical experience of a country's external milieu
5	Organizational, technological, material subsystem	National wealth (natural resources, tangible and intangible assets, technologies etc.)
4	Cognitive subsystem. Socioeconomic genotype	Knowledge creation and dissemination system. Socioeconomic genotype of society
3	Institutional subsystem	Country-specific institutional system
2	Cultural subsystem	A country's specific cultural features
1	Mental subsystem	Specific mental features of the populace

Table 3.4 Structure of key business organization and environmental subsystems

Based on the matched structure discussed here, G.B. Kleiner describes the upper layers as more controllable processes, classifying the lower levels by their degree of specificity, calling them "sandwich pyramids."[200]

As we superimpose this structure of business organization subsystems over a structure of levels of the external environment compatible with human needs (Figure 3.3), we see that every subsystem of a business organization has its opposition, corresponding with each level (meso-system) of compatibility in the macro environment (the society) (Figure 3.4).

Cognitive-scientific-spiritual level	Cognitive subsystem
Cultural / world outlook level	Mental subsystem
Religious / theological level	Cultural subsystem
Political level	Historical subsystem
Social level	Institutional subsystem
Financial / economic level	Imitative subsystem
Product / material level	Organizational, technological, property subsystem

Fig. 3.4 Possible functional correspondence

---

[200] Г.Б. Клейнер Стратегия предприятия. М.: Дело, 2008. P. 177.

If (business) organizations comprising a meso-system are at every level (in every meso-system), these organizations should consist of all the seven subsystems listed above, with some subsystems more dominant than others. We end up with a symmetrical matrix, which has a single dominant subsystem at every level corresponding to the purpose of the organization. To make sure the operating process is well coordinated at all levels and in all systems, every organization needs efficient, productive operation at any level of all the subsystems indicated. In this case, catabolism processes should be reduced to a bare minimum, just like the presence of involution processes. This would enable a mostly harmonious combination of level development with a relatively regular cyclic renewal.

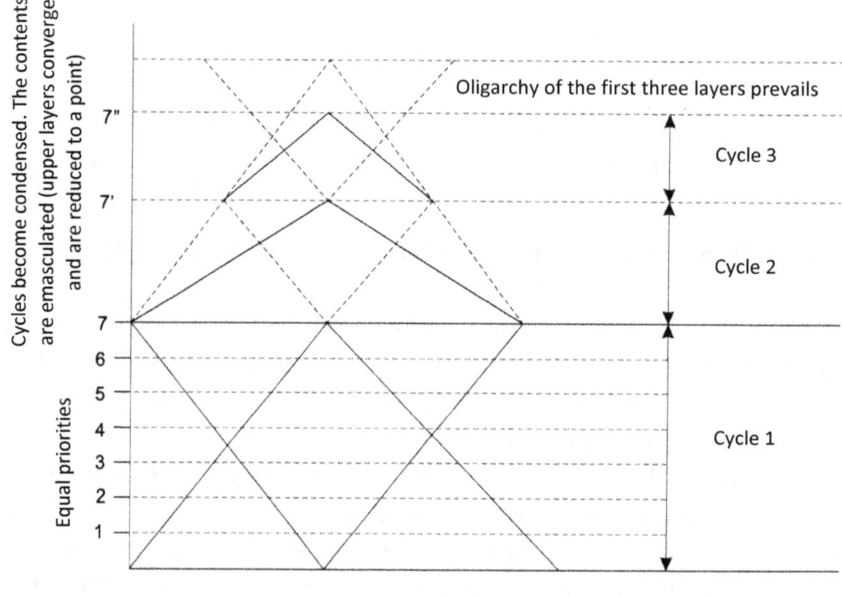

Fig. 3.5

Figure 3.5 shows the course of degradation (incompatibility) events in societal development.

When cycles are reduced because of weak involvement or inaction of the higher levels (Levels 5 and 6), they become flawed. Self-serving material (pecuniary) interests of producers of new inventions are directed into resource programs for the personal enrichment of a handful of people (and widening rifts within society). Loss of productive standards by a community results in bidirectional social contradictions between the upper and lower strata of society. This contradiction becomes the foundation for the ideology of the "uneducated haves" and for their attitude towards the integration of society. They have no use for Level 6, and can largely do without Level 5, too. They may still use the latter for isolated short-term events which help Level 4 assume the functions of Level 6. Conflicts reach a dead end; they turn into a stalemate and become non-constructive: there is no dialogue, which periodically causes international clashes and world wars. And then everything starts again.

Unfortunately, in this day and age the mainstream elite do not feel motivated for spiritual unity with other groups, or to transfer knowledge (material and spiritual) to the masses. The elite do not understand the need for this motivation because their small community is ruled purely by material considerations, while their morals are in confusion. Society is not led (governed) by conscious choice. Therefore, any sustainable growth (as we like to call it in ideological terms) is reduced to self-contraction of the compatibility level, all the way to a material point (i.e. nothingness), where a war of civilizations would result.

It is important to note that when comparing the energy levels of man, we find similar energy centers (chakras corresponding in function, direction and composition), which are responsible for functions of the human body and their interactions, which creates the set of needs we are discussing, which serves as a foundation for the compatible development of humanity. Just as a whole human body cannot exist without the involvement of moral and spiritual components, the system above cannot exist without certain essential vital subsystems.

It would make very good sense to consider situations in which the structure of societal development we are proposing slowly disintegrates from the central axis of development of all compatibility levels because the self-organization of each of the compatibility levels is inadequate. That is, these levels are not one directly above the other, but rather shifted somewhat relatively to one another, including holes or rifts in some of them (similar to holes in the ozone layer above Earth). To address this, we will use a Venn diagram. Diagrams of this kind are used in symbolic (mathematical) logic to reflect connections and interrelations between groups.

To visualize this, let us consider what the structure we are exploring looks like from below. If all seven layers are perfectly matched, perfectly overlaid over one another, we will see a single circle. If the central axis is out of perfect alignment, the picture from below will be different and could be compared to partially overlaid circles like superimposed circles of light in a circus performance, or like a portion of ice cream with multiple spherical scoops (Figure 3.6).

The first layer is that of products and property, and the last — the seventh— is that of scientific and spiritual cognition. When the circles of every layer are perfectly matched, the overall development process looks robust, effective and fully functional — it involves all organizations, with each doing its part and receiving its share from other levels. If a circle corresponding to a certain compatibility level does not cover the others, the processes are somewhat limited, faulty, because this "protruding" level is not fully engaged in civilized processes of renewal.

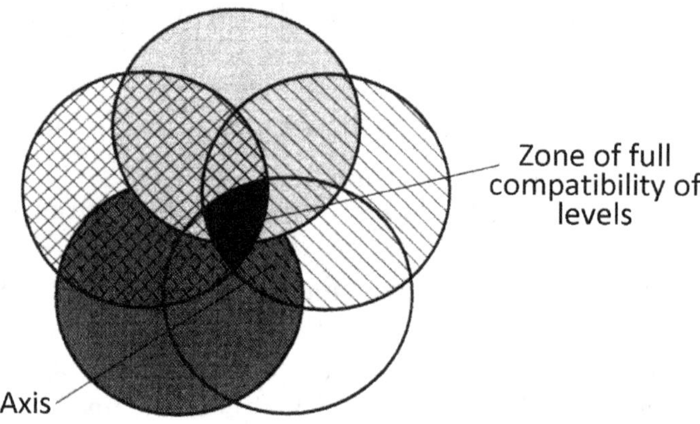

Fig. 3.6 Levels of compatibility

Globalization of this level as well as all the others is not enriched by the product of this layer, allowing all manner of problems to emerge — from a multitude of destructive conflicts to open antagonism and mutual destruction.

Let us attempt to describe a formal model of compatible development of society which we have discussed above, as seven interacting levels, using a fountain as an example. The very idea of presenting society in this way while describing the processes going on within in (the four main such processes are harmonization, evolution, reproduction and metabolism) restricts the possible simplicity of this description. When using this approach, each of the seven levels must be characterized by certain parameters directly linked to the other six. Therefore, it would be logical to represent society as a 7 by 7 matrix (Figure 3.7).

S_7^1						S_7^7
S_6^1						
S_5^1						
S_4^1						
S_3^1	S_3^2					
S_2^1	S_2^2	S_2^3				
S_1^1	S_1^2	S_1^3	S_1^4	S_1^5	S_1^6	S_1^7

Fig. 3.7

Each of the seven levels of society S j = (i = 1, ..., 7, j = 1, ..., 7) comprises seven components, i.e. is a set of seven independent variables:

$$S_j = \left\{ S_j^1 ; S_j^2 ; S_j^3 ; S_j^4 ; S_j^5 ; S_j^6 ; S_j^7 \right\}$$

and can be viewed only as a complete set of them. Therefore, using this approach, society can be represented as a set of 7 times 7 = 49 independent variables, any specific set of which would describe a specific state of society. When we have a formal description of processes at our disposal, we can describe the development of the system as a whole, forecasting its future states and testing the system for (balance, stability) compatibility.

The four main processes are described as a net of functional links, i.e. in effect every independent variable depends on others and on time (because we are looking at development of the system over time):

$$S_j^i(t) = S_j^i\left(t; S_1^1 ; S_1^2 ; ... ; S_j^{i-1} ; S_j^{i+1} ; ... ; S_7^6 ; S_7^7 \right)$$

This kind of description makes analytical investigation of the problem impossible, as we would have to consider 49 ostensibly independent variables – and this problem cannot be solved in general terms. Therefore we will try to introduce restrictions on functional links within the system that would enable us to describe the problem at least approximately in numerical terms.

We will attempt to describe interactions within the system by a simple interaction model. At first approximation, we can consider that each level S j is connected only with the preceding and the next ones, i.e. $S\,j-1$ and $S\,j+1$. Given that the system is cyclical, with $j = 1$, we will have $j - 1 = 7$ and $j + 1 = 2$, and with $j = 7$, we will have $j - 1 = 6$ and $j + 1 = 1$. This implies that each jth level element depends on the others in the following way:

$$S_j^i(t) = S_j^i(t; S_{j-1}^1 ... S_{j-1}^7; S_{j+1}^1 ... S_{j+1}^7)$$

To keep the notation simple, let us omit the dependence on $S\,j+1$ – it will be easy to account for it by analogy. Let us consider this dependence in greater detail. Let level $S\,j-1$ as a result of its operation produce a certain product $A_{j-1} = \{A_{j-1}^1; A_{j-1}^2; A_{j-1}^3; A_{j-1}^4; A_{j-1}^5; A_{j-1}^6; A_{j-1}^7\}$. This product will be transferred completely to the next level $S\,j$:

$$A_{j-1} \rightarrow S_j$$

Let us introduce a transition function for each level $K\,j$, which will depend on the outcome (the generated product) of the previous level and the current state of the function's own level :

$$K_j = K_j(A_{j-1}; S_j) = K_j(A_{j-1}^1; A_{j-1}^2; A_{j-1}^3; A_{j-1}^4; A_{j-1}^5; A_{j-1}^6; A_{j-1}^7;$$
$$S_j^1; S_j^2; S_j^3; S_j^4; S_j^5; S_j^6; S_j^7)$$

The transition function describes in what way the product (the outcome) of the previous level is redistributed at the current state of a given level. Or, rather, it shows what part of $A\,j-1$ has been used up to support the operation of $S\,j$, and what part was processed into a product which cannot be subsequently used by the system ($W\,j$, as in "waste"), and what part went towards the making of the product of the given j^{th} level $A\,j$:

$$K_j(A_{j-1}, S_j) \rightarrow S_j + W_j + A_j$$

The new product $A\,j$ will become the basis for the next level $S\,j+1$. As a reminder, each of the variables $S\,j$, $W\,j$, $A\,j$ is in fact a set of seven independent variables, and the transition factor $K\,j$ is essentially a multidimensional function.

Let us consider the following example as a way to describe development of the system.

We have the initial state of the system $S_j^i (t = 0)$ and the initial outcome (product) yielded by Level $j = 1$, A_1 ($t = 0$). We will be considering discrete steps at times $t = 1, 2, 3, \dots$. As we said earlier, when we have a full set of transition functions $K_j, j = 1, \dots, 7$, we can describe subsequent development of the system: at first, product A_1 ($t = 0$) is transferred to Level S_2 ($t = 0$), at which point K_2 comes into play, transforming the state of S_2 into $S_2 = S_2$ ($t = 1$), generating waste W_2 and useful product A_2. Now it is A_2 that is transforming S_3, and so on. Product A_7 will be transferred to Level S_1, transforming that level. This way, we will get a full picture of the state of the entire system at the next moment in time S_j ($t = 1$) and new product A_1 ($t = 1$). The cycle is complete.

For different initial conditions and different transition functions, we can solve the problems of stability, balanced existence, development, resource accumulation in certain environmental variables S_j.

Possibly, for a more precise description, we need to consider not only discrete dynamics between levels, but also to describe in detail the evolution within a single level S_j .

The complexity of this task has to do with defining functions K_j, which describe the transition processes in the system. In fact, the purpose of this exercise is to pick such functions K_j and the initial state of the system that we would get a non-contradictory stable system, the progress of whose development can be observed and analyzed. At the same time, this system should reflect processes taking place in real human society.

Speaking of different solution types, when this problem is solved, it will be possible to explore the system for relevant balance regimes.

One important regime is the regime of periodical (quasiperiodical) movement of resources within a system. This regime acts as a regime exciting oscillations. Two conditions are necessary for this regime to exist:

1) The condition of matching phases — input of resources into a system should take place at specific moments in time. Because application of an external force may not only produce a positive effect, but also (when the system is not ready from an input of energy from the outside) put the system out of its state of operation in equilibrium and stop any movement of resources and any further development;

2) The condition of matching amplitudes — the energy input should match energy losses within a system (a meso-level of compatibility).

Another mode of a similar kind is the self-reinforcing solitary wave (aka soliton) mode. This mode emerges in a medium, through which wave-type disturbances propagate. The following is the condition of its existence: if resources are diluted within a system in a uniform manner (which, on the whole, stops all movement within the system), this movement can be compensated by non-linear processes occurring during movement of resources (these processes are known to exist because the system is non-linear in principle).

When this condition is met, long-term undamped movement of resources within a system is produced, reflecting its evolutionary development.

There are different possible ways of formalizing this problem. For example, let the complex multi-parametric system S^i_j be described by parameter $W(y, x_1, x_2, ... , x_7)$. Here we understand $\{y, x_1, x_2, ..., x_7\}$ as the eight independent parameters (coordinates), relative to which the parameter W can be determined.

The parameter $W(y, x_1, x_2, ... , x_7)$ is changing cyclically along the y axis. That is, we can represent it as:

$$W = W(x_1,...,x_7)C(Sin(\omega t)+1)$$

Where $y = C(Sin(\omega t)+1)$ is the harmonic oscillator with frequency ω, acting for an arbitrary interval of time.

Consequently, $\omega t = 2\pi$ is the period of a harmonic function, and $C =$ const is a certain norm-setting multiplier which defines the area of the parameter being explored (essentially, the scale of oscillation processes).

Since external influences on parameter $W(y, x_1, x_2, ... , x_7)$ are independent (acting along a separate dimension), it would be natural to present the parameter itself as a vector sum (superimposition) of influences along a dimension in the system of coordinates:

$$W = W_0 + F_1(x_1,t) + F_2(x_2,t) + ...F_7(x_7,t) = W_0 + \sum_{i=1}^{7} F_i(x_i,t)$$

Dependence on time is manifested in that in a specific point y_i (which is time-dependent) influence $F_i(i, t)$, acting in the dimension (coordinate) of x_i, is switched on. The result of the influence remains switched on in time beyond the moment of switching on. This "switching on" can be represented as a so-called generalized Heavyside step function:

$$\begin{cases} F_i(x_i,t) = F_i(x_i)\theta\big(Sin(\omega t) + C_i\big) \\ \theta(\omega t + \varphi_i) = 0,\, Sin(\omega t) + C_i < 0 \\ \theta(\omega t + \varphi_i) = 1,\, Sin(\omega t) + C_i \geq 0 \end{cases}$$

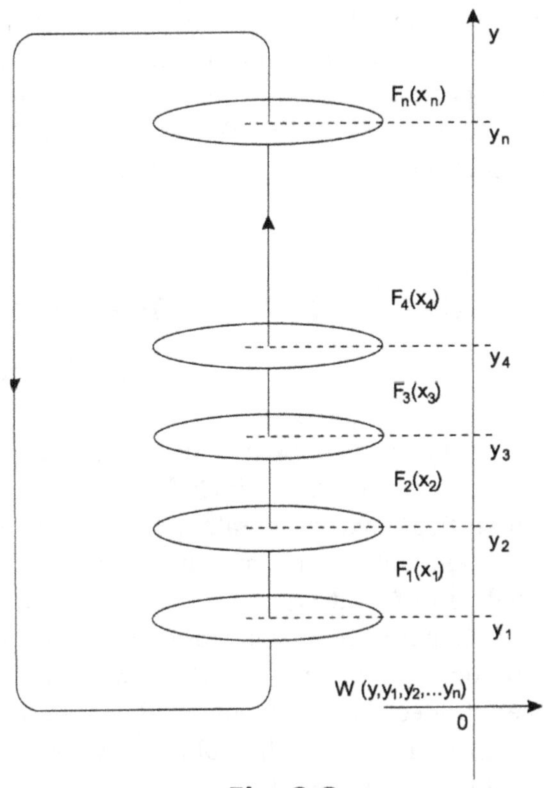

Fig. 3.8

Note that the coordinate C_i unambiguously positions the switch-on/switch-off points of a certain influence. "Turning off" (reducing to 0) the Heavyside step function and, consequently, the whole parameter $W(x_1, \dots, x_7)$ will take place on the descending slow of the "fountain", which we do not consider as a whole, as we are interested only in the area of the ascending flow. That is, by the moment the fountain is filled again (the new cycle begins), the parameter being explored will assume a value, reset to a certain initial state (at a new quality level) (Figure 3.8).

As we put together the mathematical expressions we have derived, we will have the vector representation for the parameter we are looking at:

$$W = C\big(Sin(\omega t) + 1\big)\left(W_0 + \sum_{i=1}^{7} F_i(x_i)\theta(Sin(\omega t) + C_i) \right)$$

After we assign a specific form to the $F_i(x_i)$ functions, we can track the evolution of the multidimensional parameter W (of time). This would enable us to understand to what extent it may be possible to change the value of *W (time)* periodically or quasi-periodically in a multidimensional space. We could also look at conditions for existence of this quasi-periodical change in various parameters, including those depending on the $F_i(x_i)$ function type, while observing the processes that can resolve incompatibility situations.

3.6. Compatibility as Management of Risks, Conflict and Crises

The activity of the human being, an organization or social groups (objects) comes with certain risks, including commercial, financial and economic, social, legal, environmental, natural, and others, which may come into play independently and simultaneously.

When exposed to different types of influences and impacts, an object has to adapt[201] to changing conditions, and relying on past and historical experience, knowledge gained, and intuition, with an eye to the conditions in place, make certain decisions to avoid or minimize the negative impact of the external environment on the object (which may result from incompatibility of links and actions).

The object must make rational decisions that can reduce or eliminate completely the negative consequences of risk exposure. To find adequate solutions to help the operation of an organization, one needs adequate knowledge of the risk theory.

Essentially, the majority of all theories, just like the risk theory, use their terms to describe the possible compatibilities (incompatibilities) of interaction among participants in the events they address, each theory in its field and specific area of science. Therefore, everything seems so easy when factual knowledge (facts) explain a certain interaction. However, what do

---

[201] i.e. demonstrate the ability to achieve compatibility within dynamic links between parties.

214

we know about what we know? Only that it is a small fraction of what there is to know. Things we do not know about, but only guess at, are also but a fraction of all that there is. And what is the percentage of what we don't know about things we don't know (possibly more than 95%)? How can we talk of compatibility – or even incompatibility – in this case? This is the kind of risk management (use of knowledge, intuition and future forms of thought just beginning to take shape) we should be thinking about and move towards making it a reality. As they say in the East, a battle prevented is a victory for both sides.

Given all of the above, when we make a certain decision, we have to deal with outcome uncertainty, reflecting multiple possible outcomes (favorable, unfavorable and zero outcomes), and therefore risks are seen as a consequence of uncertainty. Types of uncertainty are identical to risk types and their vectors (positive, negative or neutral).

Compatibility of development always presumes a certain risk, because development deals with overcoming a situation of inevitable choice (which can still be free of conflict). Development always involves parting with some of the old resources (one could call it also an (un)profitable loss) and receipt (or failure to receive some of) the new ones, creating the risks of deviation of the goal or achieving the goal with probable (material or cultural/spiritual) losses associated with certain compatibility levels reviewed above.

Compatibility is clearly achieved through the quality of risk management. For material levels of compatibility (the product/proprietary, financial and economic, as well as social levels) the ultimate objective of risk management is to receive the greatest possible profit at an optimal combination of risk and return or one that is acceptable for the subject (an entrepreneur, a business organization or a social group). An organization (just like a subject that is a social group as an organization) is a complex, diverse, probabilistic system. Its overall control and management system has several channels (as we know, there are seven key subsystems) of organization management, including the risk management channel. A mismatch between current and new directions of processes can reduce the overall result to zero by mutual destruction, i.e. incompatibility of action by those involved in the events.

Forecasting the occurrence of risk events, reduction and elimination of risks is based on methods and actions that together constitute risk management. Four types of risk management methods are known, including: 1) risk avoidance; 2) risk localization, as well as 3) risk dissipation and 4) offsetting risks. Risk management follows three key principles:

- You cannot put more at risk than your equity capital allows;
- You cannot risk much for the sake of little;
- You always have to consider the consequences of risk.

The development of society, social groups, organizations, as well as the fate of every man, should be deeply understood (including realization at the subconscious level). The biggest possible outcome can be achieved (while keeping the risk moderate) when the optimal combination of the best possible outcome comes at a commensurate risk, and it is possible to ensure a minimum possible risk level combined with the desired level of gain.

Compatibility of a subject's development should be constantly monitored and periodically, "rhythmically," evaluated. Every step, every stage in development implies the need for circumspection: shaping risk management objectives step-by-step; analyzing exposure to risks and selecting the methods of influencing risk; selection of controlling influences and analysis of decisions made for efficiency with (feedback-based) adjustment of management objectives to start considering the risks of the next step – and on all the way to the ultimate objective of the subject's compatible development (Table 3.5).

Harmonious development, which defines compatibility, must exclude areas of catastrophic risk and not allow for extended (or deep) sojourns in areas of critical risk. Evaluation of joint development requires constant control over correction of mutual actions in risk-free areas and areas of acceptable risk. We considered this in the previous section using metabolism processes (including catabolism) as an example and analyzing reproductive processes; we noted the importance of evolutionary process dynamism at every level of environmental compatibility. Mathematical models currently in use (determinate (non-probabilistic), stochastic, linguistic, coming from game theory), including those based on heuristic rules, are applied depending on whether initial data is available or not and on the terms of choice under certainty (determination), uncertainty and stochasticity.

Methods of achieving compatibility by regulating risks

Type of risk	Compatibility level	Ways to achieve compatibility of action
Manufacturing and commercial	Product and material	Reliably determine and maintain the ratio of financial indicators. Identify ways to improve returns on investment in manufacturing business
Economic fluctuations, changes in demand	Financial, economic	Forecast, plan for and normalize the effects in activity working plans
Financial risk from passive capital		Activate (by different methods) capital, including through participation in bidding,, shares, loans, joint projects
Employees' discontent	Social	Developing a comprehensive socioeconomic program to create a positive psychological environment
Unexpected political events leading to severe consequences	Political	Concentrating socio-ideological mechanisms and psychological resources in the community
Failure to work through and mistakes by representatives of different denominations	Religious and theological	Introduce a monitoring system, duplication of functions, to provide for constructive, respectful and polite dialogue between representatives of different denominations based on mutual trust
Risk of the chosen regional development project (without buy-in from individual participants)	Cultural, relating to world view	Negotiations focused on advantages of a given project for the party whose buy-in was not solicited, material and spiritual persuasion of the party to achieve its voluntary consent to participate in the project
Risk of implementing discoveries with potentially harmful consequences for society and the human habitat	Scientific (cognizant)-spiritual	Democratic review of results of discovery, with improvements/amendments as far as its use in society is concerned

Table 3.5

The existing parameters — the quantitative measure of results are adequate primarily for evaluation of losses from an expected positive outcome for material (the first (lowest) three) levels of environmental compatibility (and organizations that pertain to these levels). Since the parameters are interdependent, it is difficult to compare them to qualitative metrics of risk, which are typical of higher levels of environmental compatibility (cultural and worldview, and intellectual and spiritual levels). Let us use the risk of compatibility losses curve (Figure 3.9) to show critical boundaries.

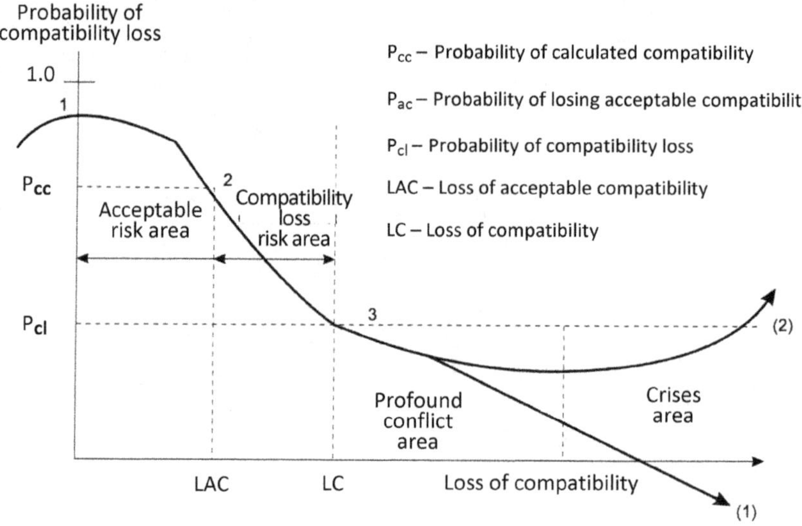

Fig. 3.9 Compatibility at risk areas

The probability of events in our case may contain three types of uncertainty (complete uncertainty / complete certainty, and partial uncertainty), which manifests itself as probability distributions, subjective probabilities and uncertainty intervals. There is a wide gamut of reasons for uncertainty: spontaneous natural processes and phenomena; mutually opposing trends, the probabilistic nature of scientific progress; incomplete compatible information; limited resources at all seven levels of environmental compatibility; impossibility of knowing an object without any ambiguity; limits to man's conscious activity, etc.

The whole range of conditions and circumstances contributing to the overall state of uncertainty makes it possible to provide only functional evaluation of risks to compatibility in the conditions of uncertainty surrounding the development of society described above. As we put the terms of development in a relatively tightly regulated framework of partial uncertainty, as shown in Figure 3.9, which identifies compatibility zones, the evaluation of risks to compatibility will be functionally expressed as follows:

$$R_c = \sum_i P_s^i P_p^i \cdot K_{CL}^i$$

where P_S is the probability of a risky situation; P_p is the consequences of compatibility loss; K_{CL} is the non-linear coefficient of compatibility levels (0.1 ÷ 0.7);[202] R_C is the risk of acceptable compatibility, and i is the number of situations.

The risk theory establishes a scale for evaluation of risk coefficients, ranking them into four categories:[203] minimal risk $K_R = 0 ÷ 0.1$; acceptable risk $K_R = 0.1 ÷ 0.3$, followed by high risk $K_R = 0.3 ÷ 0.6$ and unacceptable risk $K_R > 0.6$. Compatible decisions made at K_R values between $0.3 ÷ 0.4$ can be classified (based on a survey of experts) as risky – conflict-free situations. As the K_R coefficient gets close to $x \geq 5$, interrelationship grinds to a halt (or, on the contrary, quickly reaches termination), stagnation threatens to set in, deteriorating into antagonism and contradiction with possible conflict between the parties. Essentially, when it rains, it pours: deep incompatibility (with multiple contradictions) is coming to a head, which requires a careful study drawing on theories of conflicts and crises.

As we compare compatibility in a range of risks and compatibility in conflict conditions, we can describe it, respectively, as primarily quantitative and qualitative (with its contents refreshed after conflicts are resolved).

Any conflict (from Latin verb "confligere" which means to strike together, excite, clash, fight) is traditionally perceived as something negative, and the word is used as synonymous with violence, destruction and irrationality, which only reinforces the negative connotations of the word.

From the perspective of human relationships, conflict is a natural phenomenon for all individuals, groups and organizations. Since conflicts are inevitable in principle, the sociological view of conflict prevails as of

---

[202] Defines the weight of instances of incompatibility depending on levels at which the events are taking place.

[203] В.Н. Уродовских Управление рисками предприятия. М.: ИНФРА-М, 2011. P. 48.

something acceptable. They are impossible to avoid, and, moreover, they can contribute to improving the life of individuals and the work of groups.

From the interactive perspective, conflict is welcomed based on the assumption that a group characterized by partner relationships will inevitably become a static and apathetic combination of people rejecting all change and innovation. These considerations prompt group leaders to maintain a certain minimal level of conflict within their group, to ensure a good "tone," i.e. a healthy amount of tension within the group to keep it capable of self-criticism and creative impulses.

Reasons for conflict always have multiple layers: they are some combination of objective, subjective, obvious, hidden, immediate, remote, primary and secondary. There two types of reasons: objective — those associated with shortage of resources (material, administrative, status and other) – and subjective — psychological (perceptions, ideas of resource deficit, psychological assumptions of deficit, etc.). A possible general reason for a conflict is a social contradiction. Every conflict has a beginning and an end, i.e. a certain temporal and spatial frame, and, most importantly, temporal boundaries, which are pushed back after gaining additional knowledge through cognition, triggering further risks and conflicts.

A conflict begins as potential, possible risks become real, i.e. reach a crisis point, and ends with termination of hostilities regardless of the outcome. Spatial boundaries of a conflict are commonly seen as a "territory." Therefore, a conflict system is a combination of territorial participants.

Conflict science relies on several methods, including 1) structural and functional, 2) processional and dynamic, and 3) conflict typology (classification).

Conflict science also has some specific methods: observation, self-reflection, oral and written surveys, questionnaires, testing, business games, etc.

There are different types of systematic analysis of conflicts, including system-structural, system-functional, system-genetic and system information types of conflict analysis.

A conflict is a systematic phenomenon, a certain state of an organizational and social system — a human being, a set of groups that form a certain unity (cultural, ethnic, religious, state or governmental, etc.).

A general definition of conflict describes it as a system whose elements enter a state of structural imbalance under the influence of internal or external reasons. The resulting incompatibility blocks the effective method of its self-preservation; the system can no longer reach its objective, fulfill its function or satisfy its need.

The origin, development and resolution of conflicts follow the laws of system development, i.e. the interaction of elements is subordinated to reaching an objective useful to the system as a whole (e.g. augmentation of the system's key property). It is important at this point to introduce the concept of a constructive conflict of renewal (K_{RN}), in which a system achieves a useful result, producing positive feedback, which reinforces the compatibility of the system's operation in its chosen direction (property). When a system produces a negative effect, negative feedback results (putting a brake on and adjusting the chosen behavior mode), undermining the system's compatibility in the direction (property) it has chosen to focus on.

The positive and negative types of feedback are interrelated. Neither can exist without its opposite, bringing it into the world by its own existence. If negative feedback becomes so powerful that the system can no longer resist the growing differentiation and incompatibility between its elements without radically changing its properties, it no longer can maintain unity of its elements. In this case, conflict starts.[204]

As conflict unfolds, the system's inherent tendency to look for or create new development opportunities grows. This effect can be explained by the fact that the system development potential is not limited to one opportunity. When looking at it this way, the essence of a conflict lies in the deeper reason for structural imbalance of relationships that form the system. Functional duality of conflict stems from this (a conflict, on the one hand, undermines the current configuration of system elements; on the other, it creates an opportunity for change in the system by restructuring its elements).

Therefore, the essence of conflict is that it reinforces the urges of the system to overcome the blockade set up by old ways of development. It follows from this that conflict, just like any negative feedback, provides a form for self-regulation of systems behavior in their transition from compromised behavior formats to new objectives that they set out to achieve.[205]

As we reviewed and discussed various types of processes in earlier

---

[204] В.А. Светлов Конфликт: модели, решения, менеджмент. СПб.: Питер, 2005. PP. 18–32.
[205] Ibid.

sections of this book, we must reinforce the idea that not only is conflict a system, but it is also a combined process (that involves the dominant participants in reproduction, metabolism, evolution and harmony).

The dynamics of a conflict represent its progress over time, with changes under the influence of various internal mechanisms, as well as external factors and conditions. In the period before the conflict (the latent period), the conflicting parties evaluate their resources (material assets, information, power, prestige, etc.), as the conflicting parties consolidate their strength, and a contradiction arises which is not yet very well understood. The risk is there, but conflict actions have yet to begin.

Attempts to resolve a problem situation are essentially attempts to inform the other party — by persuasion, explanations, pleading, etc. The parties support their interests with proof and logic, and fix their positions. Each party picks a strategy or even several strategies for its actions during the conflict.

Actions in the event of conflict can be either open or clandestine. The defining moment is whether the conflict has a critical point of maximum power and intensity. Escalation is the part of a conflict that starts with an incident and ends in relaxing the struggle and transition to the conclusion of the conflict.

Matched opposition — use of force – fails to produce results, and the intensity of the struggle alleviates. The post-conflict situation is the conclusion of a conflict when searching for the solution to a problem — a settlement (compromise) or resolution (elimination of the reason for the problem or withdrawing claims on a resource by the conflicting parties). Confrontation continues until further escalation becomes pointless. From that point on, the integration process begins.[206]

On the one hand, conflicts destroy social structures, leading to unjustified costs, as we see them; on the other, they are a tool to solve many problems, to build closer teams, and are one of several multifaceted ways to achieve social, political and religious justice (mutual understanding) and unity.

The constructive content of any conflict is founded when, as a result of a quantitative increase (let us recall the material cone from Section 1.2), a contradiction with an embedded negation comes into conflict with material properties of a given subject, and in this connection a new qualitative

---

[206] А.Я. Анцупов, С.В. Баклановский Конфликтология в схемах и комментариях. 2-е изд., перераб. СПб.: Питер, 2009. PP. 84–90, 107–113, 123.

compatibility emerges (reflecting the non-material, spiritual cone of refreshed perception of the environment – see Section 1.2), as does a new life and/or operation of the subject.

Constructive and destructive paths to conflict resolution depend on characteristics of the conflict subject: its size and importance, how rigid it is, how centralized, how closely interwoven with other problems, how clearly understood.

Spatial, temporal, intra- and exosystemic conflicts can be identified.

Conflict typology has been proposed, including:

• by reasons of the subjects, including intrapersonal, interpersonal conflicts as well as conflicts between an individual and a group;

• by spheres of activity (levels of compatibility) — economic, social, political, legal, ideological, moral, religious, scientific, managerial. Different types of conflicts can be identified: 1) by duration; 2) by manifestation; 3) by organization.

Conflicts can be divided by method of resolution into antagonistic and compromise; by direction: into vertical and horizontal; by the degree of openness into open and hidden.

Compatibility can be found on the basis of mediation (internal and external) as a form of conflict resolution, which provides for involvement of a neutral third party to help the key participants in a conflict to reach a resolution. An intermediary helps conflicting parties to overcome their differences and reach a constructive resolution of the conflict through improving their communication and proposing ideas for conflict resolution.

Functionally, a mediator can perform the following functions: analytical, organizational, communicative, resource (i.e. the mediator can be a resource or a conduit of resources to the conflicting parties), creative, educational, and control.

The mediation algorithm includes: preparation, familiarizing oneself with details of the conflict; gathering information; clarifying interests; a creative search for ideas and identifying possible resolution options; selecting the best option(s); reaching and then implementing an agreement.

We will present the specifics of the role of the manager as an intermediary in Table 3.6, which draws on data from, Stephen P. Robbins' Fundamentals of Organizational Behavior.[207]

---

[207] Robbins, S. Fundamentals of Organizational Behavior. Pearson Education, 2004.

Step-by-step sequence of conflict management

Step	Nature of activity	Ways (methods) of implementation
1st	Exploring the reasons for emergence of conflict	Observations, analysis of activity outcomes, conversation, perusal of documents, biographical method (studying the bio data of those involved in the conflict), etc.
2nd	Reducing the number of participants	Working with leaders in microgroups, re-distribution of functional responsibilities, reward or censure, etc.
3rd	Additional analysis of the conflict by experts	Expert survey, bringing in a negotiator, psychologist, mediations and other.
4th	Taking decision	Administrative methods*; pedagogic methods**)

* Surface (outward) compatibility.
** Inner compatibility.

Table 3.6

If we turn to the application of compatibility models to actions of the leader of a major political party or a social group designed to resolve conflicts, it is essential to describe the key expedient steps in an algorithm of this kind.[208] Thus, S.M. Yemelyanov defines the order of conflict management steps in his practicum on conflict science.

It makes sense for a major party or group, or for an organization leader or manager to try to play the role of a mediator rather than a referee in a conflict. The referee model works best in situations when a manager has to deal with a quickly deteriorating (escalating) conflict or a short-term conflict under extreme conditions. In other cases, the mediator model may be used to resolve conflicts between peers by their position in the hierarchy, when the conflicting parties have complex relationships, or when they are highly educated and intelligent, and/or people of high culture, as well as when clear criteria for problem resolution are lacking.

Compatibility of general development is based on conflicting parties' negotiation strategies. At the same time, behavioral models used by conflicting parties in their negotiation process and the outcome of this

---

[208] С.М. Емельянов Практикум по конфликтологии. СПб.: Питер, 2009. P. 82.

process will depend to a large extent on the strategy each of them selects.

In terms of formal logic, the content of these guiding lights can be expressed as four basic alternatives: a unilateral victory, a unilateral loss, mutual loss (a lose-lose outcome) and a mutual victory (a win-win outcome). These alternatives have been covered in specific negotiating strategies in books by international and Russian researchers on this issue (Roger Fisher, William Ury, William Mastenbroek and others).

Attributes of negotiating strategies are shown in Table 3.7.

The joint development described in this book sees it as unacceptable for multilevel compatibility of life and operation to use the "winning" and "losing" outcomes as quality solutions. Constructive conflict resolution and the move to a new level in cooperation presume only mutually appealing, mutually beneficial relationships (as those of business partners).

To support mutual steps in joint development, tactical negotiation techniques are required, including:

• constructive tactical methods used at the stage when the parties' positions are clarified;

• tactical methods used at the stages of discussion and coordination of positions.

In this connection, common international material, legal, and moral and spiritual laws are required that would eliminate a deeper social and religious disengagement of civilizations.

The financial and economic level of compatibility within society, which defines the product and proprietary, social and political environment, has two typical states:

• a state of equilibrium when public production largely balances out public consumption (allowing for positive economic growth and output increasing in proportion with the growth of production factors);

• a state of disequilibrium (imbalance between production and consumption on the society scale), which can trigger an economic crisis. Incidentally, the same is true of the upper layers (the fourth, fifth and sixth levels). When these levels are in a state of crisis (which we observe approximately once every 100 years), the seventh level mostly operates to support the levels of material compatibility, and the product of the first and second levels fails to meet the requirements of the main components of the third and fourth levels of compatibility. Imbalance at the second level manifests itself as deviations in key economic parameters: production volumes, price level, level of employment, etc. Especially large deviations

Negation process strategy (based on Thomas-Kilmann model)

Strategy Type	Strategic goals	Strategy factors
Win — Lose	Winning at the expense of the opponent's loss *	Subject of conflict, conflict situation has an elevated profile, conflict reinforced by further provocation and abetting by other participants in social interaction, conflict-prone personality
Lose — Win	Conflict avoidance, giving in to the opponent	Subject of conflict, conflict situation has a lowered profile, intimidation by threats, bluffing, etc., weak will and lack of assertiveness, accommodating personality
Lose — Lose	Self-sacrifice in the name of destroying the opponent *	Subject of conflict, conflict situation has a misconceived profile, personalities of the people involved (strong inherent or situation-based aggressiveness), inability to see other solutions to the problems at hand
Win — Win	Reaching a mutually beneficial agreement **	Subject of conflict, profile of the conflict situation reflects reality, conditions conducive to finding a constructive solution to the problem at hand

* Incompatible solution.
** Compatible solution.

Table 3.7

result in a crisis, accompanied by loss of connections in production and (free-market) trade. This sort of incompatibility results in an imbalance of the economic system as a whole.

The first factor affecting expanded reproduction has been, since the latter half of the 19th century, scientific and technological progress, which belongs in the seventh level.[209] Government involvement in macroeconomic growth (a fourth-level factor) has become the second such factor.[210] The third factor is the influence of national culture and religious beliefs and affiliation of ethnicities and peoples. The West has accumulated extensive experience of implementing anti-cyclical and anti-crisis policies. As a result, economic crises have become less destructive, and business cycles are developing more gradually, with shallower troughs and smaller peaks.[211]

Crises are inevitable by their very nature: they are a necessary phase in the cyclical development of any system. They begin when the development potential of the key elements of the established current system is largely exhausted, and at the same time the elements of a new system (representing the future cycle yet to come) have already been born and joined the "battle." During this period, the over-system, according to A.A. Bogdanov's classification,[212] becomes disorganized; its efficiency plummets, because elements of the old and new systems come into conflict, absorbing some of the total available energy. A crisis creates the preconditions for system transformation — either its transition to a new qualitative state or its disintegration, whereupon it is replaced by a new, more efficient system.[213]

The depth of crises changes depending on interactions of cycles of different duration at different levels of compatibility of the social environment.

Sadly, crises are merely a form of progress. Painful though they are, they perform three essential functions:

---

[209] Scientific and technological progress must become scientific and spiritual progress; otherwise integration at levels four to six would be impossible. Modern globalization is only slowed down because politicians operate solely in economic terms of goods and services, categories more familiar to them.

[210] А. Анисимов Статистика кризиса и его механизм в России // Проблемы теории и практики управления. 1996. № 6. pp. 106–112.

[211] Braudel, F. Material Civilization, Economics and Capitalism. Quoted from: Бродель Ф.М. Материальная цивилизация, экономика и капитализм. XV– XVIII вв. Т. 3: Время мира. М.: Прогресс, 1992.

[212] А.А. Богданов Тектология. Всеобщая организационная наука. В 2-х кн. М.: Экономика. 1989.

[213] А. Виссарионов Уроки кризиса // Экономист. 1999. # 2. P. 15–22.

1) abrupt weakening and elimination of obsolete elements, which are still predominant, but have exhausted their usefulness, their potential (the destructive function of crises);

2) clearing the way for initially weak elements of a new system, or a future cycle, helping them to take root (the constructive function);

3) succession function.

A crisis goes through several of the following stages:

• a latent, hidden stage (preconditions for the crisis are coming to a head in the final stage of the stable development phase of the waning cycle, as the next cycle begins to be born within the depths of the old cycle);

• a period of collapse, as all contradictions become increasingly acute, and all parameters deteriorate. During this period, elements of the coming next, future, system gain strength and momentum and come into the fray against the old. Various delays, zigzags and false moves to end the crisis are possible at this stage;

• a period of remission, as preconditions take shape for the transition to a depression phase, which provides a respite – temporary equilibrium, followed by the transition to a livelier stage preceding a new leap of its rise and full bloom.

These stages have different durations. Crises are universal; they can affect any system of living or inanimate nature, as well as society, because without cycles there is no development, and without development a system is dead (there are practically no completely dead, stationary, static, immutable systems).

To find compatibility points in the development process, we need to consider a typology of crises, their classification by one common feature (criterion) or another.[214]

Any birth or death is a phase that has to do with transition from one state to another. This affects, upsets or destroys the system. A crisis is a period of suffering, reevaluation, rethinking, and, at the same time, a continuous process of improvement, although we are not used to looking at crises from a positive perspective.

The term "cycle" means successive rises and falls in activity over the span of several years. Cycles can vary in length and intensity. There is no precise formula for forecasting the duration or exact succession of cycles in time. Highly irregular economic cycles are rather similar to changes in

---

[214] Б. Владимиров Будет ли найден путь из кризиса? // Бизнес и банки. 1998. # 38, 39.

weather. This affects other crises of compatibility levels. However, all of them have identical phases which receive different names from different scientists.

The recession (contraction) stage: the state of the economy, social stability and cultural exchange deteriorates, reflecting a decline or slowdown in its growth and development. Business activity gradually begins to peter out and dry up. The balance of interactions is destroyed, or the equilibrium of supply and demand, as economists call it, which comes with a precipitous decline in prices, a wave of bank failures and stopped operations by manufacturing companies, rising interest rates and unemployment. This affects the upper – key – compatibility layers, which determine the unity of scientific discoveries and improvement of society's spiritual values.

Companies are wound up, markets crash. Famine, epidemics, suicides commence in the third — social – level.[215] As noted above, reproductive processes of the fourth (political) level are necessary to support the third level. Government action to support the first and second levels would guarantee the people's bank deposits, reduce debt burden and subsidize industrial production, as well as cutting unemployment through public works and introducing wage controls.

The government's more active role (i.e. action at the fourth — political – level) and anticrisis regulation have brought some results, and the market economy has not encountered any crushing shocks for more than half a century. More effective smoothing would require the involvement of the fifth and sixth levels of compatibility of society.

This involvement of compatibility levels helps relieve the decline and depression, making it possible for society to spend more time in the rally and recovery phases, when the world becomes bold enough to make new steps forward and finds out that they were justified. The rally boosts primarily the "development" sectors and industries that supply the means of production. New companies and organizations are created, pre-crisis levels are reached, and then actual net growth begins.

The new level (dual cones — material and spiritual) of the helix spans the new material and spiritual capital of society.

In the expansion phase, growth accelerates, and accelerated growth is manifested through waves of innovation and the emergence of a mass of

---

[215] Ю. Воронин Ориентиры выхода из экономического кризиса. // Экономист. 2001. # 5. PP. 11 – 21.

new products and organizations. Prosperity may be described by high demand for the skills of every man and a rising living standard. The rise often becomes overheated, causing tensions within society (just as a decline would, according to the chaos theory). Breakthrough trends are typical of the course of scientific and technical as well as spiritual progress. This exaggerates the imbalances and inequalities seeded at the recovery stage, which plants the seeds of future contradictions and risks — the elements of compatibility, the first saplings of a future cycle.

Modern cycles, both economic and social, are substantially different from cycles in the 19th and first half of the 20th centuries. General patterns are becoming less visible. Certain phases of the cycle undergo substantial transformations or disappear altogether.

The trend emerges to relative weakening of cyclical fluctuations. Crises become both weaker and more frequent, and, in a clear disruption of the classical cycle, they now dispense with certain phases.

The slower pace of social and economic life leads to intensified exploration in the field of science (the seventh level), creation of improved ("perfect") technology and concentration of capital in the hands of industrial and financial groups (at the first and second levels). All of this plants the seeds of a new expansion, and the growth cycle repeats, although now at a new level of development of the productive forces in society.

The crisis and stagnation that replaces it certainly do not enrich the people; they only exacerbate their poverty. However, every phase perceptibly improves the material condition of the people, clearing the way for mass investment, helping the economy, among other things, to move to a new phase (of material evaluation of its content).

"The nation becomes determined to follow the path of growth; in other words, the national will for progress emerges... Fluctuations of trade and industrial cycles (at the first and second compatibility levels) are the result of the clash between this will for progress with economic scarcity, which it encounters in every field."[216]

The theory of circular movement of social capital proposed by M.I. Tugan-Baranovsky explains the inability of capitalism and of the free market to achieve balanced reproduction, which leads to periodical glut in the channels of trade in goods (general over-production), sharp fluctuations

---

[216] В. Кузнецов Попытка объяснить российский кризис // Мировая экономика и международные отношения. 1996, #9, PP. 16-27.

in price, money mass,[217] credit, and to waves of unemployment.[218] Improved relationships and interactions between organizations and people at levels two and three define the mutual development of other levels of compatibility, as well as the character and rhythm of the cycles of renewal of society's material and spiritual content.

The crisis theory, according to M.I. Tugan-Baranovsky, assumes a great practical significance, as it makes it possible to make forward-looking assumptions in a very important economic and material area.

M.I. Tugan-Baranovsky's student Nikolay D. Kondratiev (1892–1938) provided the reasoning for a new type of long-term cyclical fluctuations — the longer market cycles of supply and demand (Joseph Schumpeter described them as Kondratiev cycles).

Kondratiev waves should not be restricted only to economics, as they cover practically all areas of social life (and the compatibility levels discussed in this book). These are primarily also technological cycles – long-term cycles of replacement of fixed assets and using inventions (innovation) (i.e. from the first through the seventh level of combined development of society), or, in modern terms – about the half-century rhythm of change in the prevailing patterns of technology.

Kondratiev believed that the "material foundation of all long cycles is the wear-and-tear, replacement and expansion of fixed capital goods, which have long lead times and are extremely expensive to produce. Replacement and expansion of these goods is not gradual, but rather goes in spurts, which is also manifested through long waves of change in market conditions... The rising wave of the long cycle is explained by upgrading and expanding fixed capital goods, radical change and regrouping of the main productive forces of society." This requires increased investment, capital concentration and mobilization of resources to be included in new studies and thought patterns that would provide even better material products for society. Scientific and technological inventions can be made, but would remain unused until the economic conditions are in place for them to find use... Parallel and associated long-term wave fluctuations take place in the social and political sphere, in the cultural and worldview consciousness of the people, and therefore, in the dynamics of wars and revolutions, of

---

[217] Using pure monetary theory as a guide, the economic cycle results from changes in money flows, economic activity, and alternating prosperity and depression.

[218] М.И. Туган-Барановский Периодические промышленные кризисы. Общая теория кризисов. М.: Наука: РОССПЭН, 1997.

territorial expansion: "Both wars and social upheavals are included in the rhythmic process of long cycles, and are a manifestation of this development, rather than its original driving force."[219] Kondratiev waves (cycles) are one type of historical cycles spanning the entire structure of society.

Technological development currently has the following rhythm: generations of technology (replaced every 10 years), technological patterns (upgraded every 40–50 years), and innovative technological methods of production (upgraded every several centuries).

Right now, a transition is under way to post-industrial and ecological methods of production. At the same time, development is accelerating of the first generations of the sixth pattern, which, one may assume, will dominate in advanced countries in the years 2020–2050, after which the time will come to start establishing the seventh pattern of technology.

The depth of contradiction in the transitional age will create a tidal wave of discoveries and inventions that will eventually lead to the creation of a dominant post-industrial scientific paradigm to match the radically changed world.

The main contradiction (basic incompatibility) at the financial and economic level is that the chasm between the rich and the poor nations and civilizations has expanded excessively. While in 1800 per-capita GDP in the United States was three times that of Africa, the ratio increased to 18.8 by 2000.[220] Per-capita GDP of the "Golden Billion" – 971 million people in rich countries was 59.5 times that of the poor majority (2,310 million people) in 2003. Convergence of social and economic development levels of different countries and civilizations is a pressing strategic goal for humanity in the 21st century. This goal cannot be reached successfully on the basis of the currently dominant neoliberal globalization model actively implemented and promoted by the US and the WTO. There is a different model making it possible to bridge the gaps and bring development levels closer. It is currently in use by the European Union. It would be reasonable to assume that the latter model – or one that is based on it – will dominate in the future.

Kondratiev waves still apply at material levels, but are likely to be more

---

[219] Кондратьев Н.Д. Большие циклы конъюнктуры и теория предвидения. М.: Экономика, 2002.

[220] May, В.А. Политическая природа и уроки финансового кризиса // Вопросы экономики. 1998. # 11. С. 4–20.

synchronized on the scale of the global economy, which would require the total exploration of compatibility at all levels of the manifestation of human needs at the same time.

Incompatibility receded for the first time after World War II (by the end of the 20th century), as military expenses were cut in relative terms. However, after the terrorist attacks of September 11, 2001, the share of military spending in the GDP of many countries started growing again. This indicates a crisis at the fifth – religious and theological level. Its duration is still uncertain, but all religious denominations should move more actively towards cooperation – this need is urgent and should have priority. The depth must demonstrate its unity of renewal and coordination at the general cultural and worldview level.

The generational change of political leaders has a strategic importance, especially in the clans and in the Orient/Asia, to reduce the number of asymmetrical wars and international terrorism which has become the mass-point format for clashes between civilizations.

The power of China and India (Buddhism and Hinduism) is growing, as is the power of Islamic civilization. The integration efforts of Western Europe which absorbed Eastern European civilization will start paying off. The fight over the legacy of the once-powerful Eurasian civilization will intensify. Serious problems arise as the population of the currently poorest Sub-Saharan African civilization expands. Material equalization does not happen because of demographics, and the danger of sharp incompatibility – military clashes – may rise again.

Theories of the economic cycle that are most popular and most discussed sometimes imply the existence of political and religious (cultural) cycles. They can be divided into two categories: externality and internality theories.

Externality theories see the main reasons for the economic cycle in fluctuations of factors that lie outside the economic system and include natural phenomena and political events, population growth rates and migration patterns, discoveries of new territories and resources.

Internality theories focus on the mechanisms within a system's levels (mostly evolutionary processes), which give an impetus to a self-reproducion cycle, and so each expansion creates a recession and contraction, and each contraction brings about a spike in activity and expansion, and everything ties together in a repeating, infinite chain.

A majority of modern economists tend to synthesis, or combination, of externality and internality theories. The reasons for oscillations between the two theory types are:

- technological innovation;
- population growth rates;
- discovery of new territories.

This book demonstrates that we are attempting not only to synthesize, but also to combine these theories organically into a theory of compatibility of social development.

Let us attempt to describe, somewhat superficially for now, the acceptable compatibility development (C_{AD}), taking the comments above into account:

$$C_{AD} = \int \left(R_c, K_{CCRN}, K_{AFRN} \right)$$

where R_C is the risk of acceptable compatibility; K_{CCRN} is the constructive conflict of renewal; K_{AFRN} is an acceptable forced renewal crisis.

We believe that an acceptable forced renewal crisis must be more balanced, i.e. the qualitative and quantitative changes within it must be realized in full:

C_{AD} = Material Change / Spiritual transformation $\Rightarrow$ 1.

This should delay the next upcoming crisis and reduce its severity and length.

CHAPTER 4

COMPATIBILITY OF MATERIAL AND SPIRITUAL UNDERSTANDING OF THE UNIVERSE

4.1. Compatibility of Economics and Law in Social Systems

Based on the model of the compatible development of society, in which the social, and then the political levels lie above the financial and economic level of compatibility, we propose looking at interactions of these (the second, third and fourth) levels from the perspective of interrelationships and reciprocal influences of the financial/economic and organizational/law mechanisms that territories and full-fledged countries rely on in their development.

The contemporary Russian and international research literature covers a plethora of approaches, classifications and typologies of social systems in the history of society's development. It makes sense to conduct an analysis of compatibility problems between law and economics in different systems by classifying them depending on whether or not a society has elements of a free market economy and how well developed these are.

They can be subdivided into three groups:

1) Social systems with a free market economy;

2) Systems with a rigidly planned command economy (with no elements of a free market economy);

3) Social systems with a mixed economy.

The intricacies of connections between law and economics are represented by several economic theories, including:

1) Economic liberalism and the free-market economy (Friedrich Hayek, Milton Friedman, John Hicks);

2) Institutionalism (Thorstein B. Veblen, John R. Commons, John K. Galbraith);

3) Regulated capitalism (Roy F. Harrod, John M. Keynes).

The first of these theories (Friedrich Hayek's) can be reduced to the following key principles:

• when organizing a certain area of life, one has to rely as much as possible on the spontaneous forces in society and resort to coercion as little as possible;

• personal and political freedom is impossible without economic freedom;

• the fundamentals of a planned economy require centralized control over all economic activity, over where and how social resources will be "consciously" used. In turn, competition makes it possible to coordinate (economic) activity from the inside, avoiding forced interference from the outside, and giving an individual the opportunity to make personal, independent economic decisions;

• planning and competition are compatible only when planning promotes competition, rather than working against it;

• a system based on competition needs an intelligently structured and continuously improved mechanism of legal controls. People spontaneously develop behavioral rules, institutions of property, contract, exchange, legal norms and laws, and no government can replace people's free choice in this case;

• the government and the state (i.e. the country) (as the fourth, political, level of compatibility – see Section 3.5) must restrict itself to setting general rules that encourage competition, while the law must be structured to protect and boost this competition;

• a formal equality before the law is incompatible with any actions by the government aiming to ensure the material equality of people. A political course based on the idea of equitable distribution leads to destruction of law and order.[221]

This interaction between law and economics was typical of many countries in Europe and the Americas before the 1929–1933 economic crisis.

The second theory (institutionalism, from Lat. "institutum" meaning establishment, structure, organization) represents a systematic analysis of processes and phenomena with practical recommendations for "social control" over the market economy.

The American founder and leader of the institutional economics social and psychological movement Thorstein B. Veblen[222] saw the foundation of the economy in the economic behavior of people driven by certain psychological motivations.

American institutional economist and labor historian John R. Commons believed in the primacy of the law over the economy (discussing the transaction theory). He believed that in using a transaction, i.e. a legal agreement, any contradiction can be resolved.[223] The key idea of compatibility is that the government must control and regulate the market economy, and the work of government commissions and agencies can address and resolve economic contradictions (incompatibilities).

During the Great Depression (and FDR's "New Deal"), new laws and regulations helped to smooth social and economic contradictions during that great global crisis. However, the nature and practice of development of the market economy could not tolerate this kind of government and legislative interference for long, and in the late 1930s the theory of regulatory capitalism, or Keynesianism (from the name of British economist John Maynard Keynes) took root. In the context of fast economic growth, a certain social consensus was formed after World War II, represented by a compatible block of private capital, the middle class and well-paid workers. The main idea of this theory is that capitalism is in many ways a flawed

---

[221] Hayek, F. The Road to Serfdom. Routledge Press, 1944. Quoted from the Russian edition: Хайек Ф. Дорога к рабству. М., 1992. PP. 18, 21, 34, 36, 65.

[222] Veblen, T. The Theory of the Leisure Class. Macmillan, 1899. Quoted from the Russian edition: Веблен Т. Теория праздного класса. М., 1984.

[223] Seligman, B. Main Currents in Modern Economics: Economic Thought Since 1870. 1962. Quoted from the Russian edition: Селигмен Б. Основные течения современной экономической мысли. М., 1968; История экономических учений: Учебник / Под ред. А.Г. Худокормова. М., 1994.

socioeconomic system, but if it is "managed intelligently," it can become more efficient as a way to achieve economic goals.

Government influence today (the fourth level of compatibility) is an indispensable condition for a healthy market economy (the second level).[224]

John M. Keynes' theory in its time was designed to save capitalist market relations.[225]

A socialist system based on a command economy (second group) began to assert itself in Soviet Russia, where "compatibility" of law and economics took on the following aspect: law is a condensed manifestation of politics, politics are a condensed manifestation of the economy of this compatibility within the command system.

Russian and international students of law and economics attempted to give this system a generalized description,[226] according to which:

• government property is dominant, economic players (companies, plants, organizations) have no independence whatsoever, resulting in production of goods for which there is no demand, mandatory monopoly production and mandatory distribution, freezes on capital investment and an unwillingness to implement new technologies (manifestation of the seventh level of compatibility — see Section 3.5);

• laws and regulations absolutely prohibit the exploitation of one man by another, essentially establishing the exploitation of man by the government (through ideological constructs).

The law affecting the economy not only did nothing to improve its operation, but also hampered and prevented it (through compatibility of interaction). Laws and regulations were contradictory, encouraging the practice of ignoring legislation, which came to be substituted by explicit directions by government officials.

Social (third level) security of citizens created the illusion of universal prosperity, social equality and fairness. In effect, distribution was increasingly incompatible, because it looked like redistribution in favor of the government.

---

[224] Keynes, J. The General Theory of Employment, Interest and Money. Quoted from the Russian edition: Кейнс Дж. Общая теория занятости, процента и денег. М., 1978. P. 318.

[225] Ibid. (Quoted from the Russian edition) P. 455.

[226] See, for example: Гайдар Е. Экономические реформы и иерархические структуры. М., 1990; Kornai J. Deficit. Quoted from the Russian edition: Корнаи Я. Дефицит. М., 1990; Теория государства и права: Курс лекций / Под ред. М.Н. Марченко. М., 1996. PP. 139–141; Кудров В.М. Советская модель экономики: тяжелое наследство // Общественные науки и современность. 1999. # 3.

Social systems with a mixed economy (group three) became widespread in the mid-20th century, reflecting real change in social and economic life and expanding the role of the government in the economy. There is not a single country in the world today where the economy follows the classical free market model or where market forces are completely banished. The compatible development of society identifies the most functional and most essential elements of the socioeconomic systems listed above, which could be combined in some way within a single system, potentially ensuring a certain degree of interaction.

The key feature of mixed-economy social systems is distribution of most resources through commercial transactions (i.e. via the markets), while government bodies still play a significant role. They:

• create and regulate the legal foundations of property ownership and market operation, regulating economic behavior, establishing detailed rules of operation for companies;

• are customers for and consumers of such goods and services as defense, education, roads, etc.;

• define and provide social security (social assistance if needed) to citizens;

• invest themselves through taxes and loans, using them to influence prices, interest rates and production;

• control taxes and government spending, while enforcing control over the amount of money in the economy, thereby correcting fluctuations in the economic cycle.

Compatibility of interactions in law and economics can be defined as follows: the law takes objective laws of economics into account to attempt to use social imperative to restore social and economic fairness in society. The purpose of regulation is to ensure the acceptable dignified[227] existence of all members of society, and law is a means to achieving social compromise. Dynamic development of economic relationships affects the legal foundation, encouraging changes and adjustments to it.

Different countries and regions have different models of mixed economy, distinct from each other in their unique "national mixing ratio" of free market and government regulation, capital and social aspects, economic and post-economic sides. A mixed economy is usually a "structure

---

[227] Dignified: ensuring satisfaction of the essential material, social, legal and cultural needs of a community's members.

with a dominant aspect,"[228] where one aspect or the other in the pairs above is the dominant one.

Western mixed economic models are mostly models of "mixed capitalism." The Chinese model can be described as a "mixed socialist-type economy." Compatibility in a mixed economy lies in giving "reproduction and development opportunities to every element of its structure, ensuring that each has a real weight in the overall economic system."[229]

We can use the modern social systems of Sweden, Japan, the USA and other countries, as examples of different systems.

Speaking of the Scandinavian (Swedish) system, we note that it is characterized by an overall strong influence of law and legislation on the economy for the purposes of economic stability and redistribution of income for the benefit of the poorest strata in society. The Swedish system is based on social policy, and the compatibility of the sociocultural environment rests on high taxes (accounting for more than 50% of gross national product). The government, acting as an equal economic player, undertakes to ensure a high living standard for the population.

The main characteristic of Japan is planning and coordination of actions between the government and the private sector, with planning playing a non-binding role of pure recommendation. Another feature specific to Japan is that, as wages lag productivity growth, cost of products declines, and they become more competitive on the international market. Yet another feature is that all interactions between law and economics, and all other aspects of social life, are based on a highly developed national identity, collectivism and a profound patriotism (the fifth level of compatibility).

In the US, the model of the social system gives us such an interaction between law and the economy that legislative or governmental regulation of economic relationships comes into play only in the event of extreme need: to set the rules of the game in the economic field, regulation of business and education. Economic fairness here takes precedence over social fairness, while the objective of achieving social equality is not considered at all. Compatibility within community is based on mass orientation towards achieving personal success.

The foundation is taking shape to claim that Russia today is a mixed-

---

[228] Mixed structures and their compatibility are reviewed in Section 3.4.2.

[229] В.М. Кульков Смешанная экономика (теоретико-методологические аспекты) // Вестник МГУ. Сер. 6. Экономика. 1996. # 5. Р. 26.

240

economy social system, because a free market is being established in the context of previously established traditions of collectivism, fairness and a safety net for the population.

The need remains to create a basis for developing the free market, and also, somewhat inconsistently, the positions of the government need to be established as both an asset owner (i.e. an economic player) and the source of key economic regulations for society.

As we describe the interaction (compatibility) of economic and legal mechanisms, identifying the formats and nature of the ways in which law affects the economy, we can state that they can be positive or negative: law may stimulate and support efficient economic growth and development, or it may slow it down and destroy it completely. The social systems we have looked at above demonstrate that one cannot pick a single model of interaction between law and economics for all times, disregarding changes in internal factors (community development) and external factors (development of the society as a whole).

Let us take a closer look at these types of socioeconomic systems projecting (overlaying) them against levels of compatibility in society (Fig. 4.1).

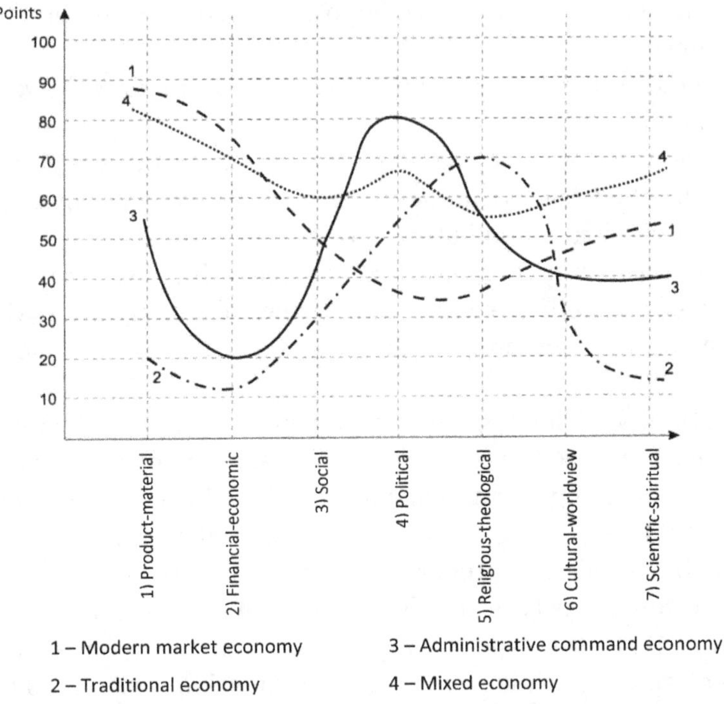

Fig. 4.1 Projection of socioeconomic system types on levels of compatibility

Every system type has its specific features, its strengths and weaknesses. Strengths are those that have the greatest meaning at a certain level, while weaknesses are those that are the least significant.

Society, as we discussed above (see Section 1.2), is developing towards a rational order, and therefore it is seeking a tolerant socioeconomic system capable of withstanding the relatively equal burden of cyclic rebirth at every level of compatibility without abrupt rises and falls.

Tolerant economics, politics, culture and science; over time, a system of these subsystems will become the most convenient format for every future period, but its principles need to be shaped today, which is why we are discussing what the compatibility is of our personal everyday urges and actions and general destiny-changing scenarios and collective action.

The system of a fountain to support harmonious processes taking place at different compatibility levels that was described in Section 3.5 above, must be actively fed (and sometimes in a single impulse) by the dynamics of the first and second material levels — the foundation of coordinated processes in a given system.

Specific characteristics of the balance between law and the economy under different social systems are expressed through the particular legal methods, means and regimes specific to that particular combination of law and economics.

A planned, command economy is characterized by pervasive top-down centralized regulation.

A market economy is characterized by decentralized regulation, as players within the economy influence the various processes by entering into contracts and performing unilateral lawful acts.

Communities with a mixed economy combine the first and second methods, the balance between which is specifically compatible with a given country given its national culture – the theological and religious component.

Compatibility of law and economics under different historical social models is characterized by the scale and predominance of certain general legal means, including permissions and denials, for example, as expressed by the formula "everything is permitted unless it is explicitly forbidden." Regulation by permission (under which everything is forbidden unless it is explicitly permitted) is typical of legal responsibility in all areas of law. It is well known that this type of regulation dominates under totalitarian government systems, while regulation by permission is also used to regulate certain economic relationships under a market economy. This kind of regulation is typical of relationships in areas of economic activity where there is a risk of uncontrolled use of technologies or insufficient control over technological processes (in production of poisonous and radioactive substances, devices containing these substances, and production of weapons and atomic energy) or in areas that have an important social function in maintaining the physical and moral health of the population (production of medical drugs, alcohol, liquor and wine, mass advertising, etc.). An example of a practical format of regulation by permission is general normative laws in conjunction with specialized – technical, medical and ecological – standards, including licenses and certificates required.

There is another condition for compatibility in addition to the features of balance between law and economics listed above for specific actual historical socioeconomic systems. The influence of the external environment often produces a mismatched combination of economic and non-economic methods of regulating economic processes through laws, which makes compatibility models significantly more cumbersome, giving the fourth (political) level of compatibility a dual color scheme in maintaining an actual economic and social course.

The key criterion for differentiating between administrative (command) and economic methods of the government's participation in the economy is their relation[230] to the economic interests of market participants and free economic choice. Formally speaking, methods of economic law (i.e. economic regulation) are also mandatory for all players in the economy.

The method of economic law may be used, for example, when setting legal/legislative bans on unfair competition (corruption or government monopoly on certain sectors). The legal plane is an indispensable element of any social system. In all social systems, law, alongside its traditional functions of ensuring public order and safety and organizing the defense of the country, addresses certain economic matters such as the organization of money circulation, tax collection, construction of roads, bridges, schools and healthcare institutions, etc.

In a market economy, the government and law are released from functions normally foreign to them, with the law focusing on things without which a society cannot exist and which the private sector tends to avoid. Transition from one socioeconomic system to another typically requires a

---

[230] The relation is seen as the condition of government during a given period of time with regard to choosing certain combinations of the said methods to achieve the best possible compatibility in producing the desired results for the community.

lot of time, and is subject to objective "natural laws," patterns of socioeconomic development. We are observing today that globalization makes it increasingly possible to combine the legal planes of different territories on different continents. Towards the end of the previous century, we witnessed a union of economic systems that were based on very different principles: the union of two countries, West and East Germany. The former German Democratic Republic (East Germany) with its planned command economy and non-competitive manufacturing industry was integrated into the market space of the Federal Republic of Germany (West Germany), and it was law that was the dominant stimulus for the unification of two very different economic systems. This once again confirms compatibility models in which ideology of law regulates the economy. Integration of the former East Germany into the market economy of West Germany came at a cost, as the industrial output of the GDR dropped 50%, the standard of living went down 20%, while the amount of social assistance to East Germans stood at 50% of East Germany's GDP). The united country allowed taxes to rise temporarily: adding surcharges to personal and corporate income tax, and increasing consumption tax. And yet, the East German economy, one of the strongest in the Eastern Bloc, ended up in deep crisis.[231]

The fifth, religious and theological (national/ethnic) level of compatibility played the crucial role for the German people. The cultural code of national unity outweighed all material privations for the sake of the unification of East and West Germany.

Even though the transition from a command to a market economy was based on a serious financial and legal footing, and although it was taking place within the stable "legal plane" of West Germany, this process still took a relatively large amount of time. This integration demonstrated that it was not enough to have a ready economic model and solid financial support; it was also important to create the right conditions and tools for a transition (for a specific society) — institutions of property, protection by law, tax law, and other aspects, for a compatible, combined operation of the unified country, ensuring equal conditions of living across the unified Germany.

Considering the great expanse of Russia's territory, and the fact that it is home to many ethnic groups, the government has always played an important role in its economy: the state has always been the largest owner of the means of production and non-manufacturing fixed assets (the

---

[231] Л.П. Ночевкина Будет ли в России «экономическое чудо?» Мировой опыт рыночных реформ. М., 1999. С. 20–21.

government owned as much as 38% of all land immediately before the first Russian revolution of 1905), and has been the largest investor in industrial fixed capital. During the Soviet period, this role of the government became absolute; this explains how private ownership came apart in the mining and resource sectors, which will define the nation's economy and legislation for decades to come.

Compatibility of interactions is particularly important for our country in the next several years, including interactions in the product/proprietary, financial/economic, organizational/law, cultural/worldview, spiritual/cognition mechanisms – levels of the development of society for the achievement of overall unity at all levels and in all areas of human need.

4.2. Compatibility of Civilizations

Civilizations, unlike countries, do not have clearly-defined boundaries. Transitional territories appear between civilizations, within which cultures constantly interact. Thus, for example, the Chinese civilization is adjacent to and interacts with the Buddhist civilization. In Russia, areas of interaction with the Islamic civilization lie in the middle and lower Volga region, while Buryatia, Kalmykia and Tuva are areas where it overlaps the Buddhist civilization. Mixed civilizations sometimes emerge if the degree of integration and mutual penetration of cultures is high. By way of example, we can take the modern Sub-Saharan African and Latin American civilizations. Civilizations come into contact with one another, and each of them is at a different stage of development.

Population growth and migration in the now emerging world will make culture, rather than ideology and economics, the main and defining source of incompatibility and conflict, although this has always been true, if to a lesser extent. The most significant future conflicts in global politics will be between nations and groups representing different civilizations. A clash of civilizations will become the dominant factor of global politics.

In the latter half of the 20th century, the world was divided into the "first," "second" and "third" worlds. Now it makes much better sense to group countries based on their dominant political or economic systems, based on cultural and civilization criteria, rather than the level of economic development. When we talk about a civilization in this context, we see it as a certain cultural entity. However, regions, ethnic groups, peoples and religious communities all have their unique culture reflecting different levels of cultural diversity. A small town in Southern Italy may have a very different culture from that of a Northern Italian village, and yet they are both Italian communities which would never be confused with, say, German communities. European countries have certain cultural features in common that set them apart from China or the Arab world. The Western world, the Arab region and China are not parts of any broader cultural unity. They represent different civilizations.

A civilization is the broadest level of unity a man can identify with. A civilization may include several nation states, as is the case with the Western, Latin American or Arab civilizations, or a single nation state, in the case of Japan. Civilizations may become mixed, overlap each other and include sub-civilizations. Western civilization exists in two main variants: European and North American, while Islamic civilization includes Arab, Turkish and Malay varieties. Boundaries between them are rarely clear-cut, but they are always real. Civilizations are dynamic: they rise and fall, they break apart and merge. And, as any history enthusiast knows, civilizations disappear; they sink into the sands of time.

The bulk of human history is the history of civilizations. According to Arnold Toynbee, there have been 21 civilizations in human history. The question about full-fledged compatibility and identity at civilization level will become increasingly important in the future. The overall appearance of the world will be largely shaped and defined by the interaction of the seven or eight major civilizations extant at this time. They include the Western, Confucian, Japanese, Islamic, Hindu, Orthodox-Slavic, Latin American and, possibly, African civilizations. The most significant manifestations of incompatibility[232] will emerge along the fault lines between civilizations.

Differences between civilizations are not just real, they are most significant. Civilizations are dissimilar in terms of their history, language, culture, traditions and, most importantly, their religion. People representing different civilizations see the relationships between God and man, between an individual and the group, between a citizen and the state, between parents and children, between husband and wife, differently, and have different ideas of relative importance of rights and obligations, freedom and coercion, equality and hierarchy. These differences have taken shape over centuries and will not disappear in the foreseeable future. They

---

232 Huntington, S. The Clash of Civilizations and the Remaking of World Order. New York: Simon & Schuster, 1996.

are more fundamental than differences between political ideologies and political regimes. Differences do not necessarily imply conflict, nor does conflict necessarily imply violence. However, over centuries, the longest conflicts have been engendered precisely by incompatibility of civilizations.

The world becomes smaller, and forms of interactions between peoples of different civilizations become more pronounced. This leads to an increasing sense of "civilization identity," a deeper understanding of differences between civilizations and similarities within a civilization. North Africans' immigration to France created considerable hostility in France, and at the same time bred and reinforced kinder attitudes to other immigrants, including "good Catholics and Europeans" from Poland. Americans (of the US) react much more defensively to investments by the Japanese than they do to much more substantial investments originating from Canada and Western Europe. Events follow the scenario described by Jonathan Horvitz: "In Eastern Nigeria an Ibo man may be an "Ibo Owerri" or an "Ibo Onicha." However, in Lagos he would be known as simply Ibo. He would be a Nigerian in London and an African in New York."[233] Interactions between representatives of different civilizations reinforce their civilizational identity, which can bring to a head disagreements and hostility going back deep into history or at least perceived as such, which lead to incompatible actions by representatives of the civilizations.

The ongoing processes of economic modernization and social change worldwide are diluting the traditional identification of people with their place of birth, and at the same time weakening the role of the nation state as a source of identity. The resulting vacuum is mostly filled by religion, frequently in a fundamentalist form. Fundamentalist religious movements are not unique to Islam; they exist in Western Christianity, Judaism, Buddhism and Hinduism. In most countries and religious denominations, fundamentalism finds support among well-educated young men, highly skilled middle-class people, professionals and business people. Revival of religion, or, in the words of Gilles Kepel, "the revenge of God,"[234] sets the stage for identification with and the sense of belonging to a unity transcending national borders to unite civilizations at a level of joint real intellectual understanding of common values as a source of life of humanity. The rise of civilization identity, dictated by the split in the role of

---

[233] А.Е. Кармин Основы культурологи: морфология культуры. СПб., 1997. Р. 346, 349.

234 Kepel, G. La revanche de Dieu: Chretiens, juifs et musulmans a la reconquete du monde. Le Seuil, 1991.

the West, leads to weakening compatibility. In this connection, non-Western civilizations increasingly return to their roots. We hear, with increasing frequency, calls for a "return to Asia" by Japan, a "hinduization" of India or statements about the failure of socialism and nationalism. In many Western countries, an intense process of de-Westernization is under way among elites educated at Oxford, Sorbonne or Sandhurst.

Cultural uniqueness and distinctions are less subject to change than economic and political ones, and therefore, conflicts based on cultural differences are harder to resolve or end in compromise. Communists may become democrats, and the rich may become poor and vice versa, but Russians will never become Estonians, no matter how much they might want to, not would Azeris become Armenians. Instilling these cultural features in the new generation as components of a complete cultural heritage is a constant goal and objective of the relevant institutions. The question of incompatibility in the past was always: "Whose side are you on?" And a man could choose sides, or change sides over time. In a conflict of civilizations the question is different: "Who are you?" This is a question about something that is a given and is not subject to change. And, as we know from the experience of Bosnia, the Caucasus and Sudan, if you give the wrong answer to this question, you can immediately get a bullet in the head. Religion divides people even more sharply than ethnic identity. A man can be half-French or half-Arab, or even a citizen of both France and an Arab country. It is much harder to be half-Catholic and half-Moslem.

Economic regionalism is gaining in power. The share of intra-regional trade has increased to 60% in Europe, 40% in Southeast Asia and 36% in North America. Apparently, the role of regional economic links will increase in the future. On the one hand, the success of economic regionalism reinforces the perception of one's belonging to a specific civilization, on the other; economic regionalism can be successful only if it is rooted in a unified civilization identity.

In turn, a common culture clearly supports very fast increases in economic connections between the People's Republic of China, on the one hand, and Hong Kong, Taiwan, Singapore and overseas Chinese communities in other Asian countries on the other. Since the end of the Cold War, common culture quickly ousts ideological differences, reverting to the previous state. Mainland China and Taiwan are becoming increasingly close. If cultural identity is a pre-condition for economic integration, the center of the future East Asian economic bloc will very likely be in China. In fact, this bloc is already taking shape. If based around

China, this strategic space will have a powerful technological and manufacturing potential (in Taiwan), skilled workers in the fields of organization, marketing and the service industry (Hong Kong), a well-developed telecommunications network (Singapore), powerful financial capital (all three countries), as well as huge land, natural and labor resources (mainland China). This influential community has a traditional clan system at its basis – the backbone of the East Asian economy.

Cultural and religious similarities are also at the basis of the Economic Cooperation Organization, which combines 10 non-Arab Moslem countries: Iran, Pakistan, Turkey, Azerbaijan, Kazakhstan, Kyrgyzstan, Turkmenistan, Tajikistan, Uzbekistan and Afghanistan. Attempts to create a broader economic community that would combine the island nations of the Caribbean and Central America have not been successful – no one has been able to bridge the gaps between the Anglo-Saxon and Latin cultures. On an interpersonal level, while defining their identity in ethnic or religious terms, people tend to see the interactions between themselves and people of a different ethnicity and religious affiliation in terms of "us" vs. "them." Although compatibility of personalities makes intermarriage possible and often successful, which is one of the defining factors of increasing full-fledged compatibility of cultures, geographic proximity also tends to encourage mutual territorial claims. However, any attempts by the West to spread its values of democracy and liberalism as general human values, preserve its military supremacy and confirm its economic interests have been met with resistance from other civilizations.

Governments and political groups are increasingly unsuccessful in mobilizing the population and forming coalitions based on ideology, and they increasingly try to gain support appealing to common religion and civilization. Incompatibility between civilizations plays out at two levels. At the micro level, groups living along the fault lines between civilizations are fighting, sometimes violently and bloodily, over land and the domination of one group over another. At the macro level, countries that belong to different civilizations vie for influence over international organizations and third countries in the military and economic spheres, trying to impose their own political and religious values.

For example, during the cold war, the hotspots of crisis and bloodshed were concentrated along political and ideological borders. At the same time, as soon as the ideological divide disappeared in Europe, its cultural divide into Western Christianity, on the one hand, and Orthodox Christianity and Islam, on the other, reemerged.

In the 11–13th centuries, Crusaders tried, with mixed success, to bring Christianity to the Holy Land and establish Christian rule there. In the 14-16th centuries, Ottoman Turkey took the initiative, spreading its dominance across the Middle East and the Balkans, capturing Constantinople and besieging Vienna twice. However, in the 19th and early 20th centuries, the power of the Ottomans began to wane. Most of North Africa and the Middle East came under the influence of Great Britain, France and Italy.

Colonial empires disappeared after World War II. First Arab nationalism and then Islamic fundamentalism asserted themselves. The West came to be dependent on the Persian Gulf nations for its energy. Islamic countries rich in oil were becoming rich in money, and in weaponry, if they felt the need. The latter exacerbated incompatibility and confrontation between the West and the Islamic world even further; incompatibility and confrontation have been occurring for a century, with no sign of abating. Indeed, they appear likely to become exacerbated further.

Many Arab countries have reached a level of economic and social development (incompatible with autocratic forms of rule), where they can be ruled democratically, and attempts to establish democratic regimes are becoming increasingly insistent.

Skyrocketing population growth in Arab countries in the 20th century, especially in Northern Africa, has been increasing immigration to Western Europe. In turn, the influx of immigrants in the context of disappearing intra-European borders in Western Europe has caused sharp political resistance. In Italy, France and Germany racist attitudes have become increasingly open in the past 20 years. Political reaction and violence against Arab and Turkish immigrants are on the rise.

The sides see a conflict of civilizations between the Western and the Islamic worlds. The history of Arab-Islamic civilization was characterized by constant antagonistic interaction with pagan, animistic, and now predominantly Christian black populations of the South (the areas south of the territories controlled by the Arabs). In the past, this antagonism was personified by an Arab slave trader versus a black slave. Now, it manifests itself through a protracted civil war. One-sided speeches by leaders of some religions can exacerbate the situation. Religion often kindles resurgent ethnic self-perception and identity. We know very well that a large part of Russian history was filled with frontier struggles between Slavs and Turkish peoples. This struggle started from the establishment of the Russian state more than a millennium ago. The thousand-year struggle between Slavs and their Eastern neighbors holds the key to understanding not just Russian history, but also the Russian character. To understand the current state of life in Russia, one must not forget about the Turkic ethnic group which absorbed the attentions of the Russian people over many centuries. Conflict between civilizations has deep roots in other regions of Asia, too. The struggle between Moslems and Hindus that goes back many centuries manifests itself today not only through rivalry between Pakistan and India, but also through growing religious strife within India, between the increasingly militant Hindu groups and the country's substantial Moslem minority. Contradictions between China and the US became especially prominent in areas such as human rights, trade and the non-proliferation of weapons of mass destruction, and there is no hope these contradictions will subside or be resolved.

Cultural differences amplify the economic conflict between the Americas[235] and the Orient (Japan and China). Each side accuses the other of racism, but at least, from the US perspective the rejection is cultural rather than racial. It would be hard to imagine two societies further apart on fundamental values, attitudes and behavior styles. Economic disagreements between the US and Europe are at least as profound, but they are less prominent politically and less emotional, because the differences between the American and European culture are much less dramatic than those between the US and Japanese civilizations.

The level of potential incompatibility in interactions between different civilizations may vary. In relations between the US and European sub-civilizations, adversarial opposition prevails in the form of economic competition, just like between the West as a whole and Japan. At the same time, ethnic conflicts have spread in Eurasia that proceed all the way to ethnic cleansing (violence), reaching complete incompatibility. Most often, conflicts take place between groups that belong to different civilizations, and these conflicts take the most extreme forms. Historical borders between civilizations on the Eurasian continent are once again gripped in the bloody throes of conflicts. These conflicts are especially acute along the boundaries of the Islamic world which spans a roughly crescent-shaped area from North Africa to Central Asia. However, conflicts between Moslems on the one hand and Orthodox Serbs in the Balkans, Jews in Israel, Hindus in India, Buddhists in Burma (Myanmar), and Catholics in the Philippines on

---

[235] М. Сиротская Американская цивилизация: восприятие в США (середина XIX в.). М.: Русское открытие Америки, 2002.

the other, also resort to violence. Conflicts flare up along the boundaries of the Islamic world everywhere where incompatibility of relationships prevails. After each war, including the Cold War, profound changes take place, establishing a new world order, and as it takes shape, belonging to one civilization, or, in the words of columnist Hugh David Scott Greenway, "a syndrome of friendly nations," replaces political ideology and traditional considerations of maintaining a balance of power as a key principle of cooperation and coalitions. All conflicts in recent time signify that "syndromes" of this kind are gradually emerging.

The world that is the stage for a clash of civilizations[236] is inevitably a world of double moral standards: one standard applied to "friendly nations (countries)," and the other – to all others. The "friendly nation" syndrome is in full display in conflicts in the former Soviet Union. Military success by Armenians against Azerbaijan in the 1990s pushed Turkey to step up its support for Azeris, who are close to Turkey in their religion, ethnicity and language. "The people of Turkey share the Azeri sentiments," a Turkish government official said. Turkey and Iran announced that they would not stand for partitioning Azerbaijan. In its last years, the Soviet government supported Azerbaijan against Armenia because Azerbaijan still had communists in power. However, as the Soviet Union disintegrated, political motives were replaced by religious ones. Now Russian troops are fighting for the Armenian side, while Azerbaijan accuses the Russian government of making a 180-degree turn away from its country to support Christian Armenia.

As for the former Yugoslavia, Germany persuaded the other 11 European Community members to follow its lead in recognizing the independence of Slovenia and Croatia. In a push to reinforce the positions of these two Catholic countries, the Vatican recognized Slovenia and Croatia even before the EC. The US followed Europe's lead. Thus, the leading countries of European civilization formed a united front to support their coreligionists. Islamic governments and political groups, in turn, chastise the West for not standing up for Bosnian Moslems.

Incompatibility which is expressed through standoff and confrontation is also possible among countries that belong to the same civilization, as well as within these countries. However, these conflicts are typically less intense and less all-embracing than conflicts between civilizations.

---

[236] Huntington, S. The Clash of Civilizations and the Remaking of World Order. New York: Simon & Schuster, 1996.

Before the 21st century, unity of civilizations was rather limited, but that process is developing, and it has significant future potential. As clashes continued in the early 21st century in the Persian Gulf, the Caucasus and Bosnia, the positions of different countries and the differences between them have been increasingly defined by their civilizational identity. Populist politicians, religious leaders and the mass media have acquired a powerful weapon here, ensuring the support of broad swathes of the population and enabling them to put pressure on indecisive governments. In the near future, the greatest threat of escalation into large-scale wars will come from local clashes, which, like those in Bosnia and the Caucasus, have been started along the fault lines between civilizations. Apparently, the next world war, if it ever comes, will be a war between civilizations.

A new tangle of inter-civilizational contradictions is forming in Crimea. A worst-case scenario development of this situation would inevitably lead to conflict; a more positive development would be preventing the conflict by developing civilization tourism in the region.

There is a tangle of contradiction in the North Caucasus and on the eastern shore of the Black Sea, where conflicts have been unfolding for over a decade at the boundary between the Orthodox Christian and Moslem segments of Eurasian civilization. The problem area includes Chechnya, Ingushetia and Dagestan, as well as Abkhazia and Karabakh, the zone where Islamic Azerbaijan overlaps Christian Armenia. The interests of Islamic countries and Russia, as well as the US are tied up in these conflicts. In a worse-case scenario, these conflicts could simmer on practically indefinitely, now flaring up, now quieting down; in a more positive scenario, a new formula of compatibility may be discovered in the next decade or two, a formula that would take into account the unique civilizational features of the conflicting parties and establish acceptable conditions for their cooperation.

Differences in the scale of power, as well as the contest over military, economic and political power are one of the sources of conflict between the West and other civilizations. Another source of conflict is differences in culture, basic values and beliefs. V.S. Naipaul[237] claimed that Western civilization is universal and should work for all peoples and nations. While many aspects of Western culture really have penetrated the rest of the world on the surface, at deeper levels, Western ideas and concepts are fundamentally different from those inherent in other civilizations. Islamic,

---

[237] Naipaul, V.S. Half a Life. London: Knopf, 2001.

Confucian, Japanese, Hinduist, Buddhist and Orthodox Christian cultures have nearly no place for such Western ideas as individualism, liberalism, constitutionalism, human rights, equality, freedom, supremacy of the law, democracy, the free market and separation of church and state. The efforts of the West to promote these ideas often elicit a hostile reaction against "human rights imperialism" and only serve to reinforce the original native values of other civilizations' culture. The very premise that a "universal civilization" is possible is an essentially Western idea. It is directly incompatible with the particularism, the strong desire of most Asian cultures to emphasize differences between individuals and groups of people.

These differences become especially clear when the US and other Western countries attempt to impose on the people of other countries Western ideas of democracy and human rights that historically came into existence in the West and have become established in some non-Western countries only as a result of Western colonialism or pressure.

In future, the standoff between the West and the rest of the World will probably become the central axis of global politics. In the event of incompatibility (confrontation), non-Western countries may follow the example of North Korea or Myanmar (formerly Burma) and take a course towards isolation, protecting their countries from contacts with the West and from Western infiltration, and remove themselves from participation in the global community, in which the West is dominant. Any attempt to achieve compatibility of development, i.e. cooperation and even partnership, would include joining the West and accepting its values and institutions. In the language of the theory of international relations, this is called "jumping on the bandwagon." And in the event of incompatibility reflecting opposition and adversarial intentions, they could try to create a counterweight to the West, developing their economic and military might and cooperating with other, non-Western countries, uniting against the West, while maintaining their indigenous national values and institutions – in other words, modernizing while avoiding westernization. If being part of a specific civilization becomes the basis for people's identity in their own eyes, countries comprising groups representing several civilizations, like the Soviet Union or Yugoslavia, are doomed to disintegration.

Split countries, in their turn, will strive to achieve unification and, if possible, create a new compatible civilization. Turkey with its internal split is a typical example of a country like this. Some elements of Turkish society support the restoration of Islamic traditions. The Turkish elite see their country as a Western society, while the political elite of the West does not see it that way. Turkey is denied accession to the European Union, and the true reason for this, according to President of Turkey Halil T. Ozal, "is that we are Moslems, and they are Christians, but they are not saying this explicitly." The collapse of the Soviet Union has opened a unique opportunity for Turkey to become a leader for a resurgent Turkic civilization spanning seven countries, covering the space between the shores of Greece and China. Encouraged by the West, Turkey is making every effort to build this new identity for itself.

Mexico has found itself in a similar situation. Mexican politicians are involved in solving a grand task of completely reformulating Mexico's identity, conducting fundamental economic reform for this purpose, which should over time lead to radical political change and transform Mexico into a North American country from one that is part of Latin America. However, Mexico, just like Turkey, has influential social powers firmly opposed to this new definition of national identity. Turkish politicians supporting integration with Europe have to make overtures towards Islam, just as Mexican leaders pushing for integration into North America are forced to make some gestures to appease those who prefer to see Mexico as a Latin American country.

Mexico is the closest split country to the United States. However, the most significant split country globally is still Russia. The tyranny of communism earlier took off the agenda and made irrelevant the historical argument between pro-Western liberals and traditionalist Slavophiles in Russia. And now, the Russian people have encountered the same argument again (Peter Savitsky wrote in the 1920s that Russia was a "unique Eurasian civilization"). The following must be conditions of compatibility for a country split from within to retain its cultural identity: unity and support of the political and economic elite of the country; consent of the people, even if grudgingly given, to assume the new identity. And, certainly, the dominant groups of the civilization the split country is trying to join must be ready to accept the "new convert." In the case of Mexico, all three conditions are met. In the case of Turkey, only the first two are.

Incompatibility preventing non-Western countries from joining the West can be of different depth and complexity. It is not particularly great in the case of Latin American and Eastern European countries. It is much more significant in the case of Orthodox Christian countries of the former Soviet Union. However, the most significant obstacles are faced by Islamic, Confucian, Hinduist and Buddhist nations. Japan is, in a way, an associated member of the Western world, in some ways very much part of the Western "camp," but certainly distinct from the West on some key dimensions. Countries competing with the West augment their own economic, military and political power through internal development and cooperation with other non-Western nations. The Confucian-Islamic bloc is a well-known example of this cooperation, which formed as a challenge to Western interests, values and power.

One of the steps towards compatibility is the West proclaiming the principle of non-proliferation of nuclear, chemical and biological weapons, ballistic missiles and other complex delivery systems for these weapons, as a universal and mandatory standard, and non-proliferation treaties as a way to implement this standard. A system of various sanctions is envisaged for those who contribute to the proliferation of modern weapons, and privileges for those who uphold the non-proliferation principle.

The goal of the Confucian-Islamic bloc is to help its members to acquire the weapons and military technology necessary to create a counterweight to the military might of the West.

Civilizational identity cannot completely supplant or replace all other forms of identity, it is impossible for all nation states to disappear and for each civilization to become politically uniform and united, and for conflict and strife among different groups within a civilization to stop. We only propose the hypothesis that: 1) compatibility between civilizations is both important and real; 2) civilizational identity is on the rise; 3) incompatibility of civilizations will become the predominant form of incompatibility, replacing ideological and other forms of incompatibility; 4) effective international political, economic and security institutions will be emerging, for the time being, within civilizations, rather than spanning multiple civilizations; 5) the main axes of international compatibility will be relationships between the West and the rest of the world, including those between Islamic and Confucian countries.

In the long term, we must focus on the following criteria. Western civilization is modern as well as "Western." Non-Western civilizations have attempted to become modern without becoming Western. Until now, Japan alone has been completely successful in this. Non- Western civilizations will keep trying to achieve prosperity, modern technology, top skills, equipment and armaments, while attempting to combine modernity with their traditional values and culture. The modern world, including the West, will need to develop a deeper understanding of the fundamental religious and philosophical foundations of these civilizations. The West will need to realize how people representing these civilizations understand their own interests. It will need to find common elements, or so-called basic compatibility of development, for different civilizations. For we should not expect a single, universal civilization to emerge in the foreseeable future. The world, for now, will consist of dissimilar civilizations, every one of which will need to learn to coexist with all the others. The world is characterized by extreme breadth and variety, richness of interactions – from standoffs and conflict to cooperation and partnership. To evaluate the compatibility and incompatibility of relationships from this extreme range, we propose formats of cooperation, including compatible formats (Table 4.1).

Forms of interaction between civilizations

Type	Levels of Interactions		
	1	11	111
Compatible	Productive dialogue	Cooperation in the fields of culture, technology, trade	Partnership
Incompatible	Stand off	Confrontation	Conflict

Table 4.1

We see the following as incompatible types of interaction:

• a clash of civilizations — military conflict at different levels, from global to a regional war. This can end either in establishing a new balance among the countries at war, or in complete destruction of the losing civilization, its removal from the historical stage or incorporation of its remnants into the winning civilization (as the Persian civilization was included in the Islamic one, or as happened after the demise of ancient American cultures);

• standoff and antagonism of civilization in the geo-civilizational space, which may last for centuries, occasionally flaring up as open (military) conflict.

Let us go back to the compatible format of interaction and note the importance of dialog in the system of interactions between civilizations. The "compatibility" of this format means that the dialog of civilizations in its different aspects gradually expands understanding between civilizations, promotes a decline in hostility, and increases tolerance and readiness for cooperation. Interactions between Eurasian and Japanese civilizations after World War II can serve as an example of this.

Civilizations resort to the format of "cooperation of civilizations" to address their common problems and achieve mutual profitability: in case of military conflict (for example the cooperation between Eurasian and North American civilizations and some Western European nations during World War II), to address common strategic goals (e.g. non-proliferation of nuclear weapons), during environmental disasters, etc. Such cooperation is achieved through the UN and other international organizations.

Partnership is the highest format of long-term stable, mutually beneficial cooperation between civilizations if they have a broad sphere of common interests, which does not exclude their differences on some matters.

What is the role of dialog between civilizations relative to other interaction formats?

A dialog serves to weaken the sociocultural grounds for a clash between civilizations in any manifestation – from wars to international terrorism. It helps to understand the nature of the other civilization better, to see the common interests and basic values of all local civilizations in the context of global civilization, promotes the development of a culture of peace that opposes the cult of war. A dialog of civilizations is, at this time, the most important instrument for preventing clashes between them, and the spreading epidemic of terrorism.

Dialog also helps to define opposition of civilizations arising from differences in their value systems, lack of understanding of any culture and civilization, their diversity that goes into creating the multi-colored palette of global civilization and adds to its vitality, the ability to adapt to radical change both in the external environment and in the internal structure of each civilization, combining heredity and variability. The dialog counterbalances the ideas of universality of any one civilization, the desires of some politicians and public figures to impose its values on the whole world, ignoring and suppressing the unique features of all other civilizations (which was typical of Western European civilization at the time of its dominance, and is typical of North American civilization at present).

The dialog of civilizations is a necessary condition for cooperation between them, addressing a growing wave of global problems that no single local civilization, no matter how powerful, can tackle on its own, and that require the combined efforts of the whole human race.

Dialog can become the foundation for the highest form of interaction of civilizations: their partnership to address global problems. Partnership assumes a deeper degree of mutual understanding and trust between civilizations, stability of a broad sphere of interconnections, combination of potentials and creation of common institutions required to solve a global problems, which, however, does not imply that one civilization is absorbed by another, or that their differences and distinctions disappear. Consistent, sustainable development of global civilization as a unified system, where the degree of the shifting out of alignment and polarization of local civilizations has reached a critical level, can be achieved only through a dialog and partnership of civilizations, through the creation of a common regulation mechanism based on economics and international law. The latter should provide, among other things, for operations of three global foundations: ecological, technological and sociocultural, funded by excess profits of multinationals and governments in the form of global resource revenues, ecological revenues and financial quasi-revenues. Development of a global or regional partnership of civilizations will require them to establish joint institutions. The experience of the European Union as a civilizational unity attests to this. The majority of citizens of nation states who defended their sovereignty and independence against the threat of losing their sociocultural identity, economic independence and independence as a state are not taking these moves positively.

The main trend of development of the compatible interaction of civilizations in modern times would be a transition from confrontation to dialog, cooperation and partnership. This process is neither consistent nor linear. In periods of transition – when historical eras, global civilizations and balances of power and world order change – it is inevitable that contradictions will come to a head and the threat of a clash between civilizations increase. This is the situation we are facing in the early decades of the 21st century, as historical supercycles change and global civilizations replace each other. However, as early as the second half of this century, we can expect a clearer manifestation of the main trend of progress – through dialog to cooperation and partnership of civilizations. This is an historical imperative, because without it not only is global compatible development impossible, but also the survival of humanity.

4.3. Compatibility of Theology and Science. Humility and Creativity

The theory of compatibility presumes the joint development of theology and science.[238] This union is defined by mutual understanding and mutual respect of science and theology, united by the mutual principle of humility, which defines the start and progress of a dialog.

Accumulation of new knowledge through science has become the fascination of the modern world. The amount of new (scientific) information is doubling every 30 months. The majority of scientists today are ready to admit that they will never reach an "end" to their education, while others are even talking of other sources of truth — philosophy and especially theology — as important components for understanding reality. This new type of humility began to find expression in the scientific community as the realization of the infinity of God's creation and the insignificance of our habitat began to set in. We can reach an understanding of the true boundless infinity of the divine intelligence through humility. Humility can help us to defeat the sin of pride and intolerance, avoiding religious clashes. Humility promotes research and progress in religion. This is a new type of humility, a new realization of an infinite, all-embracing creative spirit. It may be useful to consider the theology of humility as a set of certain key principles.

First: it recognizes that there are many mysteries that we will never resolve, because we can only perceive (and conceive of) a small part of reality, and that we may not be the only spiritual beings in the visible and invisible cosmos.

Second: this theology tells us that many miraculous concepts of God from different civilizations and cultures are only a tiny fraction of the possible ways humans can perceive and understand God. This understanding may expand by a factor of hundreds as a result of new research by scientists.

Third: the theology of humility implies enthusiasm for absorbing new spiritual information and new concepts, new ways of looking at things. It sees the desire to obtain new knowledge and freedom of research as important.

---

[238] С.Л. Франк Религия и наука. М.: Библиотека «Вехи», 2002.

Fourth: the theology of humility (the principle of openness to the achievements of science) welcomes any opportunities for obtaining new spiritual information through scientific research in both physical and spiritual realms. It also attempts to explore the spiritual laws that treat of the benefits of giving thanks, forgiveness, etc.

Fifth: the theology of humility is based on humility before God. Discoveries about the past of the Universe and its creator can lead us to a sense of wonder and gratitude.

The Center for Theology of Humility pursues two main goals: support for various research programs and creating a circle, a community of well-known and respected scientists and theologians interested in seeing progress in the process of collecting spiritual information. Scientific research today can have a great significance for theology. This section presents views of scientists engaged in the story of the so-called humility approach. This new approach represents efforts aimed at exploring the ways science can become involved in resolving theological and religious issues. The humility approach does not attempt to put down other, more traditional directions in theology. It also does not try to make a religion out of theology. This approach acknowledges that science provides fundamental knowledge about the nature of reality, and some of this knowledge may be relevant for theology, although biologist Stephen Jay Gould wrote a whole book to explain that science and religion are equal, but different realms of knowledge, representing separate and non-overlapping magesteria.

The humility approach simply gives us hope that the scientific study of reality and a spiritual quest for a deeper understanding may be complementary, possibly joining in a cooperative format, or, better yet, in a partnership format. This hope can help us avoid the dreary illusion of an unbridgeable gap between the scientific study of the universe and the need for a full, meaningful life, and, consequently, the uncomfortable feeling that one needs to choose between either nihilistic postmodernism or scientism. In fact, religion can be a friend of scientific and humanities cognition in the spirit of Enlightenment-style search for truth, as well as helping this cognition to evaluate the rich context of human culture and understand the limitations of our knowledge. Combining different aspects of intellectual life is in itself one of the reasons for having an interest in both science and religion.

Science is developing in a relatively clear direction of progress. We can expect with a very high probability that in another decade, physics of solids, cellular biology, neurology, computer science, astronomy, particle physics and other sciences will be better informed than they are today. This progress is brought about by global causes. It is a consequence of work by millions of scientists representing different cultures and different religions. Information expands and is accumulated; scientists reach general agreements on the basis of this information. Some philosophers, sociologists and other culture theorists have no wish to agree with each other. However, a majority still reach a consensus. Evidence of overall scientific progress in various fields is too obvious to deny. The experience of modern science is very different from that of religion. As Philip Brown once said[239]: "Science can only explain how something was created; religion can explain why." On the whole, science does not have canons in the sense religion does. Scientists have revised great discoveries of the past many times over. However, a majority of these efforts are of a very narrow, limited interest for active scientists. The main purpose of science is to conduct active research designed to make new discoveries, to search for new data. This makes it substantially different from religious experience, which is largely focused on tradition. The theology of humility recognizes the importance of a scientific explanation of the world and strives to create opportunities for the expansion and interpretation of results of new scientific research that has a spiritual significance.

The idea that religion will disappear in a world[240] dominated by super-intelligence has no basis in science. In effect, many scientific discoveries, especially those from the realm of physics can, on the contrary, support the idea of a great mind responsible for creating the Cosmos. Who can explore all the mysteries of modern theories such as the super-strings theory and remain untouched by the depth of reality that has puzzled the most creative and brilliant scientists and mathematicians of our time? The view of reality as a completely random coincidence is erroneous, as is the idea that the intellect has no connection to religion, like, for example, left and right halves of the human brain. Religion in the broadest possible sense is a form of a respectful response of man or society to manifestations of infinite and higher reality, to which we owe the valuable gift of life.

Let us quote Albert Einstein's dictum on compatibility of science and religion: "Religion is an age-old attempt by humanity to get a clear and full understanding of super-personal values and goals and expand their role."[241]

---

[239] At a General Synod of the Church of England. Source: BBC News, news.bbc.co.uk/1/hi/uk/8511951.stm.

[240] Р.А. Штаинзальц Наука и религия: взаимоотношения. М., 2001.

[241] Einstein, A. Einstein about Religion. (Russian translation) Эйнштейн А. Эйнштейн о

262

If religion and science are perceived in accordance with this dictum, conflict between them would be impossible. In science one can only reassure oneself of what is, but not of what should be. Religion, conversely, deals only with evaluations of human thoughts and actions; it cannot reasonably talk of facts and relationships between them. In this interpretation, famous past conflicts between religion and science will be attributed to the inability to understand the situation described.

Conflict arises in connection with religious circles' insistence that everything written in the Bible is absolutely and literally true. This means that religion is invading the realm of science.[242] This was precisely what was happening when religion fought the theories of Galileo and Darwin. For their part, scientists have often made attempts to carry out a fundamental evaluation of human values and goals using the scientific method, thereby putting themselves into opposition to religion. Although the realms of religion and science themselves are clearly demarcated, they have very strong links and mutual dependence. Religion may serve its purpose by defining goals, and yet it has learned from science, in the broadest sense, which means will help it reach the goals it has set. At the same time, science can be developed only by those who completely subscribe to the quest for truth and understanding. This quest, however, has its roots in the realm of religion. This is why we put the theological-religious and cultural-worldview at the fifth and sixth levels of compatibility respectively, and scientific-cognition-spiritual at the seventh level of societal development. The belief that it is possible that rules applicable to the material world are rational, i.e. accessible to reason, also belongs to the same level. Now we cannot imagine a true scientist without this profound faith. This situation can be expressed by Einstein's maxim: "Science without religion is lame, religion without science is blind."

The purpose of science is to establish the general principles that define interconnections between objects and events in space and time. These rules, or laws of nature, need to be absolutely universally applicable (need to have validity), but it requires no proof. It is essentially a program, and the belief that it is correct, in principle, is based on anecdotal evidence that confirms it. However, we would hardly be able to find anyone who would deny these pieces of evidence or claim they are but self-deception. The fact that we can use these laws to predict certain phenomena with great precision and

---

религии. М.: Альпина нон-фикшн, 2011.
[242] С.Л. Франк Религия и наука. М.: Библиотека «Вехи», 2002.

certainty is deeply embedded in modern man's consciousness, even if he is not particularly aware of the content of these laws. He only needs to recall that one can calculate the movements of planets in the Solar System in advance with great precision based on several simple laws. In a similar way, although with less precision, one can calculate in advance how an electric motor is going to operate, or a gear clutch, or a radio transmission system, or other contemporary designs.

Certainly, the doctrine of God as a person interfering in natural phenomena can never be rejected by science, because this doctrine can always find refuge in areas scientific knowledge cannot yet penetrate. In their crusade for the ethical good, teachers of religion probably must have the courage to forgo the doctrine of God as a person, i.e. reject this source of fear and hope that put all-embracing power in the hands of clergy. In their writings, they will have to devote themselves to the forces capable of cultivating the Divine, Truth and Beauty in the human race itself. This is certainly a much more difficult and challenging, but also an incomparably more dignified goal.

If the purpose of religion is to free humanity, as much as possible, from the servitude of egocentric drives, desires and fears, scientific thinking can help religion in one other respect. Science owes its most impressive achievements to the strong urge to unify variety from a rational perspective. "Through understanding, man achieves a very important release from the fetters of personal hopes and desires, and thereby becomes convinced of the modest place of the human brain vis-à-vis the greatness of reason fulfilled in existence, which, in all its infinite depth, is not accessible to man. Science not only clears religious urges from the dross of anthropomorphism, but also contributes to the religious vivification of our understanding of life."[243]

Can we regard theology as a science? We know that science relies on a foundation of observation and experiment. Although formulating a theoretical hypothesis can be the result of considering a certain guiding principle, created on the basis of such concepts as simplicity, economy or symmetry, the ultimate judge is still not aesthetics, but an experiment. The power of philosophic reasoning about the way the world "should" be as a matter of personal preference or personal invention always must yield to factual evidence. The final authority in matters of theology is the Bible or another set of holy scriptures (Quran, Sri Brahma-Samhita, Mahabharata). Holy scriptures, which are believed to be the word of God, are assumed to

---

[243] С.Л. Франк Религия и наука. М.: Библиотека «Вехи», 2002.

be an immutable, unassailable argument in all matters. If someone views theology in this way, then it indeed has little in common with science. Science does not acknowledge any authority from the past. However, this is not the only possible approach to theology. There is another one, more like the positions of modern science. It has come to be known as the theology of humility. It chooses, as its starting point of discourse, the human experience of the world and life (i.e. the same basis as used in science) rather than the Bible. It asks if there is any evidence of the existence of God in life, and if so, what kind of God. The theology of humility asks the question: can our entire experience be clearer and easier to understand in light of the hypothesis that God exists? Just like science, this kind of theology is modest in the sense that it is ready to accept an understanding of God that will be compatible with actual evidence and experiments. Because the overall amount of knowledge and evidence is growing, the understanding of God is expanding and becoming richer. Just like science, the theology of humility is making advances. No other field of knowledge is currently growing at the same fast pace as science, and one can expect that the theology of humility will be especially compatible with it, evaluating every new discovery from the perspective of its usefulness for expanding our understanding of God in his relationships with the created universe.

The majority of scientists currently believe that the Universe was created as a result of an explosion called the Big Bang. At first, we see that the Universe is still expanding, and we understand this as a consequence of the original explosion. At least, that's how the widely accepted interpretation goes. And yet, there is another possible explanation. A competing theory says that new matter is continuously being created in space. As all matter is moving, the space it vacates is constantly filled by newly-created matter. This way, the overall picture does not change over time, and yet, there never was an original explosion in this picture. This theory of a constant state competes with the Big Bang theory. It would have been just as widely accepted, if new evidence had not been discovered in the course of the development of science.

The Big Bang Theory claims that the original state of the Universe[244] was extremely hot, and the explosion, the "Bang," went off with a very powerful flash. This theory also claims that fragments of this primordial core must still be somewhere in the Universe, and their radiation was recently discovered. Or at least it has all the parameters that were expected

---

[244] В.Н. Демин Тайны Вселенной. М.: Наука, 1998.

of it. But there certainly are different sources of radiation. One can demonstrate that, just as expansion of the Universe is not a conclusive proof of the Big Bang theory, this form of radiation per se is not conclusive proof of the existence of these fragments. Rather, it reinforces the arguments for this theory. We can explain the Big Bang with the aid of a quantum fluctuation, but why does it have to be a quantum fluctuation? Why are we explaining this process through quantum physics, and not some other kind of physics? We can invent imaginary worlds with laws of physics different from those operating in our world. Science fiction does this all the time. Where would quantum physics come from in these very different worlds? Are we not going to need God, who created the laws of physics first; God, who selected the laws under which this world (and, possibly, other worlds) exists in a compatible manner.

In a way, this separates God from creation of the Universe. Instead of creating the world and the Universe directly, he created laws, the natural consequences of which eventually became the reason for the emergence of the Universe. Therefore, the ultimate responsibility for existence of this world is still in the hands of God – the creator of "natural" laws. This line of argumentation reflects the fact that we live in this world by some compatible laws: this world can be understood by reason. But it could have been very different. It is easy enough to imagine a world that is completely chaotic and incompatible. Maybe we should consider the source of this cognizability? Are not cognizability and evident coordination between laws in themselves a manifestation of the existence of God? The Big Bang must have had specific coordinates in Space, and its fragments should have filled the entire remaining space. But all was completely different with the Big Bang. It is not just that all matter was initially concentrated in a single point; all space was also contained within a point. There was no space around the Big Bang.[245] In fact, scientists believe that Big Bang was the beginning not only of the content of the Universe, but also of Space itself.

Why do we need to say that God created the universe? This only raises the next question: the question about who created God. Herein lies an incorrect understanding of our use of the word "God." God is a subject without existence. It is important that God is the source of everything in existence. God is the name we give everything that is responsible for existence of objects, including us. Therefore, the question the theology of humility poses is not "Is there a God?" but "Can we say something

---

[245] Большие проблемы большого взрыва // Истоки. 1999. № 1.

meaningful about God, the source of all existence, and if we can, what is it we can say?" More specifically, can we think of him as someone conscious or personal? Are we of any interest to him, or is "he" just some mindless inanimate power (the urge to have a better world)?

One of the reasons many believers refuse to accept that God did not exist before the Big Bang is that, from their perspective, this would mean that God is also a creation. How could God create himself? The problem, once again, is that our understanding of God is too small, too limited. We add to this error the mistake of thinking of God as an object subject to limitations of space and time: this point of view presumes that God exists in time. God can be in time, as we interact with him during prayer. However, God is outside time as well – he transcends time. How these two things can be compatible, we do not know. One of the reasons for humility in the kind of theology we are discussing is that God is everything we are, and also something greater than that. We must be constantly wary of having too small, too limited ideas of God, which are in our likeness. In his book *The First Three Minutes*, Steven Weinberg made some fairly bleak assumptions that if we were to travel at the speed of 300,000 kilometers per second, we would take 12 billion years to reach the farthest reaches of Space. Should we believe that God created this kind of Universe especially as a house for life? There are 100 billion stars in the Milky Way Galaxy, with several planets rotating around a significant number of those stars. Can one seriously consider the existence of life on one of them as a matter of any significance? Weinberg reached the conclusion that the Universe had no meaning, and life was only an accidental product without any significance. The theology of humility cannot ignore all this. We must answer the question: "Is the type of Universe painted by modern astronomy really as incompatible as a 'house for life' as it might appear?"

At first blush, our world seems very hostile to life, but if we observe more closely, we can see that it is quite compatible with allowing life to emerge and then supporting it. So what would be the answer to this mysterious compatibility of the Universe and life? There are three main alternative explanations. The first is to rely on science and assume that sooner or later there will be a scientific explanation for all these facts. The second is to agree that our Universe is not the only one out there.

The third alternative is simply to accept that the Universe is creation: it was created especially for life, and its creator is God.

The theology of humility gives us hope that the Universe conceals within itself compatible keys to understanding God. If God takes a personal interest in every man, this can only augment the realization of our own significance. In addition, God has worked for many centuries, through evolution, to bring us into this world. This is certainly proof of his foresight and patience. This gives us a new perspective on our own concerns about the aspects of life that do not play out the way we would like them to.

There are certain patterns to the development of the universe: it is compatible. It is beautiful: symmetry gives us a sense of harmony. A set of simple tools gives life to the endless variety of things that are. The theology of humility strives to understand what this can give us for understanding the workings of God's mind. The physical universe is not the only place in which we can find evidence of the existence of God. We must pay most of our attention to the psychic, rather than physical, world, to the world where God is within us, not outside us, to find a personal connection with Him based on love. The theology of humility in its essence is close to psychology, and we must use it to explore both compatibility of life and consciousness, and the nature of prayer.

The propensity to be religious lies at the very centre of the human mind. From Karl Jung's perspective, a well-thought through religion is a sign of a psychologically mature man; this is one of the goals he should be pursuing actively. The psychology of religion is a very rich source of information for the theology of humility. Special attention should be paid apparently to the search for potential connections and compatibility of interaction between religious archetypes and the moral sense, on the one hand, and genetically determined behavior, which evolution shapes by way of natural selection, on the other.

Religion strives to give man the fullest possible life it can. Strange though it may sound, it is weakly associated with prosperity — power, glory, money and influence. It is all about things less obvious: the need to give more than one takes, the need to forgive, rather than take revenge, the need to love one's enemies, and not fight them. If the theology of humility presumes to be a science, it must look for arguments not only supporting the idea of the existence of God. It must consider all evidence, regardless of whether it supports the hypothesis of the existence of God or contradicts it. In other words, the theology of humility must pay attention to the issues of evil and suffering, but it must not strive to give a final answer to the question of their origin. At least, it must express assumptions about possible answers, which must convince us that God is not necessarily blind or irrational if there is evil in the world. God is not going to leave us alone in our suffering, but is sharing this suffering with us with the aid of his Son.

These are just some components of an approach that could demonstrate that suffering and the presence of evil in the world do not contradict the hypothesis of the presence of God (and whether this presence is compatible?), as it may appear initially.

Even if the theology of humility is based on the principle of data exploration, rather than on strictly following the authority of the Bible, this doesn't mean that it must ignore the words of the Holy Scripture. Nobody is assuming that he will discover everything himself. We are basing our achievements on the experience of earlier generations. The Bible is a store of experience received by spiritual people of previous generations that it would be stupid to ignore. Modern science also rests on the experience of scientists of past generations. Today's' experiments are based on achievements of the past. Science accumulates knowledge. Theology can do the same. A record of changing ideas of God over centuries placed in chronological order reveals certain general development trends.

Theology, like science, is constantly developing and progressing. This goes against the traditional concept of theology as something static, carved in stone and based on the immutable Bible. The Bible itself shows very well that this is not so. Quite possibly, it will not be a mistake to say that concepts of God have changed as much as have perceptions about the structure of the world, which have been affected by science. Almost no one would want to revert to old ideas of God, just as nobody would want to accept the tenets of the science of the past. Our ideas about God may be incorrect; they are changing, they are open to correction and updates in light of new experience, and this is the way it will always be. The fact that the theology of humility, like science, is always in a state of change, should not be perceived as a sign of indecisiveness and weakness, for therein lies its strength. This openness of consciousness makes it possible to meet inevitable future changes and new issues. After all, theology and science should not be very different, as most people think.

Modern science can and must be an ally on our spiritual journey. Furthermore, this can be achieved with the help of scientific discoveries. Knowledge of the Universe[246] is also the highest degree of knowledge about its creator. The Greek word denoting humility and resignation in the context of the New Testament, denotes humility with regard to one's own opinion and meekness in one's achievement, and resignation in one's achievement. This humility is theologically based on our recognition of the

---

[246] Klecek, J., Jakes, P. The Universe and Earth. Prague: Artija, 1986.

fact that God is unfathomable and limitless. The mystery and the inevitable depth of the Universe lie at the bottom of reality. They are signs that nature is primarily a creation of God, even if he will never be understood (brought into material compatibility with science), will always be a mystery of the highest order. Theological discourse of western monotheistic religions – Judaism, Christianity and Islam – has spent centuries emphasizing the mystery of God in holy scriptures, traditions, discourse and experience. Religion and science must work together in a creative union (in an open form of dialog and partnership), to expand our knowledge of God, while at the same time understanding and accepting the inevitable incompleteness and error of this knowledge. Of particular interest is a closer combination of life and science, when scientific research begins to show the way for spiritual development, and spirituality suggests the direction to science. The very fact of the existence of the Universe, no matter how structured or infinite, is the best evidence of the existence of God, at least from the point of view of philosophical theology.

We are starting from the theology of creation, in which the Universe will be rational and ruled by cause and effect, making it accessible to scientific analysis. From here we step into the realm of science in which Einstein's general theory of relativity, and the principles of homogeneity and isotropicity of the Universe give us a time-and-space picture of the expansion of that Universe, starting from the primordial singularity $t = 0$. At the same time, observations by Edwin Hubble in 1920 and recent results of the COBE satellite confirm that the Universe is expanding and can be tracked to the original state at $t = 0$. The important thing here is that the discovery $t = 0$ serves as an indirect confirmation of theological belief in God the creator.

The standard Big Bang theory raises another question: the anthropic principle. Christian theology claims that not only did God create the Universe out of nothing, but also that he supports its existence every moment, but that God is doing this for a specific purpose: to create a being capable of self-aware, intentional and moral activity, who can understand God and establish a compatible contact with Him. Is there anything in the realm of science that would match these ideas of intentional creation by God?

Models similar to the inflation theory or quantum cosmology offer a natural explanation of the anthropic principle without using concepts of

God as the Creator of the Universe:[247] instead of this, they assume the existence of multiple universes, each of which has its own laws of nature. The inflation theory presumes that there are countless areas of a single mega-Universe, one of which areas is our Universe. Quantum cosmology provides for the infinite creation of "baby" universes similar to ours. In any case, the matter of "adjusting" the constants of our Universe appears settled: we merely live in our specific Universe, which is suitable for the existence of biological life forms. But do these theories discard the anthropic principle? For our purposes, we note that there is a certain compatible connection between the special meaning of God's creation and a scientific discussion about the features of such a possible creation, e.g. about the values of physical constants, laws of nature, etc. Clearly, if we want to use the argument of a divine concept and creation in the context of science, it must shape the ideas of theological meaning of creation and its possibility. These facts are indicative of the need for a "dialogue between science and religion." It is also important to note how the model of explanation would define the format of the question: we must very clearly understand our own theological and scientific requirements, entering into this dialogue and the subsequent cooperation on the growth of truths. Compatibility of knowledge makes it possible to see the overall movement of life everywhere, and we can finally understand its direction, as well as our place in the process of life of the Universe.

Today, the majority know the principles of identifying non-scientific factors, including religious and philosophical concepts of space, time and causality. The roots of Einstein's ideas on these factors go back to Spinoza's theory, Schrödinger's ideas go back to Hinduism, Max Planck's ideas are based on Protestantism, while Niels Bohr is ultimately based on Kierkegaard (he even picked the Yin-Yang symbol as his family arms), etc. Their works can be seen as both an analysis of modern scientific data and as a philosophy of nature, reflecting, in turn, certain theological ideas of God and nature, which are expressed in the language of mathematics and take into consideration the irremovable limitation of empirical data. As for the criterion of picking theories, scientists are increasingly finding that arguments given by researchers to support a certain theory are miraculously compatible with those used by theologians when choosing different versions of God's attitude to creation. A good example is a comparison of two possible directions of the development of quantum cosmology. In Roger

---

[247] Е.П. Левитан Эволюционирующая Вселенная. М.: Просвещение, 1993.

Penros' approach, the Universe emerges as a result of quantum field fluctuations in superspace. However, from Hawking's perspective, the Universe emerged as a result of the match of three geometries in quantum superspace, which resulted in creating a four-dimensional space and time continuum. In fact, many scientists have indicated that Penros' approach does not suit them because of its controversial question: which part of the infinite superspace is the beginning of this model, rather than another part or several parts? The Hawking model avoids this problem, and on the strength of this seems preferable. Immanuel Kant said it best: only two things can force joy and adulation: the starry sky above us and the moral law within us.

When we take into account not only the broad theological context, but also the uncompromising requirements of empirical science and verifiable thought constructs, there will be forms of progress in religion that will reflect the "humility approach," which is essentially a radical openness of our ideas to new discoveries and concepts of the Universe obtained by natural sciences. We think it is appropriate to quote here the words of His Holiness Patriarch Kirill about the compatibility of science and religion: "A scientist, just like any man, is destined to seek the truth... There are truths even more profound – moral truths, truths about our goals, our destiny and our responsibility... unlike matter, which always obeys the laws set for it, we, people, have freedom of choice. We decide on our own whether we should obey the moral law or not. And our temporary and eternal happiness, the future of our country, and the future of science depend on whether we want to follow this moral law or not."[248] This is further corroborated by Einstein's dictum: "Science can be created only by those who are utterly committed to searching for truth and understanding. However, the source of this feeling comes originally from religion. I cannot imagine a true scientist who would not firmly believe in this."[249] Compatibility may well be the meaning of our life.

---

[248] Слово Святейшего Патриарха Кирилла. Национальный исследовательский ядерный университет. МИТ. March 4, 2010.
[249] Einstein, A. Einstein About Religion. (Russian translation) Эйнштейн А. Эйнштейн о религии. М.: Альпина нон-фикшн, 2011.

NOTES

1.   Агафонов К.П. Единство физической картины мира. Неоклассическая концепция. М.: Изд-во ЛКИ, 2007.

2.   Adizes I.K. Mastering Change. Quoted from the Russian edition: Адизес И.К. Управляя изменениями М.: Питер, 2011.

3.   Айзек Г.Ю. Психология паранормального. М.: Эксмо, 2005.

4.   Амиров Ю.Д. Основы конструирования: Творчество – стандартизация – экономика: справочное пособие. М.: Изд-во стандартов, 1991.

5.   Anderson B. Imagined Communities: Reflections on the Origins and Spread of Nationalism. (Revised and extended ed.) London: Verso, 1991.

6.   Анисимов А. Статистика кризиса и его механизм в России // Проблемы теории и практики управления. 1996. № 6. PP. 106–112.

7.   Анцупов А.Я., Баклановский С.В. Конфликтология в схемах и комментариях . 2-е изд., перераб. СПб.: Питер, 2009.

8.   Апорович А.Ф. Проектирование радиотехнических систем: Учеб. пособие. Минск: Высш. шк., 1988.

9.   Arendt, H. Vita activa, or On Active Life. Quoted from the Russian edition: Арендт Х. Vita activa, или О деятельной жизни. СПб.: Алетейя, 2000.

10.   Астапенко Д.Ю. Системный анализ и синтез единого инфокоммуникационного поля на базе космических технологий: Автореф. ... канд. техн. наук. М.: Московская академия рынка труда и информационных технологий, 2006.

11.   Афанасьев В.Г. Системность и общество. М.: Политиздат,

12.   Байтурганов Х.Н. Основы теории единого информационного поля. СПб., 1998.

13.   Баньковская С.П. Другой как элементарное понятие социальной онтологии // Социологическое обозрение. 2007. № 1. PP. 75–86.

14.   Барзилович Е.Ю., Воскобоев В.Ф. Эксплуатация авиационных систем по состоянию: (элементы теории). М.: Транспорт, 1981.

15.   Барынин В.А. Теория единого первичного поля и его локальных образований: новейшая концепция фундаментальной физики. М.: Спутник+, 2008.

16.   Bateson G. Mind and Nature: A Necessary Unity. NYC: Hampton Press, 1979.

17.   Berger P, Luckmann T. The Social Construction of Reality: A Treatise in the Sociology of Knowledge. New York: Anchor Books, 1966. Quoted from the Russian edition: Бергер П., Лукман Т. Социальное конструирование реальности: Трактат по социологии знания. М.: Медиум, 1995. PP. 140 – 141.

18.   Березина Т.Н. Резервные возможности человека. М.: Когико-Центр, 2000.

19.   Берестова Т.Ф. Культура – Искусство – Образование – единство теории и практики. Челябинск, 2010.

20.   Бибихин В.В. Мир. СПб., 2007.

21.   Beer S. Management Science. London: Aldus, 1967.

22.   Блауберг И.В. Проблемы методологии системного исследования. М.: Мысль, 1970.

23.   Roger D. Blackwell, Paul W. Miniard, James F. Engel. Consumer Behaviour. 10th Edition. SW College Pub., 2005.

24.   Baudrillard J. La Societe de consommation: Paris, 1970.

25.   Большие проблемы большого взрыва // Истоки. 1999. № 1.

26.   Бондаренко О.Я. Сборник докладов по теории и философии единого поля. Бишкек, 2000.

27.   Бондаренко О.Я. Философия Единства. Бишкек, 2000.

28.   Braudel, F. Material Civilization, Economics and Capitalism. Quoted from Russian edition: Бродель Ф.М. Материальная цивилизация, экономика и капитализм. XV– XVIII вв. Т. 3: Время мира. М.: Прогресс, 1992.

29.   Bourdieu, P. Peractical Reason: On the Theory of Action: Stanford University Press, 1996. Quoted from Russian edition: М.: Бурдье П. Практический смысл. Институт экспериментальной социологии; СПб.: Алетейя, 2001. P. 268.

30.   Baron R., Richardson D. Aggression. NYC: Plenum Press, 1994.

31.   Вальков В.М., Вершин В.Е. Автоматизированные системы управления технологическими процессами. Л.: Политехника, 1992.

32.   Weber M. Basic Concepts in Sociology. Quoted from the Russian edition: Вебер М. Основные социологические понятия // Избранные произведения. М.: Прогресс, 1990. PP. 639–640.

33.   Верищагин Д.С. Параллельные миры восприятия. СПб.: Афина, 2009.

34.   Виссарионов А. Уроки кризиса // Экономист. 1999. № 2. PP. 15–22.

35.   Владимиров Б. Будет ли найден путь из кризиса? // Бизнес и банки. 1998. # 38–39.

36.   Владиславлев А.П. Идентичность и культурное многообразие: можно ли ими управлять. М., 2007.

37.   Воронин Ю. Ориентиры выхода из экономического кризиса // Экономист. 2001. # 5. PP. 11–21.

38.   Гаспаров М.Л. Историзм, массовая культура и наш завтрашний день // Вестник истории, литературы, искусства. Т. 1. М., 2005.

39.   Гель П.П., Иванов-Есипович Н.К. Конструирование и микроминиатюризация радиоэлектронной аппаратуры. Л.: Энергоатомиздат, 1984.

40.   Giddens A. The Constitution of Society. Cambridge: Polity, 1984. Quoted from the Russian edition: Гидденс Э. Устроение общества. М., 2005. PP. 45–46.

41.   Гиренок Ф.И. Удовольствие мыслить иначе. М., 2008.

42.   Гиттис Э.И., Данилович Г.А., Самойленко В.Н. Техническая кибернетика. М.: Сов. радио, 1969.

43.   Гнедов Г.М. Об актуальности и проблеме создания теории технической совместимости. Л.: Ленингр. электротехн. ин-т, 1979.

44.   Гозман Л.Я. Психология эмоциональных отношений. М.: Изд-во МГУ, 1987.

45.   Голод С.И. Стабильность семьи: социологический и демографический аспекты / Под ред. Г.М. Романенковой. Л.: Наука, 1984.

46.   Горбов Ф.Д., Новиков М.А. Краткий психологический словарь-хрестоматия. М.: Наука, 1974.

47.   Горбов Ф.Д., Лебедев В.И. Психоневрологические аспекты труда операторов. М.: Медицина, 1985.

48.   Горелик А.Л., Скрипкин В.А. Построение систем распознания. М.: Сов. Радио, 1974.

49.   Горохов В.А., Полковский И.М., Стыцько В.П. Комплексная миниатюризация в электросвязи. М.: Радио и связь, 1987.

50.   ГОСТ 22315-77. Средства агрегатные информационно-измерительных систем. Общие положения. М.: Изд-во стандартов, 1977.

51.   ГОСТ 27.002-89. Надежность в технике. Термины и определения. М.: Изд-во стандартов, 1989.

52.   Гребенников И.В. Основы семейной жизни. М.: Просвещение, 1991.

53.   Гудков Л.Д., Дубин Б.В. Институциональные дефициты как проблема постсоветского общества // Мониторинг общественного мнения: экономические и социальные перемены. 2003. # 3 (65).

54.   Goodman N. Ways of Worldmaking. Indianapolis: Hackett, 1978.

55.   Гурвич Н.С. Защита электронных вычислительных машин от внешних помех. М.: Энергия, 1975.

56.   Гуткин Л.С. Проектирование радиосистем и радиоустройств. М.: Радио и связь, 1986.

57.   Давыдов В.М., Боровиков А.В., Теперман В.А. Локальные кризисы или мировой феномен // ЭКО. 1999. № 7.

58.   Давыдов В.М., Ладанов И.Д. Психологическая совместимость в трудовых коллективах. М., 1985.

59.   Данилевский Н.Я. Россия и Европа. М., 1991.

60.	Демин В.Н. Тайны Вселенной. М.: Наука, 1998.

61.	Deming W.E. New Economics. Cambridge: MIT Press, 2000.

62.	Демокрит. Материалисты Древней Греции / Под ред. М.А. Дынника. М.: Изд-во полит. лит.,1955.

63.	Денисов А.А. Мифы теории относительности. Вильнюс: ГСП-5, 1989.

64.	Gerard R. Change Your DNA, Change Your Life! Binghamton: Oughten House Foundation Inc., 2000.

65.	DiMaggio P. Culture and Economy. Quoted from the Russian edition: // Западная экономическая социология. М.: РОССПЭН, 2004. P. 489.

66.	Дмитриев А.К. Распознание отказов в системах электроавтоматики. Л.: Энергоатомиздат, 1983.

67.	Дружинин В.В., Еонторов Д.С. Проблемы системологии (проблемы теории сложных систем). М.: Сов. радио, 1976.

68.	Дубко В.Г. Проблемы объединения наук. СПб., 2010.

69.	Евланников В.П. От последней ступени к Вознесению (теория единого поля). М.: Амрита-Русь, 2009.

70.	Емельянов С.М. Практикум по конфликтологии. СПб.: Питер, 2009.

71.	Ершов П.М. Потребности человека. М.: Мысль, 1990.

72.	General Synod of the Church of England. Source: BBC News, news.bbc.co.uk/1/hi/uk/8511951.stm.

73.	Иванов В.И., Чешев В.В. Становление и развитие технических наук. Л.: Наука, 1977.

74.   Ивин А., Никифорович А. Словарь по логике. М.: Владос, 1998.

75.   Илюхина Н.И. Теория и философия единого поля. Тула: Гриф и К, 2000.

76.   Каверкин И.Я., Цветков Э.И. Анализ и синтез измерительных систем. Л.: Энергия, 1974.

77.   Кадыров С.К. Всеобщая физическая теория единого поля и решение фундаментальных проблем естествознания. Бишкек: Шам, 2000.

78.   Camus A. The Myth of Sisyphus. Quoted from the Russian edition: Миф о сизифе. Эссе об абсурде. М.: Радуга, 1990. P. 31.

79.   Кандыба В.М. Магия Вселенной и возможности человека. СПб.: Невский проспект, 1998.

80.   Каткова Л.М. Совместимость персонала в организациях. М.: МОСУ, 2002.

81.   Kierulff S. Becoming Psychic. Pompton Plains: Career Press, 2004.

82.   Китов А.И. Психология хозяйственного управления. М.: Профиздат, 1984.

83.   Клейнер Г.Б. Стратегия предприятия. М.: Дело, 2008.

84.   Klecek, J., Jakes, P. The Universe and Earth. Prague: Artija, 1986.

85.   Ковалев С.В. Психология современной семьи. М.: Просвещение, 1988.

86.   Коллектив. Личность. Общение. Словарь социально-психологических понятий / Под ред. Е.С. Кузьмина, В.Е. Семенова. Л.: Лениздат, 1987.

87.   Коломейцев Ю.А. Взаимоотношение в спортивной команде. М.: Физкультура и спорт, 1984.

88.   Колхир К.Ф. Физическое строение мира на основе выбранной модели вакуума. М.: ВО «Агропромиздат», 1991.

89.   Комарчев А.И. Основные постулаты единой теории физики. СПб,: Деан, 2009.

90.   Кондратьев Н.Д. Большие циклы конъюнктуры и теория предвидения. М.: Экономика, 2002.

91.   Kornai J. System Paradigm. Quoted from the Russian edition: Корнаи Я. Системная парадигма // Вопросы экономики. 2002. # 4.

92.   Корсунский М.И. Оптика. Строение атома. Атомное ядро. М.: Наука, 1964.

93.   Костецкий Б.И. Фундаментальная закономерность самоорганизации технических трибосистем: докл. Академии наук УССР // Физико-математические науки. Сер. А. 1989. # 4.

94.   Кочуров М. Г. Влияние личностных особенностей на межличностную совместимость. Киров, 2006.

95.   Краткий психологический словарь / Сост. Л.А. Карпенко; под общ. ред. А.В. Петровского, М.Г. Ярошевского. М.: Политиздат, 1985.

96.   Краткий психологический словарь. М.: Политиздат, 1985.

97.   Кричевский Р.Л. Проблема межличностной совместимости в зарубежной социальной психологии // Вопросы психологии. 1979. # 5.

98.   Кузнецов В. Попытка объяснить российский кризис // Мировая экономика и международные отношения. 1996. # 9. PP. 16–27.

99.   Кузнецов В.Ю. Мир единства. М.: Академпроект, 2010.

100.   Кузык Б.Н., Яковец Ю.В. Цивилизации. М.: Институт экономических стратегий, 2006.

101.   Курбатов В.И. Конфликтология. Ростов н/Д: Феникс, 2007.

102.   Лапко А.В. Непараметрические методы классификации и их применение. Новосибирск: ВО «Наука». Сибирская изд. фирма, 1993.

103.   Лачинов Ю.Н. Ноология и миссиология. М.: Центрополиграф, 2004.

104.   Левитан Е.П. Эволюционирующая Вселенная. М.: Просвещение, 1993.

105.   Леонов А.А., Лебедев В.И. К проблеме психологической совместимости в межпланетном полете // Вопросы философии. 1972. # 9.

106.   Лийк К., Нийт Т. Интимность и взаимоотношения в семье // Человек, общество и жилая среда / Под ред. Ю. Орна, Т. Нийта. Таллин, 1986. PP. 154–163.

107.   Ломов Б.Ф. Методологические и теоретические проблемы психологии. М., 1984.

108.   Лощинов В.И. Информационно-волновая медицина и биология. М.: Аллегро-Пресс, 1998.

109.   Lewis C.S. Out of the Silent Planet. Quoted from the Russian edition: Льюис К.С. Соч.: В 2 т. За пределы Безмолвной планеты. Т. 1. М.: ЛШ, Вече, 1993.

110.   Любимова Н.М. К вопросу о совместимости инфекционных форм. М., 1999.

111. E. McConkey. How the Human Genome Works. Sudbury, MA: Jones & Bartlett Learning, 2004.

112. Максимов Г.Ю. Теоретические основы разработки космических аппаратов. М.: Наука, 1980.

113. Малинова О.Ю. Гражданство и политизация культурных различий // Политические исследования. 2004. # 5.

114. Марков А. Эволюция человека. М.: Аст: Астрель, 2011.

115. Maslow A. Motivation and Personality. 3rd Edition. 1997.

116. Мау В. Политическая природа и уроки финансового кризиса // Вопросы экономики. 1998. # 11. PP. 4–20.

117. Медведев А.В. Элементы теории параметрических систем управления // Актуальные проблемы информатики, прикладной математики и механики. Ч. 3. Информатика: Сб. научн. тр. / Отв. ред. В.В. Шайдуров. Новосибирск – Красноярск, 1996. PP. 87–111.

118. Медведев В.В. Экспериментальная установка для исследования согласованности групповых действий и рационального подбора групп // Вопросы психологии. 1967. № 2. PP. 166–169.

119. Межгосударственный стандарт. Совместимость технических средств электромагнитная (термины и определения). Минск, 1995.

120. Межгосударственный стандарт. Техническая совместимость (термины и определения). ИПК издательство стандартов. Минск, 2003.

121. Методологические проблемы научно-технического прогресса. Новосибирск: Наука, 1987.

122. Методология исследований по инженерной психологии и психологии труда / Под ред. А.А. Крылова. Л.: ЛГУ, 1974. Ч. 1.

123.   Mintzberg, H. Structure in Fives: Designing Effective Organizations: Prentice Hall, 1992.

124.   Михайлов Н.Н. Социализм и разумные потребности личности. М.: Политиздат, 1982.

125.   Морозов В.А. Предприятие и внешняя среда: уровни взаимодействия // Российское предпринимательство. 2012. # 8 (206).

126.   Морозов В.А. Совместимость стилей (ролей) управления организацией // Креативная экономика. 2012. # 7.

127.   Морозов В.А. Формирование конкурентных преимуществ отрасли // Маркетинг. 2011. # 5.

128.   Морозов В.А. Экоуправление развития (территории, сектора экономики, человек). М.: Креативная экономика, 2008.

129.   Мунипов В.М., Зинченко В.П. Эргономика: человекоориентированное проектирование техники, программных средств и среды. М.: Логос, 2001.

130.   Неизвестный Э.И. О синтезе искусств // Вопросы философии. 1989. # 7. PP. 74–75.

131.   Неумывакин И.П. Биоэнергетическая сущность человека. М.: Диля, 2012.

132.   D. North Institutions, Institutional Change and Operation of the Economy. Quoted from the Russian edition: Норт Д. Институты, институциональные изменения и функционирование экономики. М.: Фонд экономической книги «Начала», 1997. PP. 111–112.

133.   Носенков А.А. О методологической концепции теории технической совместимости // Микроэлектронные устройства. Проектирование и технология: Межвуз. сб. / Отв. ред. А.А. Левицкий; КрПИ. Красноярск, 1990. PP. 100–103.

134.   Носенков А.А. Совместимость как первооснова качества техники // Проблемы обеспечения качества изделий в машиностроении: Матер. междунар. научн.-техн. конф. КрПИ. Красноярск, 1994. PP. 423–430.

135.   Носенков А.А., Медведев В.И. Теория технической совместимости как новая дисциплина системного анализа // Вестник САА имени академика М.Ф. Решетнева. Вып. 2. Красноярск, 2001. PP. 231–236.

136.   Носенков А.А. Техническая совместимость: практика, наука, проблемы / Сиб. гос. аэрокосмич. ун-т. Красноярск, 2005.

137.   Носенков А.А., Медведев В.И., Мулин А.М. Совместимость технических систем. Красноярск, 2005.

138.   Обозов Н.Н. Межличностные отношения. Л.: Изд-во ЛГУ, 1979.

139.   Обозов Н.Н., Обозова А.Н. Три подхода к исследованию психологической совместимости // Вопросы психологии. 1981. #6.

140.   Обуховский К. Галактика потребностей. Психология влечений человека. СПб.: Речь, 2003.

141.   Общая психодиагностика / Под ред. А.А. Бодалева, В.В. Столина. М.: Изд-во МГУ, 1987.

142.   Олейник Ю.Н. Исследование уровней совместимости в молодой семье // Психологический журнал. 1986. Т. 7. #2. PP. 59–67.

143.   Ордынская Т.А. Волновая терапия. М.: Эксмо, 2008.

144.   Орлов В.В., Васильева Т.С. Человек, ускорение, научно-технический прогресс. Красноярск: Изд-во Красноярского ун-та, 1989.

145.	Основы инженерной психологии: Учеб. для техн. вузов / Сост. Б.Ф. Ломов, Б.А. Душков, В.Ф. Рубахин и др. М.: Высш. школа, 1989.

146.	Основы социально-психологической теории / Под общ. ред. А.А. Бодалева, А.Н. Сухова. М.: Международная педагогическая академия, 1995.

147.	Павлов В.П. Волновая форма человека: исцеление с помощью мыслеформ. Пенза: Золотое сечение, 2009.

148.	Панов П.В. Институты, идентичности, практики: теоретическая модель политического порядка: Учеб. пособие. М.: РОССПЭН, 2011.

149.	T. Parsons. The Concept of Society: Components and Their Interactions – quoted from the Russian edition: Парсонс Т. Понятие общества: компоненты и их взаимоотношения // THESIS. 1993. # 2.

150.	T. Parsons. The Structure of Social Action. 2nd Edition. Free Press, 1969. Quoted from the Russian edition: Парсонс Т. О структуре социального действия. М.: Академический проект, 2000.

151.	Патрушев С.В. Институционализм в политической науке: Этапы, течения, идеи, проблемы // Институциональная политология: Современный институционализм и политическая трансформация России / Под ред. С.В. Патрушева. М.: ИС РАН, 2006.

152.	Перегудов Ф.И., Тарасенко Ф.П. Основы системного анализа. Томск: Изд-во НТЛ, 1997.

153.	Планк М. Единство физической картины мира. М.: Наука, 1966.

154.	Платонов К.К. Личность как объект социальной психологии // Методологические проблемы социальной психологии. М.: Наука, 1975.

155.   Платонов К.К. Общие проблемы теории групп и коллективов // Коллектив и личность. М.: Наука, 1975. PP. 6–11.

156.   Проников А.С. Параметрическая надежность машин. М.: МГТУ им. Баумана, 2002.

157.   Психология. Словарь. 2-е изд. / Под ред. А.В. Петровского, М.Г. Ярошевского. М.: Политиздат, 1990.

158.   Рукавишников А.А. Опросник межличностных отношений. Ярославль: НПЦ «Психодиагностика», 1992.

159.   Светлов В.А. Конфликт: модели, решения, менеджмент. СПб.: Питер, 2005. PP. 18–32.

160.   Семенкин Е.С., Семенкина О.Е., Коробейников С.П. Адаптивные поисковые методы оптимизации сложных систем. Красноярск, 1996.

161.   Семенов Н.Н. Наука и общество. Статьи и речи. М.: Наука, 1973.

162.   Сетров М.И. Организация биосистем. Л.: ЛГК, 1971.

163.   Сетров М.Л. Методологические принципы построения единой организационной теории // Вопросы философии. 1969. # 5. PP. 28–41.

164.   Сиротская М. Американская цивилизация: восприятие в США (середина XIX в.). М.: Русское открытие Америки, 2002.

165.   Системный анализ: Проектирование, оптимизация и приложения / А.Н. Антамошкин, М.А. Воловик, А. Торн и др.; под общ. ред. А.Н. Антамошкина. Красноярск, 1966.

166.   Скобельцын Д.В. Парадокс близнецов в теории относительности. М.: Наука, 1966.

167.   Слово Святейшего Патриарха Кирилла. Национальный исследовательский   ядерный университет. МИТ. 4 марта 2010.

168.   Совместимость и последовательность применения лечебных физических факторов: Метод. рекомендации / Под ред. А.А. Шатрова. Ялта, 1986.

169.   Социальная психология: история, теория, эмпирические исследования / Под ред. Е.С. Кузьмина, В.Е. Семенова. Л.: Изд-во ЛГУ, 1979.

170.   Спицнадель В.Н. Основы системного анализа. СПб.: Бизнеспресса, 2000.

171.   Справочник конструктора РЭА: Общие принципы конструирования / Под ред. Р.Г. Варламова. М.: Сов. радио, 1980.

172.   Татарчук А.С. Современные возможности предварительного исследования. М., 2011.

173.   Teltscher F. Biorythmustheorie. Quoted from the Russian edition: Тельчер Ф. Теория биоритмов (трех биоритмов). Инстург, 1997.

174.   Templeton J. Worldwide Laws of Life. Radnor, PA: Templeton Foundation Press, 1998.

175.   Therborn G. Being Part of a Culture, Place within a Structure and Human Activity: Explanation in Sociology and Social Science // THESIS. 1994. Issue. 4. P. 9.

176.   Титов К.В. Чакральные коммуникации. СПб.: Афина, 2007.

177.   Toynbee A.J. A Study of History. Oxford University Press, 1987.

178.   Туган-Барановский М.И. Периодические промышленные кризисы. Общая теория кризисов. М.: Наука: РОССПЭН, 1997.

179.   Фатхутдинов Р.А. Инновационный менеджмент. М.: Интел-Синтез, 2000.

180.   Feyerabend P. Against the Psylib Method. Quoted from: Фейерабенд П. Против метода PSYLIB. (http://psylib.org.ua/books/fayer01/txt03.htm).

181.   Фетискин В.В. Потребности. Деятельность. Личность. Социально-философское исследование. М.: РГАЗУ, 2001.

182.   Флейшман Б.С. Элементы теории потенциальной эффективности сложных систем. М.: Сов.радио, 1971.

183.   Франк С.Л. Религия и наука. М.: Библиотека «Вехи», 2002.

184.   Франтов Г.С. Единство мира природы. СПб., 2004.

185.   Fromm E. Psychoanalysis and Religion. The Art of Loving. To Have or to Be? Quoted from the Russian edition: Фромм Э. Психоанализ и религия. Искусство любить. Иметь или быть? Киев: Ника-Центр, 1998.

186.   Huntington S. Political Order in Changing Societies. Yale University Press, 1969.

187.   Huntington S. The Clash of Civilizations and the Remaking of World Order. New York: Simon & Schuster, 1996.

188.   Hermann R. God, Science, and Humility. Ten Scientists consider Humility Theology, 2000.

189.   Хлопин А.Д. Российский социум: границы общностей и парадоксы их институциональной интеграции // Институциональная политология / Под ред. С.В. Патрушева. М.: ИС РАН, 2006.

190.   Цветков В.Д. Системно-структурное моделирование и автоматизация   проектирования технологических процессов. Минск: Наука и техника, 1979.

191. Церковь призывает к единству. Святейший Патриарх Кирилл. Минск: Белорусская Православная церковь, 2010.

192. Цзинь Це. Универсальная цигун терапия. Киев: Пересвет, 2000.

193. Чугин-Русов А.Е. Единое поле мировой культуры. Кижли-концепция. М.: Прогресс-Традиция, 2002.

194. Шатров А.А., Троценко С.Я., Соколов Б.А. Методические рекомендации методов лечения НИИ им. Сеченова. Ялта, 1986.

195. Шевандрин Н.И. Психодиагностика, коррекция и развитие личности. М.: ВЛАДОС, 1998.

196. Шибутани Т. Социальная психология. Ростов н/Д: Феникс, 1998.

197. Shils, E. Society and Societies: A Macrosociological Approach. Quoted from the Russian edition: Шилз Э. Общество и общества: макросоциологический подход // Американская социология: Перспективы, проблемы, методы. М.: Прогресс, 1972.

198. Шмитт К. Понятие политического // Вопросы социологии. 1992. # 1.

199. Spengler O. Der Untergang des Abendlandes. DTV Deutscher Taschenbuch, 1993.

200. Штаинзальц Р.А. Наука и религия: взаимотношения. М., 2001.

201. Щеглова Л.В. Культурология: единство и многообразие форм культуры. Волгоград: Перемена, 2009.

202. Эйдемиллер Э.Г., Юстицкис В. Психология и психотерапия семьи. 2-е изд. СПб.: Питер, 1999.

203.   Einstein A. Einstein About Religion. (Russian translation) Эйнштейн А. Эйнштейн о религии. М.: Альпина нон-фикшн, 2011.

204.   Ashby W.R. Design for a Brain. New York: Wiley, 1960.

205.   UNCTAD. World Investment Report, 2004. UNCTAD.org, 2004.

206.   Языки как образ мира. М., 2003.

207.   Якимова Н.Н. Дыхание Вселенной (Единство мира). М.: Дельфис, 2010.

208.   Яковец Ю.В. Циклы. Кризисы. Прогнозы. М.: Наука, 1999.

209.   Ясина И. Человек с человеческими возможностями. М.: Эксмо, 2010.

210.   Cross-Cultural Studies of Individualism and Collectivism // Nebraska Symposium on Motivation. 1989. Vol. 37.

211.   Eisenstadt S., Roninger L. Patrons, Clients, and Friends: Interpersonal Relations and the Structure of Trust in Society. Cambridge; N.Y.: Cambridge University Press, 1984. P. 25.

212.   Lane J.-E., Ersson S. The New Institutional Politics: Performance and Outcomes. L.-N.Y.: Routledge, 2000.

213.   Lechner N. Politics in Retreat: Redrawing Our Political Maps // The End of Politics? Explorations into Modern Antipolitics / Ed. by A. Schedler. N.Y.: St. Martin's Press, 1997.

214.   Lewis B. The Roots of Muslim Rage // Atlantic Monthly. Vol. 266. 1990, September. P. 60; Time. 1992. June, 15. PP. 24–28.

215.   Mahbubani K. The West and the Rest // National Interest. 1992. Summer.

216.   Murray S.L., Holmes J.G., Griffin D.W. The Benefits of Positive Illusions: Idealization and the Construction of Satisfaction in Close Relationships // Journal of Personality and Social Psychology. 1996. Vol. 70 (1). PP. 79–98.

217.   New York Times. 1990. December. P. 41.

218.   Offe K. Designing Institutions in East European Transitions // The Theory of Institutional Design / Ed. by R. Goodin Cambridge: Cambridge University Press, 1996.

219.   Parsons T. Prolegomena to a Theory of Social Institutions // American Sociological Review. 1990. Vol. 55. # 3.

220.   Pierson P. Increasing Returns, Path Dependency, and the Study of Politics// Amcrican Political Science Review. 2000. Vol. 94. #2.

221.   Roland J. Psychological Pattering in Marriage // Psychological Bulletin. 1963. Vol. 60 (2). PP. 98–112.

222.   Roosevelt A. For Lust of Knowing. Boston, 1988.

223.   Schneider D.A. Russian Movement Rejects Western Tilt // Christian Science Monitor. 1993. February.

224.   Scott W.R. Institutions and Organizations. Thousand Oaks: Sage Publications, 1995.

225.   Sharpley C.F., Khan J.A. The Relationship between Marital Adjustment and Self-Concept for Married Individuals and Couples // Individual Psychology Journal of Adlerian Theory, Research and Practice. 1982. Vol. 38 (1). PP. 62–71.

226.   Stankevich S. Russia in Search of Itself // National Interest. 1992. Summer. PP. 47–51.

227.   Stets J.E., Burke P.J. Inconsistent Self-Views in the Control Identity Model // Social Science Research. 1994. PP. 236–262.

228.   The End of Politics. Explorations into Modern Antipolitics / Ed. by A. Scedler. N.Y.: St. Martin's Press, 1997.

229.   Tolli C. Political Identities in Changing Polities // Social Research. 2003. Vol. 70. # 2.

230.   Wallace K. Direct First-Order Experiment on the Propagation of Light from a Moving Source // Journal of the Optical Society of America / 1962. Vol. 52. N. 9. September.

231.   Weidenbaum M. Greater China: The Next Economic Superpower? // Washington University Center for the Study of American Business. Contemporary Issues. Ser. 57. 1993. Feb.

232.   Wissenburg M. Political Pluralism and the State: Beyond Sovereignty. Milton Park, Oxford: Routledge, 2008.